MEMOIRS OF A WILD GOOSE

MEMOIRS OF A WILD GOOSE

CHARLES BEWLEY

Irish Minister in Berlin, 1933-1939
Detainee at Modena, Verona, Terni, etc., 1946
author of HERMAN GOERING AND THE THIRD REICH *(1962) etc.*

Foreword by Lt-Col (retd) John P. Duggan
author of NEUTRAL IRELAND AND THE THIRD REICH *(1989, 2nd ed.)*

Edited and with an Afterword by
W. J. Mc Cormack

THE LILLIPUT PRESS
1989

Copyright © The Lilliput Press Ltd, John P. Duggan, W.J. Mc Cormack

All rights reserved. No part of this publication
may be reproduced in any form or by any means
without the prior permission of the publisher.

First published in 1989 by
THE LILLIPUT PRESS LTD
4 Rosemount Terrace, Arbour Hill,
Dublin 7, Ireland.

ACKNOWLEDGMENTS

Thanks are due to the late Dr Geoffrey Bewley (Dublin),
brother and executor of Charles Bewley, and to
Dr David Bewley (London), his nephew. John Duggan
came across the 'Memoirs of a Wild Goose' MS while
doing research for a thesis on Dr Hempel, the German Minister
to Ireland (1937-45), for Trinity College, Dublin.

A CIP catalogue record for this title is available from The British Library.

ISBN 0 946640 42 4

Jacket design by Jole Bortoli
Set in 11.5 on 13 Bembo by
Seton Music Graphics Ltd of Bantry
and printed in England by
Billings & Sons Ltd of Worcester

Contents

	A Note on the Text	vii
Foreword	The Career of a 'Sport' by John P. Duggan	ix
	Introduction	3
One	The Golden Egg	7
Two	Towards Irish Independence	39
Three	In Germany and France	76
Four	The Law of Ireland	89
Five	Minister in Rome, 1929	100
Six	'We in Berlin'	117
Seven	Eamon de Valera	156
Eight	A Conversation	179
Nine	South Tyrol in Wartime	186
Ten	1945 — Under Arrest	212
Eleven	Meeting John Amery	247
Twelve	Dispersal	264
Afterword	Camp Literature by W.J. Mc Cormack	283

A Note on the Text

Memoirs of a Wild Goose derives entirely from a typescript prepared by the author shortly before his death in 1969. As Bewley left it, the work was not ready for publication — many of the chapters were impractically short. Chapter-headings were provided for the first half — he had orginally divided his book into two Parts — but not for the second. The text contained repetitions, *longeurs,* misspellings, and occasional unrevised contradictions. (In the present Chapter 8, for example, a conversation ostensibly taking place early in 1939 concludes with what one can only take to be a reference to the post-war state of Israel.) The editor, in consultation with Colonel John Duggan who brought the typescript to light, has submitted the text only to the kind of copy-editing which would normally be effected with the author's consent. (Bewley's spelling of names has been retained, however, and no attempt has been made to verify or correct his statements of fact.) Chapter-titles are the editor's, though the author's title for the work as a whole has been retained. (The editor's preferred title, at times, was *Memoirs of a Wild Goose-Step!*) Scholars anxious to consult the original typescript should apply in writing to the Department of Manuscripts, Old Library, Trinity College, Dublin 2.

FOREWORD

The Career of a 'Sport'

Charles Henry Bewley (1888-1969) began life in a blaze of contradictions and reversals. Born into colonial Dublin, he rejected the Protestant and Unionist values of his family even before going up to Oxford where he converted to Catholicism. At school in Winchester, he became prefect of the library, won prizes in English, and his maiden speech in the debating society was much praised. But, in the second speech, he went a-coat-trailing and mocked the national anthem. Having won another scholarship which took him to New College, Oxford, in 1910, he won the Newdigate Prize and, under the influence of the charismatic chaplain, Father Martindale SJ, joined the Catholic Church. Back in Dublin by Michaelmas term 1911, he was admitted as a student to King's Inns. Called to the Bar in Hilary term 1914, he was ready and waiting to defend rebel prisoners at summary trials in Dublin Castle in 1916. In addition to his work in the Sinn Féin courts – brilliantly recollected in these memoirs – he stood unsuccessfully as a Sinn Féin candidate. Against the English interest, he is credited (by Oliver Gogarty) with composing General Sean Mac Eoin's death-sentence speech, but during the Civil War, under the aegis of John A. Costello, he vigorously prosecuted republican prisoners.

In 1929, despite Sean T. O'Kelly's opposition in Dail Éireann, Bewley was appointed resident Minister to the Holy See. He would have preferred Berlin, but this posting was given to the reluctant Daniel A. Binchy. Complex diplomatic disagreements between Britain and Ireland affected the official arrival of Bewley in Rome. In his presentation speech he invoked the long line of Irish soldiers of Christ, continued with a disquisition on the diaspora of the Irish race, and edgily recalled that it was almost three hundred and sixty years since a pope had sent a nuncio to Ireland. These themes alarmed the British who saw that the principle of diplomatic unity, as between dominion and mother-nation, was at risk. In July 1933, Bewley further irritated the British by acceptance of a decoration from the Pope without obtaining prior permission from London. Yet officials in Dublin were also treated cavalierly by their representative in Rome when they inquired about the matter.

Transferred to Berlin in 1933, Bewley drove the whole way from Rome to the capital of the Reich in his own car. Addressing Hindenburg in German which the President found impeccable, Bewley omitted all reference to the King (whom he officially served), but praised instead the importance of Celtic studies and commerce in fostering links between Ireland and Germany. In the course of this diplomatic induction to his new posting, he took great liberties with an English text supplied for him, introducing positive reference to the 'rebirth' of a new Germany, and undermining his predecessor Binchy. His enthusiasm for the Nazis was undisguised, as his account of the Party Day rally at Nuremberg on the 2nd and 3rd of September 1937 illustrates. The Irish Minister in Berlin gave a series of interviews to German newspapers, ostensibly about trade but never failing to stress the centrality of one issue in Irish eyes – for or against England. Meanwhile, he managed to fall out with the tax authorities in Dublin, and the man with a reputation for being 'as mean as cats' meat' had met his match.

Bewley used his uncle, Sir Arthur Pim, a retired colonial administrator living near Oxford, to introduce him to the right circles in England. Yet, after Bewley had boycotted the King's jubilee celebrations in 1935, English opinion of the Irish maverick was unambiguous. An official of the Foreign Office wrote in a memorandum:

I am not surprised altogether to hear that Mr Bewley's manners have deteriorated from his residence at the Vatican to that at Berlin. At his former post I understand that he was fairly friendly personally but difficult officially. He had the reputation of being very pro-German and anti-Jewish and so, having got to Berlin, he no doubt felt he could let himself go.

When de Valera's new constitution was introduced in 1937, Bewley's attitude towards his superiors in the Department of External Affairs led to his being reprimanded for a report of the

7th of September in which he stressed that the British still dominated Ireland. In November 1938 he refused to attend a dinner at the South African Legation on the grounds that the British *chargé d'affaires* would be the only other diplomat present. Reprimanded again by Dublin, Bewley was unabashed. In January 1939, he complained bitterly about a report that Minister MacWhite and another Irish diplomat were to meet the British Prime Minister Chamberlain at Rome railway station during the latter's quest for appeasement. (After the war, he records sardonically in these memoirs, MacWhite did little to help him during his detention by the Allies.)

Bewley had made up his mind about which side he would support in the coming war. In 1938 the British Embassy in Berlin reported:

For internal political reasons he is careful to associate himself as little as possible with this Embassy. I gather that although a professional admirer of Germany he is not popular with the Ministry for Foreign Affairs where he is described as being too sharp-witted and anxious to strike a hard bargain.

Is reported to have declared his intention to resign if Mr de Valera had in the September crises joined Great Britain in the war against Germany. (Emphasis added.)

When de Valera finally forced Bewley's retirement, the former Minister was given no pension for his fifteen years' service. Embittered, he made his way back to the Axis block where his aspirations, both personal and national, could be realized only in a total victory by his hosts. Details about Bewley's wartime activities are elusive. The Americans claim that they gave all the relevant documentation to the British. They, for their own reasons, have 'retained' the intelligence files. But the former Minister can be spotted in Stockholm in the spring of 1940 disseminating disinformation. One of his pronouncements sought to publicize Hitler's intention to attack the Maginot Line and to refrain from embroiling the Low Countries. Of course, the opposite was to happen. Michael MacWhite, Irish Ambassador in Italy, enigmatically reported that Bewley's paymaster in all this had a club foot. Apart from the Devil himself, this might indicate Goebbels or Veesanmeyer, Ribbentrop's specialist on Irish affairs, who used the code-name

'Clubfoot'. Captured at the end of the war, Bewley's survival was the result of Sir John Maffey's intervention (at de Valera's instigation).

After his release, Bewley settled in the Parioli district of Rome, but travelled extensively – to Vienna, Munich, Paris and Madrid. (He had somehow missed Spain during the great era of fascism.) He came to London and Dublin once a year, and received his Irish relatives in return in Rome. Like his wartime activities, his financial affairs were a mystery to his family. His continuing journalism could not have generated enough to support his style of living. A year or two before his death he took out a large endowment policy with a Swiss company, suggesting that his normal source of income was drying up. At the time he failed to find a publisher for *Memoirs of a Wild Goose*. His caste-conscious biography of Goering (originally published in German in 1956) sold 10,000 copies in its American edition (published in 1962). Did Bewley have homosexual leanings? His relations with his chauffeur, Agostino, may point this way for he left his main legacy (two million lire) to him, and left nothing to his female servant Rica. Bewley never lived up to his Oxford promise as a writer. These wartime reminiscences of rogues and vagabonds, pimps and high-class prostitutes, have been turned into neither a Joycean epiphany nor a Bondian thriller. Yet they have their value in providing insight where much still remains cloaked.

John Duggan
Dublin, September 1989

Memoirs of a Wild Goose

Introduction

As few but the Irish know, the Wild Geese were those Irishmen who some three hundred years ago left their native land to seek in the service of the European monarchs that career, or at least that possibility of living, which was denied them by misgovernment at home. Among them are reckoned the O'Donnells, the Taaffes, the Nugents and a dozen other families which rose to fame and distinction in the Catholic states of Europe; from their numbers were recruited the Irish brigades which fought at Fontenoy and Cremona and in countless other battles 'from Dunkirk to Belgrade', as the Irish ballad has it.

They were compelled no doubt in the first place by economic necessity, just as later generations were driven by hunger to seek a new life in the American Republic; but in the imagination of the Irish people they have come to be regarded as the symbol of Romance insurgent against the commonplace of everyday existence. And so, when recently a friend wrote to me from Ireland of the banality of modern life in comparison with the heroic age through which we had lived in our youth, and of the incomprehensible satisfaction of the majority with conditions which to him meant the abandonment of an ideal, I replied:

Another distinguished Irishman has expressed the same thought in the lines –

> *Was it for this the wild geese spread*
> *The grey wing upon every tide;*
> *For this that all the blood was shed,*
> *For this Edward Fitzgerald died,*
> *And Robert Emmet and Wolfe Tone,*
> *All that delirium of the brave?*

INTRODUCTION

Speaking as a contemporary Wild Goose (others are, of course, Oliver Gogarty and Donald Hales of Genoa; our friend X.Y. does not, I think, deserve the adjective), I can only say that in my opinion it emphatically was *not*, but I have no doubt that the vast majority of your colleagues would disagree, and am convinced that they consider the Rising of Easter Week and the sufferings of our War of Independence to have been more than justified by the fact that they have got jobs which they would not have got, were the English still in possession. But, as you know perfectly well, there is no being so futile as the Romantic, even though he may derive a certain egoistic satisfaction from his romanticism.

The words were written at random in response to the mood of my correspondent; but, when I considered them later, they seemed to me genuinely to express my fundamental attitude towards life in general and towards the history of Ireland in the last two generations in particular. Nearly fifty years ago a handful of Irishmen deliberately sacrificed themselves in order that their country might become, not merely politically independent, but 'a nation once again' in every sense of the term: in their own words, they gave their lives to save the soul of the nation. The vast majority of Irishmen, myself among them, recognized the nobility of their sacrifice and continued the struggle until political independence had been attained. But, once a native government had been established in Dublin, their efforts relaxed: they considered that the fight had been won once and for all, that the former enemy had become a friend, and that we were in no danger of losing our nationality.

Never was there so fatal an error; my reasons for saying so will be apparent in the course of this book. The Irish people today are anglicized more than ever in the course of their history – to such a point that one is often tempted to despair of the establishment of a native culture or mentality or language. No political party has made any serious attempt to stem the flowing tide of anglicization: it may well be that at the present day any such attempt would be foredoomed to failure.

Nor, while blaming the politicians, do I wish to claim any

credit for those who like myself and my correspondent have seen the mortal danger: it may be that we are even more to be condemned than they, because, being aware of the peril, we made no determined effort to arrest it.

But the truth in all probability lies deeper: the harm was done before they or we came into existence – in the middle years of the nineteenth century, when the Irish people abandoned their language in favour of English, and nothing that politicians or romantics could later do would ever have availed to dam the flood of English influence. The Rising of 1916 was a last flash of national spirit in combat with the inevitable; subsequent developments have only been further strides in the direction of complete assimilation to the country which it has become an anachronism to call 'the hereditary enemy'.

ONE

The Golden Egg

Time: one of the last years of the nineteenth century.

Place: a house in Lower Baggot Street in the professional quarter of Dublin.

Characters: my Father (a doctor in his late thirties – no politician, but loyal by tradition to British rule in Ireland and elsewhere); my Mother (endowed with a peculiarly feminine disbelief in the various systems devised by man for the betterment of the world and an infinite charity which never failed to find good in the deviser); myself (a precociously intelligent, opinionated, highly objectionable urchin with a vague hankering after romance). We are sitting before the fire on an autumn afternoon; my Mother is reading Hans Christian Andersen's story of the Goblin and the Huckster to me, my Father the *Irish Times* to himself.

My Mother (reading): 'There was once a poor student, he lived in the attic and had no possessions; there was a rich huckster, he lived on the ground floor and owned the whole house.'

The silence is broken only by my Mother's voice, while I see myself (perhaps prophetically) in the role of the goblin who tried to have the best of both worlds. My Father lays down the paper with a sigh.

My Father: Things aren't going well out there.

My Mother: We must hope for the best, dear.

My Father: It's extraordinary they can't drive the Boers back. I would have thought – (he breaks off in the fear of criticizing too harshly the forces of Her Majesty).

My Mother: I expect it'll be over soon.

My Father: I hope so. But things are going badly.

Myself (with horrible perkiness): I hope the Boers'll win!

My Father (thinking his ears have misled him): What's that?

Myself (with less perkiness): I hope the Boers'll win!

My Father (losing a heaven-sent opportunity of exposing my complete ignorance): There are some things I won't allow to be said in my house –

My Mother: Harry! He's very young.

My Father: Yes, but that's too much.

My Mother (to me): Would you like me to go on reading?

Myself: Yes, please, Mother.

My Mother (reading): 'It's wonderful here,' said the goblin. 'I would never have expected it. I think I will stay with the student!' – and then he thought it over and became sensible and said with a sigh, 'But the student has no jam!'

My Father gets up to leave the room. My vanity tells me I have cut a poor figure, but I do not venture to repeat the offending statement. Finally I hit on a phrase which I hope will not sound too flat a defiance, while at the same time saving to some small extent my self-esteem.

Myself: I don't see why I shouldn't say I hope the Boers'll win.

My Father goes out.

My Mother (reading): 'I'll divide myself between the two!' thought the goblin. 'I can't quite give up the huckster – because of the jam!'

Myself: I think the goblin was right, Mother. Don't you?

I find it now difficult to say why at the age of nine I considered it necessary to champion the cause of the Boers. I knew nothing whatever about them except that everyone seemed to regard them as monsters of iniquity who were flying in the face of Providence by defying the forces of England – and of course the temptation to oppose the general opinion was too strong to be resisted.

I had always had the inclination to back the beaten side. One of my favourite books was an old edition of Pope's translation of the Iliad with Flaxman's illustrations: I had never ceased to deplore the defeat of the Trojans and to resent what I considered to be the unjustifiable turning of the scales of war by the Olympian deities in favour of the self-righteous Greeks. And I sympathized deeply with the Amalekites, Amorites,

Hittites and the other tribes with the exotic names who were doomed to vanish from the earth before the hosts of all-conquering Israel.

There is no more exhilarating sensation than that of standing alone against an overwhelming majority – especially, as a cynic might suggest, when no personal risk is involved. Only a saint like Athanasius could be immune from vanity on finding himself *contra mundum*. Yet I do not think it was only vanity which made me espouse platonically the first unpopular cause which came to hand. A Quaker lady called Miss Emily Hobhouse had started a campaign against English methods in South Africa: the grown-ups by whom I was surrounded, most of them Quakers, as were my parents, regarded her as an unpatriotic, interfering, ridiculous busybody who would have been better employed in knitting socks for the soldiers. Only my Mother gave her credit for good intentions. I could not help admiring Miss Hobhouse, who seemed to be in one boat with myself.

And perhaps through the servants or the coachman some hint had leaked through to me of the general sympathy with the Boers in the Nationalist Ireland by which we were surrounded. I had seen Queen Victoria driving in her open carriage through Lower Baggot Street, a little huddled-up figure in black, her bonneted head lolling forward on the black silk of her mantle, amid the indifferent silence of the few casual spectators. A young woman had contrived to hang out a black banner with skull and crossbones over the street through which Her Majesty was to pass on her triumphal entry of the Irish capital. My relations shook their heads over the exploit and exclaimed 'Scandalous!', but never failed in the next breath to mention Maud Gonne's extraordinary beauty, and it was not hard to see that they regarded her with the indulgence due to a spoilt child. At my age the fact of personal beauty had little importance: it was no more than one of the conventional story-book attributes of heroines and princesses; but I had heard, I know not on what authority, that she had the habit of walking through the Dublin streets with a monkey on a leash.

Politically, then, we, the Irish Unionists of the 1890s, were a class apart. The English connection was regarded as a safeguard against anarchy and the rule of the mob. A native government meant little less than 'red ruin and the breaking-up of laws'. It was thought scarcely possible for a gentleman to be a 'Home Ruler': the rare exceptions were put down unhesitatingly and with complete sincerity as eccentrics or opportunists. But in sentiment, as distinct from politics, Irish Unionism was largely, if not completely, Irish.

There were few homes in which could not be found copies of the *Spirit of the Nation* or John Mitchel's *Jail Journal*. My mother used to tell me how her grandmother as a young girl had seen Robert Emmet led off to Kilmainham Jail by the British soldiery. I knew the melodies of 'O'Donnell Abu' and 'The West's Awake' long before I had heard of 'Rule, Britannia' or 'Hearts of Oak'. From my governess I learned of the Wars of the Roses, the Spanish Armada and the battles of Trafalgar and Waterloo, but I cannot remember when I first heard of 'Ninety-Eight' and 'Young Ireland' and the stories of Lord Edward Fitzgerald and Pamela or Robert Emmet and Sarah Curran: about these I did not need to read in books – I learned about them from casual references in conversation; they were in the air I breathed, in the bricks and mortar of my native city of Dublin.

For it was a romantic sentiment – akin to the romantic sentiment felt for Mary Queen of Scots or Bonnie Prince Charlie by many Scottish men and women who for all that have not the slightest desire to see an independent Scotland. The Irish unionist felt himself at liberty to admire the national heroes of the past, so long as it was understood that they remained safely buried in the past and would not emerge to disturb the tranquil present. What was heroic in 1798 would have been insane and criminal in 1900: while the sentimental part of his nature did homage to Wolfe Tone or Thomas Davis, his commonsense led him to reject John Redmond as a dangerous revolutionary. It was a curious example of divided loyalty, a struggle between the head and the heart in which the head invariably won.

My great-grandfather, who was for some years a Member of Parliament for the City of Dublin, had travelled through the West of Ireland on one of the Famine Relief Committees in the years 1846 and 1847. I have never read the report of his Committee, but what he saw must have profoundly impressed him, for a few years later he purchased a small estate on the shores of Clew Bay in the County Mayo.

The property consisted of two long grassy promontories running out into the bay together with a few of the small islands surrounding them. At the time of the purchase it was occupied in part by some fifty families of tenants, the rest consisted of grass-land in the direct occupation of the landlord. My great-grandfather built a rambling, one-storeyed house on one of the promontories, planted a belt of ash and fir trees to shelter it from the havoc of the west wind, laid out a little fruit and flower garden, and spent as much of his time in Rosbarnagh as he could spare from parliamentary and business duties.

My great-grandfather had little regard for the laws of economics; on the other hand, he had a strongly developed sense of social justice. Consequently, one of his first acts after taking possession of the estate was to announce to his tenantry a general reduction of their rents. His liberality earned him widespread popularity among the small-holders of the County Mayo, but was regarded by his fellow-landlords as a gross betrayal of the interests of their class. One of them actually drove twenty Irish miles in his carriage and pair over the rutty roads of the West of Ireland in the forlorn hope of opening his eyes to the consequences of his rash act. History does not relate the conversation which took place between the two, though it is not difficult to imagine the scene – the courteous remonstrances over a glass of my great-grandfather's sherry giving way gradually to indignant protests as the full extent of his obstinacy was revealed. But the close of the dialogue has been handed down by family tradition: my great-grandfather in the Quaker 'plain language' put to his uninvited guest the unanswerable proposition, 'Thee spends thy money on thy horses and thy hounds: if I spend my money on my tenants, what is that to thee?' The unsuccessful remonstrant drove back the twenty Irish miles in his carriage and pair, no doubt cursing the new order of things under which a damned Quaker tradesman could open the door to social revolution.

In my childhood Rosbarnagh had little changed from the date of its building. The rooms were still filled with the middle-Victorian furniture of the Fifties and the bookshelves still crammed with the 'yellow-backs', Ouida and Nat Gould and Charles Lever, which had delighted an earlier generation. The fuchsia hedges which enclosed house and garden had grown to more than man's height, and the hydrangea bushes displayed in ever greater profusion their pink and blue chintz-like blooms. The constant storms from the Atlantic had begun to ravage the belt of trees on the West: the salt spray had burned away the green needles of the firs, while the ash trees, twisted and deformed by the winter gales, seemed like beasts in a circus cowering before the ringmaster's lash. But they still gave sufficient shelter to the apple trees and strawberry beds in the box-bordered garden, from which the eye passed over the undulating slopes of the islands and the blue of their intersecting channels to the Holy Mountain Croaghpatrick silhouetted against the southern sky.

There is little worth relating in the details of a small boy's days – the rowing and sailing and fishing in the charge of the old boatman who except for a short interval on the cattle-boats between Westport and Glasgow had spent his life half a mile from Rosbarnagh Lodge. My particular delight was to be allowed to accompany him when he set the herring-nets in the warm summer nights when the herring had come into the bay. I can still see the phosphorescence of the water that dropped from the oar-blades in flakes of silver light and the black outline against the starry sky of the fir-trees on the neighbouring island and the rosy glare of his pipe as we sat on the deck of the yacht in the windless dark; I can still hear his voice as he sang in an undertone, as though unwilling to disturb the silence of the night:

>'Oh, then, tell me, Shawn O'Farrell,
>Tell me why you hurry so?'
>'Hush, ma bouchal, hush and listen,'
>And his cheeks were all aglow.
>'I bear orders from the captain,
>Get you ready quick and soon,
>For the pikes must be together
>At the Risin' of the Moon!'

I knew nothing of Shawn O'Farrell or the Rising of the Moon, but the words and the melody and the nocturnal scene filled me with a pleasant sense of excitement and mystery. A curlew cried somewhere in the air; a shooting star traced its fiery way across the firmament; a heron flapped drowsily out of the trees and vanished once more into the darkness of the branches. An almost imperceptible luminosity over the hills in the East told of the end of the short summer night and of approaching dawn. And gradually my eyes grew heavy and the landscape dim, and the song and the nightbird's cry and the plashing of the little waves against the prow of the yacht were mingled in my consciousness into one vast harmony which swept me away into the gulf of sleep. The last thing I remember was being carried down to the cabin and covered with a blanket: then I slept a dreamless sleep which lasted until morning.

★ ★ ★

When I had reached the age of ten, my parents sent me to a boarding-school in England.

Park House, like other English schools for the 'sons of gentlemen', was a little world in itself; we were strictly forbidden ever to pass the boundaries of our playing-fields. Above all, it was prohibited to enter into conversation with the boys of the village: the teachers feared that their charges might acquire a cockney accent or pick up vulgar expressions and so get the school a bad name. Only on Saturday afternoons we sometimes went to play cricket or football against neighbouring schools, and on Sundays we marched to church morning and evening under escort of the master: our Eton suits and top hats created a solemn impression well befitting the sacred character of the day and emphasized the invisible barrier which divided us from ordinary mortals.

The Boer War still dragged on, but in the whirl of new sensations I had almost forgotten my former interest. In the England of sixty years ago wars were regarded as a sporting event involving, it is true, a certain degree of personal risk, like big game hunting or polar exploration, but never as catastrophes which might lead to national ruin. The boys therefore took little interest in the campaign beyond hoping that someone would send them stamps from the South African Republics for their collections. Mr Gilbert, the mathematics master, thought it his duty to read out to his class the reports from the new halfpenny newspaper, the *Daily Mail,* and to mark the advance of the British Army with little flags on a map; it was a welcome interruption in the wearisome course of quadratic equations and isosceles triangles, but when the mathematics hour was over, I do not remember that any of us devoted another thought to the events in distant Africa.

When British troops relieved the town of Ladysmith from the besieging Boer forces, we were allowed for once to leave the school premises and take part in the celebration on the neighbouring village green. Like the other boys, I had stuck a red, white and blue rosette in my buttonhole and cheered without conviction when cheering seemed to be required. Boys of twelve – especially those educated in an English school – are the tamest creatures in the world, and it never occurred to me to run counter to my companions. But in the following year a change came about in my feelings.

It was partly that my bewilderment in the strange milieu and my shyness of the thirty English boys by whom I was surrounded had begun to wear off, and I felt once more the inclination to be different from the others. It was partly that they found me more than a little ridiculous and my Dublin accent highly diverting – and did not scruple to tell me so with all the brutality of youth. The only revenge I could think of, being one against so many, was to say something which would outrage their sentiments. I realized even at the age of twelve that they were a conventional lot and would be shocked at the slightest departure from the pattern of their prejudices.

But there was more in my attitude than mere vanity or exhibitionism, although on looking back I can see that I was both vain and exhibitionistic. Lured by curiosity, I had begun to read the Dublin Nationalist press in my holidays: the consideration that my relations certainly disapproved was an extra inducement. But what had begun in a spirit of bravado soon developed into something more genuine. I realized that war was not merely a game, but bitter earnest for those who were caught in its grip. And I found something ignoble – I would have said 'caddish' in the manner of the English schoolboy – in the sneers of the *Daily Mail* at the farmers who were struggling to defend their homes against an immensely stronger enemy.

I made a remark in this sense to Young, a boy of my own age and my greatest friend in Park House, but he entirely failed to see my point of view.

'Do you think', he asked me severely, 'that you know better than the people who write in the papers?'

'No, of course not,' I said hurriedly, for the assumption of 'knowing better' than the generality was for us one of the unforgivable sins.

'Well, then,' he retorted, 'I don't know what you're kicking up all this row about.'

The discussion ended; for my friend the question had been finally settled. For me, on the other hand, it had only begun to become interesting. I dropped the subject, but determined to bring it up again when I was better prepared with arguments to meet the disapproval which I would certainly have to face.

The advance of the Boers into the colony of Natal had long since been driven back, and they were spending their last cartridges in a hopeless cause. The British command had inaugurated the policy of burning their farmhouses and interning their families in concentration camps. From the *Freeman's Journal* I learned of the sufferings of the populations of the Transvaal and the Orange Free State, and began to realize that the little flags which Mr Gilbert moved so jauntily backwards and forwards on his map were not merely the pieces on a chessboard, but human beings, men and women and children, who lived and suffered and died. I also learned that two Irishmen, Colonel Lynch and Major MacBride, were fighting on the side of the Boers. I understood for the first time that President Kruger, the Oom Paul of the top hat and umbrella and Bible and shaven upper lip, was no figure of fun, but a hero who had dedicated himself to the service of his people. And the thought occurred to me, 'I must tell them I'm a pro-Boer!'

It was a serious consideration: in the England of 1900, and most certainly in Park House, a pro-Boer was a scoundrel, a sneak, a traitor – something worse than all these put together. I had never met one, nor, I am confident, had any of my schoolfellows. They were a category outside the pale of human society, which one knew to exist, but with which one never expected to be brought into contact. And now I discovered that I belonged to this pariah class!

Elementary commonsense told me to keep quiet about my newly acquired convictions, to avoid all arguments about the Boer War, to say nothing which might wound the susceptibilities of my companions. But even at the age of twelve that most dangerous of attributes, the propagandist instinct, was strongly developed in me: I could not let sleeping dogs lie nor leave the others in what I held to be their erroneous belief in the justice of England's cause. I considered it a point of honour to inform them that I differed from them in this most fundamental tenet of their faith, and told myself that it would be cowardly to sail under false colours. And of course I promised myself a certain satisfaction in upsetting their self-sufficiency.

I did not go out of my way to seek an occasion for my profession of faith but one soon offered itself. We were seated in the dining-hall at six o'clock tea, chattering about the opening of the cricket season and the peculiarities of the new French master, when someone took it into his head to remark, 'Well, the War'll soon be over now.'

'We shan't be long in taking Pretoria and hanging old Kruger,' said another.

'On a sour appletree,' a third contributed facetiously.

The moment had come: I endeavoured to master the tremor in my voice, as I said, 'I don't think it's anything to be so proud of if the whole British Army succeeds in beating a few thousand half-armed farmers.'

The sentiment was taken directly from the articles in the *Freeman's Journal,* though of course the others did not know it. They stared at me in silence for an instant, while they strove to grasp the full significance of my words. Finally one of them asked in a voice laden with incredulity, 'Then you're pro-Boer?'

Conscious that I had burned my boats, I hesitated. I should have proudly proclaimed my faith and waited for the heavens to fall, but my nerve failed me. The best I could do was to mutter confusedly, 'I suppose so.'

THE GOLDEN EGG

It was not glorious, but it was sufficient. A whisper passed down the long table, as the shocking news was communicated by one to another. I wondered what was going to happen to me when we left the tea-table. But I did not have to wait so long: suddenly and unexpectedly I received a violent kick on the shin from the boy sitting opposite me.

My first instinct was to return the kick, my second to draw back my legs as far as possible in the hope of avoiding further hostilities. It was useless. The boys who were sitting left and right of my first assailant joined him with vigour in delivering kicks in the direction in which they thought my legs should be. The eyes of the whole table were fixed on me. At last one of the masters, whose duty it was to sit at the head of the table and preside over our meals, noticed the excitement and, I imagine, the redness of my face.

'What's up?' he shouted.

They all shouted together, 'Bewley's a pro-Boer, sir!'

'Nonsense!' said the master. 'Why do you say that?'

'He admits it himself, sir.'

The idea of a twelve-year-old pro-Boer obviously appealed to Mr Sykes' sense of humour. He inquired with an expression of amusement, 'Well, supposing he is – ?'

The answer came in swift and indignant chorus: 'It's a rotten thing to be a pro-Boer, sir! Sir, isn't it a rotten thing to be a pro-Boer? Tell him it's a rotten thing to be, sir!'

But Mr Sykes evaded a direct answer. 'Five against one's not sporting,' he said. 'Where's your fair play?'

They said no more, but they were clearly unconvinced: even the doctrine of fair play, they felt, has its limits.

Finally they decided to send me to Coventry for a day as punishment.

I knew nothing about their intention: consequently it was a complete surprise to me when on getting up one morning and asking my neighbour in the dormitory the time I received no answer but a blank stare.

'What's the matter with you?' I asked. 'Are you deaf or dumb?'

He looked at me with an air of contempt in which there was also a certain embarrassment; then he called to the boy beyond me, 'Franklin, have you seen my comb? I can't find it anywhere.'

Gradually it dawned upon me – they did not wish to speak to me. Very well, I was not going to give them the satisfaction of speaking to them. The day passed in silence; even at meal-times no-one spoke to me and I spoke to no-one. For the others it must have been a disappointment: I do not believe they had intended to keep up the ostracism for twenty-four hours.

Next morning one of them asked me, 'How did you enjoy yourself yesterday?'

'I enjoyed myself all right,' I said with all the indifference I could muster.

'Would you like the same again today?'

'I don't care.'

I wondered whether they would keep it up and for how long: it was an alarming prospect, but I was not going to give in. However, during breakfast my neighbour said shyly, 'Salt, please!' And after that I knew that life had become normal once more.

I was at this time first in the school and received special coaching for the scholarship at Winchester. The examination took place in June 1901; to my surprise my name appeared at the top of the list.

It was a great event for Park House: every scholarship won by the boys under his tuition was a feather in the cap of the headmaster. A whole holiday was announced for the school, and on the first Saturday after my return we set out in two charabancs with hampers of food and the other requisites for a picnic. The day was spent in a pine wood: in the heather-covered clearing we could play rounders and chase butterflies to our hearts' content.

I was naturally the hero of the hour: everyone was anxious to sit next to me, to play with me, to do me all the honours. Our former differences were forgotten: all, masters and boys alike, were resolved that my last days in Park House should be spent in a blaze of glory.

I found my sudden popularity hard to understand: I was still very young, and it was my first lesson in the truth of that most ignoble of proverbs, 'Nothing succeeds like success!'

★ ★ ★

THE GOLDEN EGG

Since the years which I spent in Winchester two wars have passed over the world, bringing to less fortunate nations a ruin and devastation whose like humanity has never seen and to England a displacement of the social centre of gravity. I have never returned to visit my old school and have no idea how far it has been affected by the shifting of values in English society, but I cannot believe that the emergence of a new ruling class has left the public school system entirely untouched, or that our changing times have not given a new interpretation to William of Wykeham's old motto 'Manners makyth man'.

If such a shifting of standards has taken place, it will not have been the first in the century-long history of the school. Founded as a Catholic institution in the days when a Catholic bishop could still be Chancellor of England, it had yielded together with the rest of the country to the pressure of the new ideas of the Reformation and devoted itself to the production of the type of English gentleman which first emerged in the reign of Elizabeth and has persisted, allowing for the inevitable modifications of time, down to our own day.

In many countries the object of a school is considered to be the imparting of that instruction which will enable the pupils in later life to earn a living and take their places as useful members of the community. In the English 'public schools' of fifty years ago this was very far from being the case. With the exception of those who, like myself, had won scholarships and did not belong to the 'leisured classes', the boys regarded their class-work as a tedious necessity and those who took an interest in it as harmless eccentrics. Such an attitude was natural enough in schoolboys: more remarkable is the fact that it was shared by the majority of the masters.

For masters and boys alike the serious business of life consisted in games – football and cricket, which were supposed to have a beneficial effect on the character and to build up what was known as the 'team spirit'. The Duke of Wellington obviously took the same view when he asserted that 'the battle of Waterloo was won on the playing-fields of Eton': it would never have occurred to him to ascribe the victory to any knowledge acquired in the class-rooms. And a recent Poet Laureate could find no more urgent message to the youth of

England than the exhortation 'Play up, play up, and play the game!'

It is not easy now to think oneself back into the spiritual atmosphere which then existed; but, if one succeeds in doing so, one is forced to the conclusion that the masters were not altogether wrong from their point of view. Apart from the seventy Scholars, almost all the boys who were sent to Winchester for their education were the sons of well-off parents. The majority of them would later be in possession of an income sufficient to protect them for the rest of their lives from the danger of having to work for a living. Others expected through the influence of their families to obtain posts which would enable them to live the life of a gentleman without excessive mental strain. Some would perhaps spend a few years in the Army – in one of the crack regiments in which technical qualifications were less sought after than a steady income, good family connections and a talent for shooting, cricket and polo: parents who planned a serious military career for their sons sent them, not to Winchester, but to one of the more modern and less exclusive public schools.

Why, then, should the masters plague the gilded youth entrusted to their charge by excessive insistence on Latin or Greek or mathematics? The boys themselves would have resented it, and their parents would not have been grateful. All were united in the view that lessons were a tiresome convention to be supported so many hours a day, after which the pupil could devote himself with a clear conscience on the playing-fields to the real business of life. In a word, the school aimed at turning out young men of a definite pattern, amiable, well-intentioned and healthy, *mens sana in corpore sano,* as it had done ever since the reign of Elizabeth.

Not, indeed, that there was any deliberate policy of forcibly crushing recalcitrant members of the community into one intellectual mould: anyone who had original ideas and was prepared to affront an adverse popular opinion was at liberty to develop them as best he could. Neither Sir Stafford Cripps nor Sir Oswald Mosley corresponded to the ideal of the country gentleman or the athletic housemaster, and in an earlier generation Winchester had counted among its pupils Dr Tanner, one of the group of Irish Nationalists who had supported Parnell in his obstructionist campaign in the British House of Commons, and Lionel Johnson, the County Sligo poet and friend of William Butler Yeats. But these were exceptions, as they would have been in any community: their very divergence threw into relief the standardization of the Winchester finished product.

It would be superfluous to attempt to draw a pen-picture of the landscape surrounding the school: it at least has not been changed by the years or war or social upheaval. In the transparent chalk-streams the water-weeds still wave gently in the languid current and the trout rise lazily to the fly. 'Hills' are still spangled, as in my memory, with buttercups and harebells, and the cottage gardens are bright with nasturtiums and larkspur and marigolds. In the water-meadows kingcup and spearwort flaunt their golden globes; like an immense park the pasture-lands undulate to the horizon, broken only here and there by a lonely and majestic oak or chestnut tree. So it must have been when William of Wykeham founded the College of 'Seinte Marie by Wynchestre' for the purpose of educating 'poor scholars' in the Catholic and Apostolic faith; so it will be when in the centuries to come Winchester College has long been transformed to a centre of technical instruction for the sons of the proletariat.

But fifty years ago no concession had yet been made to the claims of progress. Clad in our black trailing gowns we Scholars attended Anglican prayers twice a day in the Gothic chapel; morning and evening we ate our bread and butter from the wooden platters in the oak-panelled hall hung round with the portraits of bewigged and beribboned Wykehamists of the past; before and after our midday dinner the Prefect of Hall pronounced the Latin grace of medieval tradition; in our speech there lingered certain words – the famous Winchester 'notions' – handed down from the days before England dreamed of greatness and jealously preserved by the successive generations. And yet, when I now look back on our life in College, it seems to me that the tradition was a purely outward one, that there was but little sense of continuity with the past.

In the six years of my life at Winchester I cannot remember that any endeavour was made to render us familiar with the history of the school, or that any of the masters ever spoke of William of Wykeham and his aims in its foundation. We did not know who lay under the gravestones in the Gothic cloisters, nor what artist had designed the medieval windows in 'Chantry'. Even of the portraits in 'Hall' which we gazed at every day we knew nothing: familiar to us was only that of the 'Veal Lady' – an eighteenth-century benefactress who out of the kindness of her heart had bequeathed a sum so that on Sundays in summer we might in perpetuity eat veal instead of the conventional English mutton and beef. In a word, we were little more conscious of our connection with the past than is the twentieth-century American of his connection with the Redskins who inhabited the continent before the white man's landing.

At first sight such neglect of the past would appear to be in crass contradiction to British love of tradition: only on closer consideration does one come to see why it was not only natural but inevitable. The reformers' zeal which had broken up the statue of Our Lady in 'Chamber Court' was no isolated outburst; through the length and breadth of the land similar zealots did their utmost to root out every trace of the Ancient Faith, to destroy every work of art which could remind posterity that England had once been Catholic, and to adapt the architectural monuments which they could not destroy to the uses of the new religion.

So it had been with those who set the tone for Winchester College. After the Reformation every link which bound it to the Catholic past had been deliberately broken; it had been re-formed after the pattern of the English Protestant gentleman. And through the generations, consciously or unconsciously, those who had the moulding of the youth of England in their hands shrank from the knowledge that the founder of the institution with which their lives were bound up had belonged to a faith which they distrusted and that the buildings which he had erected and the endowments which he had furnished were being put to uses to which he could never have consented.

No: a thousand times better to let William of Wykeham rest in peace, to relegate him to the realm of myth, to resuscitate him briefly as a figure-head on ceremonial occasions, but on no account to investigate too deeply the ideals for which he strove or the hopes which he had cherished when he laid the foundations of the College of Seinte Marie by Wynchestre. It would only have disturbed the comfortable English philosophy of three centuries and set the thoughts of the new generations wandering on ways which are definitely not those of the English gentleman.

I can look back on six happy years at Winchester. I no longer felt myself in opposition to my surroundings, as I had done at Park House: I had for practical purposes taken over the ideas of my fellow-Scholars, and was perfectly content with the world of school. It was, as I now see, a very small world – far more limited than that of the state schools of other countries, whose pupils come into daily contact with the population surrounding them. Our interests were confined to the trifling events of school life – games and work and the peculiarities of the masters: we had no contact with the world outside, and desired none. It is true that, when I came back to Dublin for the holidays, I still read the Nationalist press and made an effort in the summer in County Mayo with the help of an Irish teacher and O'Growney's grammar to learn the Gaelic language, but, when I returned to Winchester, I wondered whether such interests were more than a personal and even presumptuous eccentricity.

Education in Winchester was the most effective propaganda imaginable for English ideas, English standards, the English way of life. Many years later when I saw the youth of Germany succumbing almost without a struggle to National Socialist ideals, I could not share the surprise of many foreign observers – I remembered how I myself had undergone the same process. But the Nazi propaganda, like all German propaganda, failed through over-emphasis and over-saturation of its objects; inevitably, once the first fervour of the proselyte had died down, it aroused a feeling of opposition, even of nausea, in the more intelligent. The Nazis were in a hurry; the English, with three centuries of tradition behind them, could afford to wait. They knew instinctively that no propaganda, however able, could be one half so efficient as the tranquil and well-mannered assumption that their philosophy of life was the Absolute, and all others deviations from the right road. They never argued; they regarded the ideas of others with the casual and courteous indifference with which they might have regarded a Negro passing in the street. Their complete self-assurance was more impressive than the most violent protestation, and their disregard of the existence of other points of view more annihilating than the most irrefutable logic. However sure one might feel of oneself, one's faith was nevertheless shaken by that placid and unreasoning certainty: one felt oneself like a small dog helplessly and frantically yapping at a majestic and benevolent St Bernard in a picture by that most English of all painters, Sir Edwin Landseer.

★ ★ ★

I obtained one of the scholarships reserved for Wykehamists at New College, Oxford, William of Wykeham's other foundation. It was my introduction to an English life larger than the confined existence of school.

The peculiarity of life in New College which struck me most forcibly was the sharp dividing-line drawn between the different categories of undergraduates. We lived in the same building, the doors of our rooms opened on to the same staircase, we dined seven times a week in the same hall; and yet, if two undergraduates did not belong to the same 'set', they could easily pass through the three or four years of Oxford life without ever exchanging a word with one another. Even on the evening of our arrival, groups had been formed, partly of previous acquaintances, but even more in virtue of some mysterious law of magnetism which drew like to like and repelled the unlike. After a few weeks everyone had found his appropriate place in the social structure of the College.

The most prominent class was without a doubt that of the 'Bloods' – magnificent creatures who bought their clothes from the best London tailors, often wore rings, tie-pins, monocles and other adornments unusual in young men of our age, and gave themselves the greatest pains to look and behave like 'men about town'. Some had brought with them from their schools the fame of special exploits on the football or cricket field; these knew from the first moment that Oxford – and the world – belonged to them. They were received with open arms by the athletes of previous years; they had the consoling certainty that during their University career no professor would insist on their attendance at his lectures. Like the lilies of the field, they needed neither to toil nor to spin.

It was the same worship of sport as at Winchester – and yet, as I soon observed, there was a difference. The height of good form was the Bullingdon Club – an institution which to the uninitiated possessed some quality of mystery. It had no premises; the members met in one another's rooms, where we heard with awe that they played roulette and baccarat for stakes which equalled our yearly incomes. They had the right to wear a pale-blue and white ribbon around their straw hats and along the seams of their white flannel trousers. Once a year they held a club dinner at which legendary quantities of champagne were consumed.

It was obvious that many athletes would have felt out of place in such a company: they lacked the philosophy of the man of the world – and the income which made such a philosophy possible. On the other hand, there were members of the Bullingdon who never took any part in the organized sport of the College and had little interest even in polo, hunting or racehorses. The most conspicuous example was a young man from Eton called Cooper.

Cooper was anything but an athlete: he was fond of saying that with the exception of roulette he considered all ball-games childish – possibly because he had no aptitude for them. He dressed, so far as it was possible for an undergraduate, like a drawing-room version of the Quartier Latin: his long fair hair almost concealed the collars of his rose-pink or apple-green silk shirts. He composed lyrics in the style of Oscar Wilde and Ernest Dowson and was said to be a brilliant historian. He spoke excellent French (an almost unheard-of thing in England), and had the love of Parisian life and manners which became the vogue under Edward VII. His friends spread the report that he had spent a week-end with Polaire – a French actress then playing in London with, if her press agents could be believed, the smallest waist and the ugliest face in Europe. The story was probably untrue, but it was sufficient to win him a certain prestige among his fellow-students. He was also a keen politician, and everyone predicted for him a brilliant career in the Conservative Party.

In the robust atmosphere of Winchester he would have been considered impossible: his affectations, no less than his genuine qualities, would have doomed him to permanent unpopularity. In every respect he was the direct contrary of the semi-illiterates of the Bullingdon Club – and yet they had overlooked his peculiarities and admitted him to their exclusive ranks. I asked a friend who had known him at Eton for the explanation.

He looked at me with astonishment and said, 'His mother is Lady Agnes Duff.'

'Who is Lady Agnes Duff?' I asked.

His astonishment gave place to pity for my ignorance. 'Don't you know', he asked, 'that Lady Agnes Duff is a daughter of the Duke of Fife, so that he is closely related to the Royal Family?'

I ventured on no further question: it was unnecessary, for I understood that the standards applied in judging one's fellows in Oxford had their origins in considerations very different from the schoolboy's ingenuous worship of sport. It was the first time that I had learned from experience that money and family connections were keys to open every door in English life. For Alfred Duff Cooper they opened many doors besides that of the Bullingdon Club.

At the opposite pole of life in New College were the 'Highbrows'. These consisted of the Scholars and those others who attached more importance to intelligence than to good form. We worked for our examinations because our tutors expected it of us and because many of us needed a degree with first-class honours for our subsequent professions. The majority were painfully inclined to priggishness: they rejected all music other than that of Bach and Beethoven and turned up their noses at those who played bridge or admitted a preference for operetta. A few strove to awake interest through deliberate eccentricity: the White Rose Society was dedicated to the restoration of the Stuart dynasty to the throne of England. Its members hung in their rooms a portrait of King Charles I, laid yearly a wreath of white roses at the foot of his statue and sent a telegram of homage to the Crown Princess of Bavaria as legitimate ruler of England.

With the 'Bloods' we had practically no intercourse of any kind: there was no common interest to bring us together. There existed no hostility between us and them – it was merely that, while living in the same college, we lived in different worlds. They regarded us with faint and indifferent contempt; we looked on them with vague and reluctant admiration, which we knew to be illogical, but which we could not resist. It was the tribute of mind to matter, the homage of the incomplete to the complete.

Between these two extremes came the average undergraduates from the public schools who were neither particularly wealthy nor athletic nor intellectual, and far below them, if the diagrammatic representation of society be persisted in, the few who had been educated in grammar schools or similar institutions. These formed a class apart; they had no contact worth speaking of with the remaining members of the college. It was not that they were Socialists (the word Communist was unknown): the Fabian Society existed only as a pardonable eccentricity of the wealthy. They were for the greater part genuinely convinced Conservatives who believed firmly in the established order of things. What separated them from their fellows was a combination of little significant details – accent, choice of words, clothing, table manners. They were genuinely regarded as belonging to another race of beings; it would never have occurred to an undergraduate from one of the public schools to invite one of them to his rooms or stroll with him in the quadrangle. They themselves seemed to find this state of affairs perfectly natural and made no attempt to break down their isolation.

Sometimes, after a particularly animated dinner, one of the 'Bloods' would bethink him of a face, an accent or a suit of clothes which had not met with his approval. The word of command was given, and the *jeunesse dorée* marched with songs and hunting cries to the rooms of the offender. Here, in spite of their victim's protests, they smashed whatever was smashable, after which they marched back in triumph, carrying with them whatever trophies they had selected from his possessions. One might have thought them British soldiers liberating a European town.

At the moment of the attack the victims had of course no possibility of defending themselves. But it struck me as extraordinary that they took no steps when it was over to secure elementary justice: so many courses were open to them, had they been possessed of a little courage. If they had had a taste for dramatic situations, they could have chosen some public occasion to slap one of their tormentors in the face. Or they could have awaited a suitable opportunity to make reprisals on his property. They could have formally placed the matter before the college authorities and demanded a public apology under threat of ventilating their experiences in the public press. But they did none of these things: they meekly accepted a five- or ten-pound note as compensation, as if the damage were due to some inevitable cataclysm of Nature. No apology was either tendered or asked for. It was clear to me that, if the young men who presumably represented the most intelligent and enterprising elements of their class submitted with such incredible and unworthy patience to personal insult, the social revolution in England, predicted by so many writers from Cobbett to Chesterton, would never come about.

Even more strange to me were the Oxford Dons. At Winchester the masters had been without exception orthodox Church of England Conservatives, or, if they had other opinions, they took care not to create a scandal by obtruding them on their pupils. At New College there were many of the same type – Diehard Tories who appreciated with equal gusto a well-turned Latin period and a glass of vintage port and regarded with equal horror a false quantity and a heterodox opinion. But 'progressive thought' was beginning to make its inroads into the Oxford colleges, and in New College there was more than one who diverged widely from the type to which Winchester had accustomed me.

There was, for instance, Zimmern, a little man with a bald head and spectacles, who (as I see now) with considerable moral courage proclaimed himself a member of the then inconsiderable and unpopular Labour Party. There was the Most Reverend Hastings Rashdall DD, who, though a divine of the Church of England, made no secret of the fact that he rejected the Thirty-Nine Articles of his Church and a considerable portion of the Apostles' Creed; the parts which he did not reject were accepted by him of course in a strictly symbolical sense and not in their literal crudity. He was fond of informing his pupils that his religious beliefs were approximately those of the Unitarians, but did not for that reason think it necessary to resign his present position. And there was Professor Gilbert Murray.

Gilbert Murray was for nearly two generations so well-known a figure in English public life that it would be difficult to find anything new to say of his career. Born of an Irish-Australian Catholic family, he had at an early age come to England and adopted a religion of humanitarianism, of which his wife Lady Mary Murray was a devoted adherent. In politics, he was an enthusiastic supporter of the underdog, in whatever continent the dog-fight happened to be taking place. It was the old English Liberal tradition: he would have shared to the full Gladstone's righteous wrath over the Bulgarian atrocities or the persecution of the Armenians by the Turks. It must also be admitted that he was always ready to acknowledge the wrongs done by England in the past, which he put down to the Tory or Imperialist governments then in power. I remember him telling me with genuine horror of the Australian settlers of his youth, who in the course of their shooting-parties fired casually at any native who might have the misfortune to cross their way. He was also willing to concede the injustice of the Boer War – and, if the wrongs in question lay too far back in the past to admit of a remedy, that was in no way Murray's fault.

He was of course in favour of Home Rule for Ireland: self-government with the necessary safeguards for British interests formed a part of the Gladstonian, as well as of his humanitarian, tradition. And, as I was his pupil and he was extremely hospitable and he had heard that I was an Irish Nationalist, he asked me to lunch. When lunch was over, I found myself sitting on a sofa next to Lady Mary in the drawing-room. She plunged at once, as was her habit, into the heart of the matter. 'And what do you Irish propose to do when you get Home Rule?'

It was probably sheer imagination on my part, but I fancied I could discern a shade of condescension in her tone, as if she had said, 'And now, my little man, what do you propose to do with your nice new toy?' I answered, 'I expect our government will be strongly national and will do its best to keep out international socialism.'

It was no doubt unpardonable, but I had not expected to be taken too seriously. There was a short and icy silence; then Lady Mary said with solemnity, 'Mr Bewley, I worked for Home Rule before you were born. But there are some things which I cannot allow to be said in my house. I think it would be better for you to go home.'

Highly embarrassed, I said goodbye and made for the door. As I was putting on my coat in the hall, the Professor appeared. I apologized as best I could, and assured him I had not meant to be in any way insulting. He shook his head and said sadly, 'My wife takes politics very seriously.' I could not contradict him.

In spite of this unfortunate episode, my good relations with the Murrays were soon re-established, but it had taught me that the underdogs whom they championed were expected in return to dance to a Gladstonian and humanitarian tune. And, as I later discovered, Murray, for all his detestation of Tory Imperialism, was a devout believer in Britain's imperial mission, for which of course he would have found some euphemism such as 'apostolate of democracy'. Willing, as I have mentioned, to admit the iniquities of British policy in the past, he was much less ready to see them in the present – or, rather, he was invariably convinced that Britain was on the side of righteousness.

Like Broadbent in *John Bull's Other Island,* Murray believed himself to be entirely honourable, sincere and idealistic; like Broadbent, he had his blind side where British interests were concerned. His transparent sincerity and idealism made him the most useful of instruments in the hands of those who possessed neither idealism nor sincerity. As a moulder of the ideas of the youth of England, he was unequalled: of the generations of Oxford undergraduates who came into contact with him, there were few who remained unaffected by his influence. At a time when the crude jingoism of the Boer War had gone out of fashion, he revived in a modern form the evangelical zeal of the previous century. The Victorians had urged the expansion of British rule as a means of spreading Gospel truth; Murray urged it as a means of spreading the gospel of democracy. He would have shuddered at the idea of an Empire on which the sun never sets, but he believed with all his soul that the interests of the backward nations were best served by placing them under a British protectorate.

It was not surprising that his influence on the youth, first as an Oxford professor, afterwards as President of the League of Nations Union, finally as delegate of South Africa at Geneva, was tremendous. There can be no greater moral satisfaction than that caused by the discovery that one's nationalism is no mere lust for imperial power, but an aspiration for the greater good of humanity – and this discovery was the lesson imparted by Murray to his disciples. In pursuance of this doctrine Germany was deprived of her colonies by the Treaty of Versailles; it was one of the main obstacles to the return of colonial territories to Italy and Germany in the years before Hitler's rise to power. In a sense, it may be said to have been one of the chief contributory causes of the Second World War and the enslavement of half Europe.

But Murray would never have conceded that his well-intentioned doctrine could have any share of responsibility for the catastrophe of the world. He was a pure idealist, whose motto was *fiat justitia ruat coelum,* and if in the back of his mind there was always the comfortable assurance that no part of the sky would fall on British territory, I am certain that such an idea was never allowed to emerge from his subconsciousness. He was possessed of exceptional personal charm; he was a scholar of world-wide reputation. All the more regrettable was it that he should have embarked on a political career in which his influence did so much to destroy the prospects of that peace which he so ardently desired. It would be hard to imagine a more striking example of the melancholy truth that in this world the greatest harm is often done by the best-intentioned of men.

★ ★ ★

If Winchester had gone some way towards converting me by its calm and unquestioning self-sufficiency to the English way of life, Oxford effectively undid its work. Moreover, I was beginning to think for myself as an adult, and logic was taking the place of boyish conventionality.

I had for a long time felt the attraction of the Catholic Church. I find it now difficult to say what it was that, humanly speaking, first turned my thoughts in that direction. It certainly was not any influence to which I was exposed in Oxford: the effects of the 'Oxford Movement' and the tradition of Cardinal Newman had long since died out, and none of my friends was in the least interested in religious problems. Nor do I think that my conversion was induced by the fact that the vast majority of the Irish people belonged to the Catholic faith: I was personally acquainted with no Irish Catholic sufficiently well to discuss questions of theology with him. Possibly Belloc's writings influenced me more than I suspected at the time: he had the art of presenting religion not as a thing to apologize for, but as a banner to be flaunted in the face of a hostile world.

It is often said that it is natural for the young to deny the existence of God. I cannot say whether that is so; I only know that I myself never had any such inclination. Starting from an oasis of Christian belief, my only problem was therefore to ascertain what form of Christianity was that of its Founder. My parents were Quakers, that is to say they did not recognize the sacraments and denied the necessity of an ordained priesthood; at the same time they frequently attended Divine Service in the Protestant Church of Ireland, which counted among its tenets certain sacraments and an ordained priesthood. I began to wonder at an early age which was right: the necessity or non-necessity of the sacraments and a priesthood could not be treated as a matter of indifference, and it seemed to me illogical to take part in the worship of two bodies which contradicted each other on an essential dogma of faith.

The doubt had arisen in my mind: it became more acute in consequence of a controversy which involved the fundamental beliefs of the Society of Friends. An English Quaker, a certain Edward Grubb, had in his addresses and writings expressed the opinion that the Divinity and Resurrection of Christ were not to be understood as literal historical facts: his views apparently enjoyed some support in the Society of Friends in England. The Dublin Quakers on the other hand were scandalized; in their view Edward Grubb had denied the fundamental doctrines of Christianity. They protested against his coming to Ireland to preach heresy in the Dublin Meeting House: if I recollect right, his proposed visit was abandoned. But the fact that such differences could exist and that within one religious body people could be found to assert and to deny the same doctrine with apparently equal sincerity, had started a train of thought which led me farther than Edward Grubb could ever had intended.

If Christianity was a divine institution, then, I reasoned, it was logical to suppose that its Divine Founder had given to humanity some method of distinguishing the true from the false and some person or body to whom the individual could appeal for a decision. It was the orthodox argument for authority, as it presented itself to my immature mind. But the authority for which I was seeking was obviously not to be found in the Society of Friends, which possessed no hierarchy and believed in the direct inspiration of the individual. That belief, as I early realized, was purely theoretical: the fact that the Friends who preached in Meeting on Sunday mornings were speaking 'as the Spirit moved them' did not protect them from criticism or even from good-humoured imitation when their hearers were assembled at the Sunday dinner. But, if neither authority nor direct inspiration existed, how could I tell whether Edward Grubb or the Dublin Quakers were right? And how could I tell that both were not wrong in their rejection of the sacraments and the priesthood which other Christian bodies recognized?

Nor did the situation seem very different in the Protestant Church of Ireland. A distant cousin of mine, the Reverend Joseph Bewley, was rector of the parish of St John's, Sandymount, in the Dublin suburbs, where he conducted Protestant services in a manner described by many of his parishioners as 'popish and ritualistic'. It was alleged that he lit unnecessary candles on the communion-table (which he insisted on calling an altar), that he turned towards the East when reciting the Creed and that he had placed crosses and images in his church. Members of his flock booed and hissed him at the church door;

his Archbishop issued from time to time a severe reprimand and condemned his practices. At the same time I knew that identical practices were tolerated without protest in many English dioceses.

Where, then, lay the truth, and where the authority? After studying the subject to the best of my ability, I came to the conclusion that the only possible answer to my question was the Catholic Church.

I tried to explain my position to the Reverend Hastings Rashdall, who had heard, I know not how, of my dilemma and had invited me to discuss my religious difficulties with him in the course of a walk along the banks of the Isis. Unfortunately our minds seemed to move on different planes: the idea of authority appeared to be meaningless or actually repugnant to him. His approach to the problem was a totally different one. He warned me that the Catholic Church insisted on a belief in miracles. I told him that I was aware of the fact, adding that I had always believed that miracles were accepted also by the Protestant Churches.

'But,' he objected, 'you are studying philosophy – you know that there can be no effect without a cause. Do you not realize that a miracle is an alleged effect without a cause? And, if so, how can you possibly believe in it?'

He was putting me in a difficult position – I knew nothing of philosophy, and his first proposition seemed incontrovertible. I grasped at the only plank in sight. 'If God is almighty,' I said, 'I suppose He can work miracles.'

I now see that I was unintentionally placing Mr Rashdall in an even more awkward dilemma: as a clergyman of the Church of England, he could not very well directly deny the omnipotence of God. So he said, 'I suppose you mean that a material effect may result from a moral as well as from a material cause?'

'I do,' I said thankfully.

Mr Rashdall abandoned the question of cause and effect in favour of another line of argument. 'How can you get over the Forged Decretals?' he asked me.

I had never heard of the Forged Decretals, and said so.

'And Pope Honorius?'

I knew nothing of Pope Honorius.

During our walk he bombarded me, though in the kindest manner, with the usual anti-Catholic arguments; at its end he lent me Salmon's *Infallibility*. Abashed at my own ignorance, I asked a Catholic friend about the Decretals.

'I know nothing whatever about them,' he answered, 'but of course the Church has an answer.'

'And you think it doesn't matter that you and I don't know it?'

'Of course. We can't know everything. I don't believe in the Church because it gives the right answer about the Decretals; I believe its answer about the Decretals is right because I believe in the Church.'

He at least had given me the right answer: I returned Salmon and the other anti-Roman propaganda to Mr Rashdall with thanks. We had no further discussion on religious questions. Some days later I began instruction with Monsignor Kennard, the chaplain to the Catholics in Oxford.

It only remains to say that, in spite of the grief which my change of religion must have caused them, neither my father nor my mother ever made me the slightest reproach. If I was inarticulate in expressing my gratitude to them, at least I hope that they understood . . .

It must have been about the same time that I began to feel an increasing irritation at the sort of politics favoured by my fellow-undergraduates. They continually debated current questions in the Oxford Union and belonged to little clubs (the Pitt, the Shaftesbury and many others) which held bi-monthly meetings and an annual dinner. If they had any idea beyond that of finding a vehicle for undergraduate wit, it was that of later making a career in one of the two great English political parties. It was all harmless and natural enough, but there was about it an air of smugness which got on my nerves. I could not help thinking that politics should be more than a pastime or the ladder to a job.

It was the moment when for the first time in Ireland doubts had risen on the efficiency of parliamentary agitation. The nationalist party under John Redmond had set its hopes on the fall of the Unionist Government and the assumption of power by the Liberals: now, the long-desired change had taken place, and we were no nearer to the attainment of our ends. Arthur Griffith pleaded in his weekly paper for the boycott of the British parliament and policy of self-help after the Hungarian model. Under the motto *Sinn Féin Amháin* (Ourselves Alone) he founded a new party and contested a number of bye-elections. But the people were not yet ripe for so radical an alteration of their political course: a European war and an Irish rebellion were needed before the Irish Parliamentary Party could be dislodged from its position of supremacy.

But in the tranquil decade which followed the Boer War who thought of an Irish rebellion? Such romantic adventures belonged to a remote past; in a century of progress and reason humanity believed in its parliaments. The small nations, the oppressed classes (the Marxist term 'proletariat' was as yet seldom heard), the discontented minorities submitted their modest claims to the constitutionally elected representatives of the people: they were discussed in due form – and in due form rejected. It was a pleasant game, in which the party that had made the rules always won. The vanquished had no right to complain, because the constitutional forms had been scrupulously observed.

I could not believe that we would make any progress by means of speeches at Westminster. But, on the other hand, I could not see that we could hope to gain much by the mere abandonment of the House of Commons. The principle of self-help was unexceptionable, but we lacked the numbers and the material resources. I saw no possibility of realizing our national aspirations for many years, perhaps many generations, to come. But suddenly all was changed.

The Entente Cordiale had come into existence in 1905; in the following years the tension between the Western democracies and Imperial Germany increased alarmingly. For the first time for generations people in England thought of the possibility of a European conflict in which the British Empire might be involved. The shadow of coming war lay over the land; many believed that war itself was imminent.

I was standing with a group of friends in the New College Quad: it was a summer evening; the fading light still gilded the gables of the College buildings, and clouds of starlings chattered in the sunset sky. We stood on the grass where countless generations of students had stood before us, and talked of war. My thoughts went back to the discussions on the Boer War in Park House. It would be a pity, I reflected, if I had less courage now than when I was twelve years old.

'If the war really comes,' I said, 'I will be on the other side.'

I do not know whether I had wanted to make a sensation; certainly I made none. One of the group looked placidly at me and said, 'You know you don't mean that.'

'I do,' I retorted. 'I mean it seriously.'

'No,' he replied imperturbably, 'you don't mean it. Perhaps you think you do, but when the time comes you'll see that it's all a nonsensical idea.'

His unshakable conviction that there could be no point of view but his own impressed and infuriated me at the same time. I could only try to show a conviction as strong as his own.

'We'll leave it to time to see who's right,' I said.

It was a proof that Irish nationalism was regarded as a picturesque relic of the past, like the legitimism of the White Rose Society, or as a family quarrel to be put aside in the face of a common danger. Ten years later, when England had discovered that there were Irishmen ready to transform their romantic aspirations into action, another Irish undergraduate, Lord Longford, proclaimed his nationalism under similar circumstances: as a reply, he was thrown by his fellow-students into the Christchurch fountain. It was the first step towards understanding the Irish question – the recognition that one existed.

The War did not come, and my life at Oxford drew to an end. I went up for the necessary examinations without undue enthusiasm and was more than satisfied with second-class honours. I had little regret on leaving Oxford; the four years which I had passed there had been undeniably agreeable, but I could not help thinking them more or less wasted time. I felt that, when one has reached the age of twenty-two, a knowledge of Plato and Thucydides is an insufficient mental equipment for facing life. The friends whom I had made in England I did not expect to see again save at rare intervals; our paths in the future seemed unlikely to cross. Despite all its poetic tradition Oxford was for me a stately façade with little behind it, a beautiful voice which spoke only of trivialities, a gramophone record which repeated over and over again the words of some long-forgotten song.

It was with a feeling of relief that I prepared myself for my new life in Dublin.

TWO

Towards Irish Independence

The War had come after all, but nothing had turned out as I had expected. Instead of making use of it to win our liberty, John Redmond – the leader of the Irish national cause – had assured England of our complete loyalty in face of the 'common foe'. Sir Edward Grey had declared Ireland to be the 'one bright spot' in the international scene. The Irish Parliamentary Party had called on the youth of Ireland to fight for their freedom in the trenches of Flanders, and tens of thousands of young Irishmen had taken them at their word and were flocking into the Irish regiments of the British Army. Even the Volunteers, recruited like Grattan's and Charlemont's Volunteers in 1782 to defend our rights against English aggression, were placing themselves at England's disposal: only a small minority had refused to follow their leaders into the Empire.

It was 1915, and a mass meeting was to be held in the Mansion House in favour of recruiting. Asquith was to be present, and the Chief Secretary for Ireland Augustine Birrell, and John Redmond, and a host of minor speakers. The Dublin Metropolitan Police, who kept order outside the building, were reinforced by a battalion of the Redmondite Volunteers. I could see by their embarrassed manner that they were far from easy in such unaccustomed company. Inside, the great hall and the passages swarmed with secret service men. I made my way in and looked round me at the audience.

It was not the usual Mansion House audience: there were few of the Dublin citizens who habitually came to applaud the orators of the nationalist party. Instead, well-dressed men in tweeds, ladies in furs occupied the foremost rows. Black-coated professional and business men gave a serious tone to the assembly. And I could see a sprinkling of the other Ireland – the nationalist majority – exhilarated by the exalted company they were keeping and at the same time a little shamefaced – like the Volunteers in the street.

The speakers came in and took their places on the platform. They were greeted with frantic cheers. Asquith gave once more his oft-repeated pledge not to sheathe the sword until justice had been re-established on the earth. Birrell praised the British Empire which knew no distinctions of race, creed or colour (I could see eyebrows raised as he compared by implication the Irish race with the dark-skinned tribes of England's equatorial colonies). Redmond with his polished, eighteenth-century eloquence exhorted the youth of Ireland to combat for liberty on the battle-fields of Europe. Their oratory was received with enthusiastic applause. At the start of the First World War people were less sceptical and more easily carried away by high-sounding periods than the disillusioned audiences of today.

The meeting came to an end, and I walked down the corridor towards the entrance. As I went, I heard a voice behind me saying, 'Thank God that I have lived to see this day!'

It was the voice of a man under strong emotion. I looked round and saw a Protestant clergyman – a mild-looking little man, whom I could imagine pottering round the roses and dahlias in his vicarage garden. Come up from his country parish, I thought, specially for the meeting.

He was greeting a friend, and the tears were standing in his eyes. 'Thank God I have lived to see this day!' he repeated. 'At last we have a united Ireland!'

I could understand his feelings, I could not but feel a certain sympathy with him. For years he had cared for the souls of his small and dwindling flock, but always he had known himself isolated from the vast majority of his neighbours, barred from them by the invisible wall of conflicting ideals. Possibly he had a son in the British Army.

I left the Mansion House, walked up Dawson Street and turned to the right. At the corner of Stephen's Green and Grafton Street a small crowd had assembled: a man was speaking from a car. Members of the DMP stood idly about: the bystanders were too few to threaten disorder. It was the Labour leader James Connolly. The bayonets of his bodyguard from the Citizen Army glittered white in the light of the arc-lamps. I heard the cold incisive tones of the speaker, as he said in his Ulster accent, 'England's war is not our war. The Irishman who joins the British Army is lost to Ireland.' But his voice was soon lost in the tramping of the crowd and the hooting of the motors coming from the Mansion House.

I had settled down to earn my living as a barrister, and toiled around the local courts of Quarter Sessions in the province of Connacht in the hope of picking some stray brief from a kindly disposed solicitor. Recruiting was still going strong: public men urged their constituents to join the colours, and a few young ladies in Dublin distributed white feathers to the youths of military age who dared to appear in public in civilian clothes. It was a profoundly discouraging situation for those who, like myself, believed that an Irishman's first duty was to his own country and that it would be time enough to talk of the freedom of Belgium when we had won freedom for ourselves. But there was little headway to be made against the war-propagandists. Every day brought a new story of German atrocities; every street-corner flaunted a placard: 'Join the Army and avenge Catholic Belgium!' And our people were so simple, so unworldly, so idealistic that they never doubted the reports of Reuter's agency and the subsidized press.

It must have been in the autumn of 1915 that I arrived at the Quarter Sessions of the little town of Carrick-on-Shannon. There was not much doing – the usual disputes about the right of way to a well and the trespass of a neighbour's cow. At the end of a tedious day we adjourned – barristers, solicitors, land surveyors and engineers – to the local hotel. We were crowding into the bar for a drink after the labours of the day when we became aware that a man in uniform was holding the floor. He was in the middle forties, solidly built, weighing perhaps eighteen stone, red of face, with lungs of iron. To an audience consisting of the barmaid, the boots of the hotel and half a dozen farmers he was delivering an oration on liberty, democracy, the rights of small nations and the horrors of German militarism.

'Nobody is safe from them,' he repeated in a voice which had become lachrymose, 'nuns nor priests nor innocent children. They have it all planned. They have their maps of the

County Leitrim, and I can tell you, there'll be little left for the Irish farmer when each one of them has made his choice.'

'My God!' whispered a colleague next to me. 'It's Johnny O'Donnell!'

I had heard of Johnny O'Donnell and read his name in the papers – the ex-Sergeant-Major of the British Army who had been promoted Captain for the purpose of recruiting. The British authorities presumably considered that one so racy of the soil would prove an efficient propagandist: he spent his time going from fair to fair and from bar to bar pleading the cause of the British Empire. Occasionally his patriotic feelings had run away with him, and the local police had been obliged to charge him with being drunk and disorderly and to bring him before the Resident Magistrate, but he had always got off with a smiling caution and a warning not to do it again. The Resident Magistrates, it may be recalled, were popularly known as Removable Magistrates, because they could at any time be removed from their office by Dublin Castle if their decisions did not find favour with the Government.

Nobody seemed inclined to give in his name to the Captain; several of the younger farmers edged to the door and disappeared before he could get hold of them. I felt his eye lighting on me.

'I'd like to know why Irishmen should fight for Belgium and not for Ireland,' I said mildly.

Johnny O'Donnell glared at me for an instant – he had reached a stage which does not willingly tolerate contradiction. His face grew even redder than before; he emitted an inarticulate snort. Then, putting down his head like a bull, he made a rush in my direction. He had the advantages of weight, physical strength and a riding-whip, I those of sobriety and speed. It did not take me a second to decide that my best policy was flight. I sprang to the door, closely followed by the Captain brandishing his riding-whip. Once in the street it was not difficult to evade his pursuit; he soon realized the uselessness of the chase and returned to the bar.

It would undoubtedly have been more glorious to stand up to him, but there are circumstances in which courage becomes foolhardiness, and I knew that I had not one chance in a thousand in a row with Johnny O'Donnell. I had no wish for a black eye or the loss of a couple of teeth. On my return to Dublin I issued a writ against him for assault. He paid five pounds into Court, which I accepted. The publicity of a trial would have helped neither him nor me in our respective careers.

And all the time, unknown to me and to nine-tenths of my fellow-countrymen, things were in preparation underground which were to prove the turning-point in Irish history.

For the last fifty years the man in the Dublin street had voted nationalist from tradition or, if you will, from force of habit, but he had taken, and had wished to take, no active part in politics. The freedom of Ireland had been to him an ideal to be aimed at in a distant future; his immediate concern had been the support of wife and family, the maintenance of his personal comfort and social position. It would not have broken his heart if the attainment of his ideal should remain in abeyance for another generation. And therefore it was a shock when on the morning of Easter Monday 1916 the green, gold and white of the Irish tricolour was hoisted on the roof of the General Post Office and soldiers in the green uniform of the Irish Republic patrolled the streets of Dublin.

I strolled out from our house in Merrion Square towards the centre of the city. It was a sunny spring morning, and the streets were deserted. I went on along Nassau Street, past College Green with a glance at the closed gates of Trinity College, across O'Connell Street, where I could see the flag floating against the blue April sky. No-one was about but a few loiterers like myself. Of British troops there was no sign.

Suddenly from the direction of the GPO a man came running. He held in his hand a bundle of little oblong sheets of paper, which he distributed to all whom he met. I took one and glanced at it. It was the Declaration of Independence of the Irish nation.

'In the name of God and of the dead generations . . .', it began; and, as I read on, I realized much that I had vaguely felt, but never dared to look on as reality. I understood for the first time that I myself and my generation were in the lineal succession of those who had witnessed the heroisms of 'Ninety-

Eight'. The epic past had been reborn overnight. What had been a vaguely cherished but half-forgotten tradition was suddenly a glorious reality. The historic drama of Ireland's fight for freedom was being re-enacted before my eyes. I apprehended, as I had never before apprehended, the continuity of history: for the first time Lord Edward Fitzgerald and Wolfe Tone ceased to be the romantic, semi-mythical figures of an epoch as irrevocably past as that of Cuchulainn or Fionn MacCumhaill and were once more alive in the world of the twentieth century.

What would come afterwards, I knew not. It was clear that the handful of badly equipped, scarcely trained Volunteers could never hold out against the forces of an Empire. Yet I felt that their sacrifice must leave an imperishable trace in the hearts and in the lives of those who had witnessed it. It had opened the way towards possibilities which few had even for a moment considered seriously. It had done away with the fatalism which was another name for despair become a habit. The veils of indifference were torn down; henceforth life would have a burning interest even for those who made no pretence of personal heroism.

Near me stood a little man in shabby black clothes – probably a clerk or a shop-assistant taking advantage of the holiday to stroll around the city. Like me, he was reading the Declaration of Independence. He looked up at me, and I saw that tears were standing in his eyes. Then, with an air half-defiant and half-apologetic, he said, 'Thank God I've lived to see this day!'

★ ★ ★

My own part in the Movement, as I have hinted, was in no way glorious. I had once been induced by a friend to attend a Volunteer drill with dummy rifles, but I had felt and looked so entirely incompetent that I did not repeat the experiment.

I came to the conclusion that in my case the pen was, if not mightier, at least more effective than the sword. Another friend had started a weekly paper with more literary pretensions than the average Sinn Féin weekly. I became a regular contributor in prose and verse.

TOWARDS IRISH INDEPENDENCE

A writer of the time, one Conal O'Riordan, had published a poem entitled 'A Song for Irish Soldiers in the Great War'. Its quality may be seen from the following lines:

> *We live, we live now with Young England.*
> *Do we forgive Old England? No!*
> *But with Young England, noble Young England,*
> *Ready are we to march on the foe,*
> *The foe that of old was the friend of Old England,*
> *Tyrannous Germany, Hessian and Prussian,*
> *That was the friend of Old England!*

Unfortunately, so far as I can ascertain, the distinction between unforgiven Old England and noble Young England proved too subtle for the Irish soldiers in the Great War, who continued to sing 'Tipperary' and 'Keep the Home Fires Burning', as they had done before.

It occurred to me that my muse should take up the challenge launched by the muse of Mr O'Riordan, and in the pages of *New Ireland* I published a series of rhymes which, though obviously strongly influenced by Belloc and Chesterton, then at the height of their fame, I still find quite creditable.

The following ballade in the Bellocian manner was provoked by the photograph in an illustrated paper of 'Mr John Redmond chatting with Her Majesty the Queen at the distribution of shamrock to an Irish regiment on St Patrick's Day':

> *Where'er the realms of thought extend*
> *And culture has its devotees,*
> *Wherever* Sketch *and* Mirror *blend*
> *Pictorial art with journalese,*
> *Between 'Miss Plumpton's Pekinese'*
> *And 'Huns' Nefarious Machine',*
> *With throbbing heart the patriot sees*
> *John Redmond chatting with the Queen . . .*

Redmond was in my view responsible for sending thousands of young Irishmen to certain death, and that therefore any weapon was legitimate in attacking him. In addition, it is only right to point out that the followers of Redmond with equal lack of justification accused Sinn Féiners of personal cowardice and of being the paid servants of Germany, and that in the bitterness of controversy no charge was too wild or too ill-informed to be resorted to.

More personal were the attacks on Maurice Healy, a young barrister who in a moment of eloquence had called on the young men of County Wexford to join in the war against Germany and avenge the outrages committed by the Hessians in Wexford in 1798. As the Hessians had been in the service of His Britannic Majesty King George III, and as their conduct had been in no way better or worse than that of the British regiments engaged with them in putting down the rebellion, Healy's appeal struck me as a piece of outrageous dishonesty, and I published a 'Come-all-ye' in the appropriate style of the country ballad, such as is sung at Irish fairs and markets:

> *Gather round me, kind friends, and I'll sing yez a song,*
> *'Tis a loud lamentation and a history of wrong,*
> *Of the woes and the griefs that to Ireland came o'er*
> *With the cruel barbarian from Germany's shore.*
>
> *O, once there was peace and content in our land,*
> *And an Irishman ruled in the highest command;*
> *There was happiness and plenty, as all will agree,*
> *Till a German called Strongbow came over the sea.*
>
> *The Prussians did plunder, did rob, and did slay,*
> *Till the people of Ireland near vanished away,*
> *And those that escaped from the murderous foe*
> *To Hell or to Connacht they bade them to go.*
>
> *The Germans destroyed us with force and with guile,*
> *Killing children and priests in the true German style,*
> *And Cromwell the Prussian he reddened the sod*
> *With women's blood shed to the glory of God.*

TOWARDS IRISH INDEPENDENCE

They robbed us of cattle, they robbed us of wheat,
They stole all the land that is under our feet,
They stole away the Parliament that we did win,
And sent us religion and laws from Berlin.

Then here's to brave Healy, the valiant in fight,
Who battles from Bray to Dundalk for the right,
And tells us our duty's to die for our race,
While he does his bit down in Beresford Place!

May his prospects be bright, as his conscience is clear,
And he get a good job at a thousand a year,
For he's keeping us safe till the War will be o'er
From the cruel barbarian from Germany's shore.

Healy naturally paid no attention to my scurrilous rhymes: to the questions of hecklers why he was not himself in Flanders, he replied that he would prefer to be at the Front, but the authorities needed him as a speaker, and he had to do as he was told.

Maurice Healy was after some months sent to the Front, where he served with considerable distinction; but in the feverish atmosphere of wartime Ireland, where charges and counter-charges were bandied with complete recklessness and each side believed the other to be committing an unpardonable crime against the country, such injustice was not uncommon. After the War Healy decided not to return to an Ireland in which Sinn Féin was supreme: he was called to the English Bar, where he enjoyed a flourishing practice until his death in 1946.

Of my more serious verses I have mostly lost trace. One has survived with the title 'In Winter Twilights'. It seems to me to express not too inadequately the sentiment which lay behind the Movement:

In winter twilights
Under the rain
Christ is walking
By moor and plain.

*From East and South
They have driven Him forth;
He finds no home
In the bitter North;

But here in the West,
When day grows dim,
A faithful people
Is waiting Him.

A candle is set
In every home
To shed its light
If the Christ should come,

And none dares turn
The poor away,
For Christ on earth
Was poor as they.

And if He comes,
What should He find
But the drip of the rain
And the winter wind,

And the love of the poor
Before Him spread,
And the earth made rich
With the sainted dead.

In winter twilights
By moor and plain
In holy Ireland
Christ walks again.*

★ ★ ★

The Armistice with Germany was proclaimed.
On that evening I happened to go through the city. The

people were in a strange mood – glad that the War was over, anxious what the peace might bring to Ireland. Only a few of the Unionists had hung out flags; there was no exultation in the streets. Everyone knew that dark days awaited us.

As I passed by the Mansion House, I saw a small crowd before it. I went towards the steps on which the speaker was standing; as I approached, I heard him say 'Today the Great War has ended, but our War is only beginning.' His hearers were silent; his words had only expressed what all were feeling in their hearts. The men of 1916 had led us on a road on which there was no turning back.

At the election of December 1918 seventy-three Sinn Féiners were returned, of whom thirty-seven were in prison. The remainder at a meeting in Dublin of Dáil Éireann, the Irish Parliament, formally ratified the declaration of a republic made on Easter Monday 1916. It also passed a democratic constitution and an appeal to the nations of the world; a provisional government was formed, and a deputation sent to the Peace Conference.

None of the Sinn Féin leaders of course expected seriously that any of the Great Powers would let themselves be distracted from their manoeuvres for the leading place in the councils of the world in order to play the role of a guardian angel to Ireland; but the tradition of American friendship was strong among the people, and it would have been criminal to neglect even the slenderest chance of reaching our goal by peaceful means. There were some who genuinely believed that President Wilson would apply the principle of the self-determination of small nations to Ireland: in anticipation, his portrait by Sargent was hung among those of our national heroes in the National Gallery.

All the more bitter was the disappointment of the optimists when the Irish delegates found every door in Paris bolted and barred against them. No state would run the risk of offending a victorious Great Britain. It speedily became clear that the blessings of self-determination were reserved for Poles and Czechs, for Estonians, Letts and Lithuanians, and that none of the principles so loudly proclaimed by the victorious states would apply to Ireland or the other subject states of the British

Empire. If the Irish people desired its freedom, it must adopt other means to attain it.

Griffith's original plan had been based on the theory of passive resistance, and many of the measures adopted by the Provisional Government of the Republic would have well fitted into a campaign of non-violence. But, if it takes two to make a quarrel, it also takes two to avoid one, and a policy of passive resistance can only be logically carried out if the other side abides by the rules and equally abstains from the use of force. But the British Government, not unnaturally in the circumstances, so far from limiting itself to constitutional methods, had immediate recourse to more drastic measures: it declared Dáil Éireann illegal, as well as all other associations suspected of Sinn Féin sympathies. Public meetings were only allowed by permission of the police; even the weekly cattle-markets were often prohibited. The national press was seized and destroyed. Anyone who played a prominent role in the movement was in danger of arrest and deportation; members of the Dáil were permanently 'on the run'.

Against such methods it was clear that passive resistance had no hope of success. Consequently, in addition to and in defence of the numerous non-military institutions set up by Sinn Féin, it became necessary to train and equip more efficiently the already existing Irish Republican Army. And, as even the most indispensable arms could not be legally imported, methods of violence were of necessity employed almost from the first: rifles and revolvers were carried away from barracks or obtained by force or purchase from individual British soldiers, and dynamite was plundered from the quarries under Government supervision. It could not yet be said that we were in a state of war, but from the month of January 1919, when two policemen were shot in an attack on the quarry Soloheadbeg in the County Tipperary, it could even less be maintained that we were at peace.

In every case of the shooting of a police officer or Government servant by the Republican forces the local authorities were condemned to pay compensation from the rates; the dependants of those shot by the Government forces received no compensation, even when the murdered man was proved to have no connection with the national movement. The

Provisional Government issued an order prohibiting payments from the rates to the British authorities. As a reprisal, the Mayors of Cork and Limerick were murdered by the police; the Chief Secretary for Ireland, Sir Hamar Greenwood, told the House of Commons that they had been shot by extremists of their own party.

The chief activity of the IRA was directed against the members of the police force who were acting as spies in the anti-national interest. The people looked on them as traitors, their own comrades despised them. The demoralization in the Royal Irish Constabulary made rapid progress: some retired from the service, others established relations with the IRA. Most of them, in the hope of preserving their pension rights, confined themselves to the prosecution of lightless cyclists and the owners of straying cattle.

It was not long till their ranks were strengthened by 15,000 discharged British soldiers, whose only qualifications for keeping order were their years of experience at the Front: the khaki tunics which they wore at first over their black police trousers earned them the name of 'Black-and-Tans'. In order to prevent them from reoccupying the country barracks which the RIC had evacuated, three hundred and fifty of these were burned down in one night by the IRA. We were in open warfare.

In July 1920 a further contingent of sixteen hundred Auxiliary Police was sent to Ireland to assume the leadership of the Black-and-Tans. They were mostly young men with more education than the average soldier; many had been officers in the War, others had had experience in the colonies of the methods to be employed against rebellious tribes. They had received from the Chief Secretary for Ireland the order to break the national movement by force and the promise that the Government would under no circumstances let them down. They made full use of their privileges.

In the greater part of Ireland there existed a reign of terror such as Western Europe had not seen for centuries. The life of no man suspected of sympathizing with Sinn Féin was safe: even the peasants in the fields were in danger when the Black-and-Tans passed by. The creameries to which the farmers delivered their milk and which were essential to the economic life of the country were systematically burned down. The hosiery factories in Balbriggan were similarly burned by the police. Masked policemen burned down the main public buildings in Cork: Greenwood announced that the incendiarism was the work of the Sinn Féiners themselves.

It is obvious that, if the British Government had been prepared to use its force ruthlessly, it could have broken the movement in a short space of time: it would have been as impossible for us to resist as it was for Czechoslovakia in 1938 to resist Hitler or for the Baltic States in 1939 to resist Stalin. All that was necessary was to proclaim martial law for the whole of Ireland, to suspend all constitutional guarantees of the liberty of the subject and to declare the law courts incompetent to deal with any offences committed by the forces of occupation. Such was in fact the policy advocated on military grounds by Sir Henry Wilson as Chief of Staff of the British Army.

But the British Government was unable to determine its policy on purely military grounds; it had to pay regard to public opinion in America and elsewhere. The only justification of its policy in the past, of its continual denial to Ireland of self-government down to the shooting of the national leaders in 1916, had been the theory that an Irish nation did not exist and that Ireland was no more than an English province. The fiction had been assiduously maintained that the better elements in Irish life were hostile to the national movement, which according to the English official theory was kept alive by professional agitators in the pay of whatever state happened at the moment to be hostile to Great Britain. Therefore it must be presumed that such a criminal conspiracy could be put down by the methods of the ordinary law, whereas, if it was necessary to abolish civil law and the constitutional guarantees of the liberty of the individual, the inference must inevitably be drawn, as Lloyd George well understood, that the movement, so far from being a mere criminal conspiracy, was a nation-wide struggle for independence such as Great Britain itself had done so much to foster in the nationalities subject to the Russian and Austrian Empires.

For political reasons, therefore, the British Government permitted the functioning of the law courts and the presence of representatives of the international press in Ireland. Though the activities of both were restricted, they still continued to play an important part in influencing public opinion both in and outside the country. In consequence, both sides endeavoured to make the best use of them for propagandist purposes.

The propagandist efforts of the British forces were not always happy. It is true that they had much to contend against, for in a fight between David and Goliath the sympathies of the on-looker will always tend to be on the side of David. But, even after making all due allowances for the difficulties of their position, they frequently showed a surprising ineptitude. Thus, an English illustrated paper published photographs of members of the IRA butchering wounded British soldiers after an ambush in County Kerry. It was in itself a remarkable fact that the assassins had so obligingly consented to pose for the photographer, but the authorities had presumably a low opinion of the intelligence of the British reader. Unfortunately, a few days later the Director of Sinn Féin publicity was able to show to the assembled representatives of the international press the landscape which formed the background to the photos: it was not in Kerry, but in Killiney some ten miles from Dublin where no ambush was ever suggested to have taken place. The question of who had posed as the IRA assassins was left to the journalists to conjecture.

Meanwhile the British Government began to be seriously disquieted at the increasing interest taken by American public opinion in the Irish war. Leading Americans of Irish descent formed a White Cross Commission for the purpose of relieving distress in Ireland and at the same time of obtaining first-hand information from the scene of action. Lloyd George and Greenwood understood that mere denials coupled with assurances that all outrages had been committed by the Sinn Féiners themselves against their fellow-countrymen were powerless to conceal the truth. The British forces were ordered to redouble their efforts to break our last resistance.

A fresh wave of terrorism swept over the land. Members of the RIC who had resigned rather than take part in atrocities were tracked down and murdered. Even the clergy came under suspicion. The possession of a photograph of the Pope was considered an incriminating circumstance; the officers who commanded the midnight raids declared His Holiness to be 'disloyal'. Masked police broke by night into the palace of the Bishop of Limerick: the Bishop had received a warning and was gone. The White Cross Commission had invited a young priest Father Griffin to give evidence on the occurrences in his parish: he failed to present himself at the sitting, and three days later his body was found in a bog with a revolver-shot through the head. The sixty-year-old Canon Magner was shot dead on the public road by a young English officer.

Such outrages had an incalculable effect on the opinion of the man in the street in Ireland. At the beginning of the campaign there had been many who, while fully sympathizing with the National cause, yet regarded with misgiving the methods employed by the IRA. It was natural enough: while all but the most extreme pacifists are prepared to excuse the taking of human life if it is taken by men in uniform fighting for a just cause according to the recognized rules of warfare, it was more difficult in those days when 'partisans' had not yet received the official approval of the Allied authorities to justify the shooting of an enemy by one who wore no uniform. Many had overlooked the fact that the wearing of a uniform was in itself an offence involving the death penalty, whereas those who did not wear it were shot with or without trial or killed 'while attempting to escape' – a practice which continued until two British officers had been executed as a reprisal for the hanging of two IRA prisoners in Cork jail. (It may be of passing interest to note that twenty-five years later the same action was taken under similar circumstances in Palestine by Irgun Zwai Leumi.)

But after the intensification of the Black-and-Tan terrorism in the autumn of 1920 there was no longer room for misgivings: the people were united as never before in their history. It realized that we were engaged in a struggle for life or death, and that those who served the enemy deserved their fate.

★ ★ ★

On a Sunday morning in November 1920 I had gone to eight o'clock Mass. As I was returning to my flat in Fitzwilliam

Square a little before nine, I found some thirty people assembled before a house on the same side of the Square. I asked an acquaintance what had happened.

'Haven't you heard?' he said. 'They've just shot an English spy here. I expect he's not the only one.'

He was right: it was not long before we heard that there had been shooting in Baggot Street, Morehampton Road, Upper and Lower Mount Street, Earlsfort Terrace, in all the better-class districts. At midday special editions of the Sunday papers were issued: fourteen officers had been shot in the city and suburbs and five wounded. It was officially admitted that the harmless-looking engineers and writers who had been peacefully practising their professions in Dublin apartments had belonged to the Information Service of the British forces. A few days later they were buried with full military honours.

All that Sunday armoured cars patrolled the streets. The other agents, whose hour had not yet come, were taken into Dublin Castle. Small groups stood at the street corners and asked themselves what would be the next move; at the coming of a military car they sprang asunder and ran for shelter. Certain streets were cut off, their inhabitants held up, searched, often beaten. A football match was being held at Croke Park in the afternoon: the ground was surrounded by military and police, and machine-guns turned on the spectators. There were twelve dead, over sixty wounded. Even in the night there was no peace, the armoured cars thundered through the streets until dawn. Many prisoners were brought to the Castle: some were shot in the early morning hours – 'while attempting to escape', as the official report announced.

The police had found a list of the members of the Dublin Brigade of the IRA. As it believed that the Brigade was responsible for the shootings, it arrested every member on whom it could lay its hands. They were examined, threatened, sometimes tortured, but none betrayed his comrades. In the end the Chief Secretary for Ireland decided to bring to trial before a court-martial all those against whom evidence could be procured. Sinn Féin had long enough been using the law courts as vehicles of propaganda: now there was an opportunity for the British authorities to employ them for counter-propaganda.

The prisoners were tried in batches of three or four. At the first trial I was briefed to defend one. With colleagues engaged on the other cases, I made my way to Dublin Castle.

The Castle had all the appearance of a beleaguered fortress. When the sentry had admitted us through a side-door and searched us for concealed weapons, we had to thread our way through a series of barbed wire entanglements before reaching the slope of the Lower Castle Yard. The Yard was full of police and soldiers; it was their only exercise-ground, as they could never leave the precincts except on an occasional punitive expedition. We passed under an arch into the Upper Castle Yard, which had been laid out in makeshift tennis-courts for the officers. My solicitor Michael Noyk pointed out in a corner of the Yard the notorious 'News Room', in which prisoners were tortured. He was Jewish by descent and religion, but no-one could have served the Irish cause with greater courage and devotion.

We went on to the City Hall, where the court-martial was to be held. On three sides of a long table sat five officers of ranks varying from general to lieutenant. With them sat a Judge Advocate, whose sole function was nominally to advise them on questions of law: in a case of such importance as the present one, the Judge Advocate General had been sent expressly from England. With him had arrived four Crown Counsels. These latter had been met at the landing-stage by an armoured car which carried them to the Castle: during their stay in Dublin they did not set foot outside the Yard until the armoured car stood ready to carry them back to the steamer. They were inclined to start at any sudden noise: one could see that only a strong sense of duty, a proportionate fee and the prospect of speedy promotion could have induced them to accept so perilous a task.

The back of the room was occupied by officers' wives and typists, whose knowledge of Ireland was limited to the wearisome life in Dublin Castle; it was a welcome distraction to them to look at the mysterious and terrible Sinn Féiners. They giggled and whispered to one another, but always with a cautious eye on the presiding General. From time to time an officer appeared through a door at the rear, glanced round the room, as if he wished to assure himself that everything was in order, and disappeared once more. His slender figure, the admirably cut uniform and the pale unhealthy face with the watery, red-rimmed eyes caught my attention: I asked Noyk, 'Do you know who he is?'

'That's Major T——,' he answered. 'He's the man who personally conducts the examinations in the News Room.'

'Judging by his appearance,' I said, 'it seems quite likely.'

'He's said to be of good family,' said Noyk. 'I don't know anything about his past career, but they say he takes morphia. But of course that may be an invention.'

The trial took its course. The prisoners were charged with the murder of Lieutenant Angliss of the Royal Inniskilling Fusiliers, who had been living in a flat in Lower Mount Street under the name of Mr McMahon. It was testified by another officer who had shared his room as well as by the servant-girl employed on the premises that a number of men had burst into the bedroom and shot the lieutenant; both, though with some hesitation, identified my client Teeling as one of their number. A few minutes later a body of police on the way from their barracks had heard firing and entered the house: in the garden they had found Teeling with a revolver in his hand, apparently waiting to cover the retreat of the others. One of the police had fired and wounded him; he had then been arrested.

It was a hopeless case to defend. All I could do was to attempt to make clear the point of view of the IRA by underlining the subjective justification of Teeling's act and the provocation which had brought it about. Accordingly, when 'Mr C.', who had shared Angliss' room, appeared as witness, I put the question to him whether he too had been in the employment of the British Government.

He admitted it without hesitation.

'In what capacity?'

Crown Counsel objected to the question, and the Judge Advocate ruled that it was inadmissible.

'Did you know anything of the activities of Lieutenant Angliss?'

'You need not answer that question,' intervened the Judge Advocate.

'Are you aware', I continued, 'that a number of persons have been arrested and sentenced as a result of his activities?'

But the patience of the Court was exhausted, and I was informed that no further cross-examination on those lines would be permitted. I sat down under protest: it was clear, if anyone had previously doubted it, that both the deceased man and the witness had been members of the Secret Service – not that the fact could have any influence on the result, but it was important for the judgment of the public.

Teeling was asked if he desired to make a statement. It was impossible not to admire the calm with which he replied, 'Well, gentlemen, I am going to tell you that these other people who have been arrested for this affair, I honestly swear, were not there at all and had nothing to do with it. I therefore don't like to see them suffer when wholly innocent. That's all I have to say.'

It was a remarkable exhibition of courage: unfortunately it did not leave me much to say when I was called upon to address the Court on his behalf. I suggested unconvincingly that he might have only accompanied the others in order to keep watch outside: the Judge Advocate replied correctly that, even if there had been evidence for my theory, he would still have been a member of a conspiracy to commit a felony and so according to English Law guilty of the murder committed. The Court withdrew to consider its decision. On its return it announced that one of the accused had been acquitted on all counts, the others were found not guilty of manslaughter, which meant that they had been convicted of murder. One of those found guilty was of course Teeling, who however did not undergo capital punishment, as a few days later he was rescued from Dublin Castle through the instrumentality of a bribed warder.

On the next day I appeared for two of the four IRA men charged with the shooting of a Captain Baggallay. Unlike Teeling, none of them had been arrested on the scene of the shooting; their defence was an alibi, of which it is not now of interest to give the details. Suffice it to say that in at least one of the cases it seemed to have been proved by highly respectable witnesses who could not be suspected of the slightest sympathy with Sinn Féin that the accused was far away from Baggallay's lodgings at the time of the shooting. It might have been expected that the Judge Advocate, whose sole function was to advise the Court on points of law, would display in his address at least an outward impartiality. Instead, he analyzed the evidence of the witnesses in a manner which even in a prosecuting counsel might have been considered excessively one-sided.

Some of the witnesses for the defence had seen the accused in church, but had not looked at their watches to fix the exact minute; their evidence was useless, as they might have mistaken the time. Others had happened to look at a clock; such an allegation was so clearly a proof of bad faith as to deprive their testimony of all value. It was as ingenious an application of the principle 'Heads I win, tails you lose,' as can ever have been heard in a court of law.

But the Judge Advocate's arguments did not seem to have convinced even himself, for he continued: 'Finally there is one thing which I must add. Although I have gone through the evidence of the witnesses for the defence in detail, this Court is not necessarily bound to do the same. One cannot overlook the fact that men who are capable of committing so atrocious a crime are also capable of inducing their friends to commit perjury on their behalf. It is open to the Court to come to the conclusion that such evidence can have no weight against that of the witnesses called by the Crown, who have no object in coming before this Court except to tell the truth.'

It was too much to let pass without protest: as soon as an opportunity offered itself, I rose to my feet. 'I wish to refer', I said, 'to certain observations made by the Judge Advocate. He informed the Court that it was not necessary to consider the evidence for the defence, because men who were capable of committing such a crime were also capable of suborning their friends to commit perjury on their behalf. In other words, you are asked to assume that the accused are guilty and that in consequence it is a matter of indifference what evidence may be given in their favour. I wish to protest as strongly as I can against such an assumption. It amounts to poisoning the wells of justice at their source. If you are to accept that principle, these trials are a mere farce, and the accused might as well be condemned without a hearing.'

The Judge Advocate said nothing, and the Court looked at me in wooden silence: it would have been hard to say whether its members understood my protest or not.

My client was declared guilty of murder.

★ ★ ★

It was anything but a favourable omen for the next two prisoners who were brought to trial for the murder of a Lieutenant Ames in a house in Upper Mount Street. One of the two, Patrick Moran, was gravely compromised from the start by the fact that he was known to be a captain in the IRA. On the other hand, the evidence of identification was weak: an officer who had been called by the Crown admitted under cross-examination that he had only seen him from the upper window of a neighbouring house and could not swear to his identity. In addition, there was a considerable volume of apparently unimpeachable evidence that during a period which covered the shooting he had been seen three miles away in Blackrock. Two ex-soldiers swore to having met him at and after eight o'clock Mass; MacCabe, the Chairman of the Blackrock Town Commissioners, had seen him after the conclusion of Mass; he had then gone to breakfast, and towards 9.30 a tram conductor had issued him a ticket in his tram from Blackrock to Dublin.

The defence relied above all on the evidence of MacCabe, an ancient supporter of the Irish Parliamentary Party and a bitter opponent of Sinn Féin, who had made recruiting speeches for the British Army. To anyone familiar with Irish life and conditions it was inconceivable that he should perjure himself in order to save the member of an organization which he condemned as whole-heartedly as even the prosecution could have desired.

'How can you be so certain that it was Moran whom you saw?' Crown Counsel asked him. 'Did you know him before?'

'Yes,' said MacCabe, 'I knew him before.'

'How is it that you who profess to be opposed to the IRA

knew this young man who is admitted to have been one of its members?'

'I had often seen him in the shop where he is employed,' said MacCabe.

As I left the Castle with Charles Wyse Power, Moran's counsel, I asked him, 'What do you think of the prospects?'

'It's hard to say,' he replied. 'It all depends whether they pay any regard to the evidence. If they do, I think they are bound to acquit. Any judge would warn a jury that it could not possibly hold that there was no reasonable doubt. No-one listening to him in Court could possibly believe that MacCabe was lying. But the prosecution and the Judge Advocate seem to look on everyone in this country as implicated in a conspiracy to perjure themselves in favour of murderers.'

'I noticed that,' I remarked. 'Even the counsel engaged in the case were attacked by the prosecution because they spoke of the 'shooting' instead of the 'murder'. They don't seem to realize that there is any difference between a soldier of the IRA and a thug who cuts a woman's throat in a London slum.'

'So that', Wyse Power continued, 'it's impossible to know what they will do. All I can say is that, if they make any attempt to be fair, they must acquit Moran. A judge would direct a jury to bring in a verdict of 'not guilty'.'

But the Judge Advocate took a different view. In order to get over the difficulty presented by the obviously respectable alibi witnesses, he developed the theory tentatively suggested by the prosecution that the murderers had had at their disposal a high-powered car which enabled them, if not to be in two places at the same time, at least to approximate to that idea sufficiently for the purposes of his case: the fact that a constable stationed on the road over which the 'high-powered car' would have had to pass swore that none had in fact passed did not in the least disturb his theory. Moran was duly found guilty of murder and sentenced to death.

The Secret Government of the Irish Republic authorized Wyse Power and myself to put the cases of Moran and Whelan before such English circles as were in favour of a more moderate policy in Ireland. Teeling and two other prisoners had meanwhile escaped from Dublin Castle; we heard later that

Moran who at that time had not yet been brought to trial, had had the opportunity of joining in their flight, but had refused to do so on the ground that they would never condemn an innocent man.

We had not much confidence in the success of our mission, but there was a possibility that the civil authorities would not confirm the sentences of the military. A number of Conservative members of Parliament had founded a 'Peace with Ireland Council'; we asked the Secretary to put us in touch with any personalities likely to have influence with the Government. He agreed to do his best, but warned us that it was out of the question to expect any interference with the Supreme Command in Ireland. 'Another great difficulty', he added, 'is the Chief Secretary, who has made the suppression of the Sinn Féin movement a question of personal prestige. Four of his predecessors – Birrell, Duke, Short, Macpherson – have failed to solve the Irish problem. Lloyd George has given him full authority to break the movement by force. All will depend on him.'

It was not encouraging, but we were bound to try everything which could conceivably be of use. For three days we visited the various personages on the Secretary's list. All without exception received us with the greatest kindness – the Archbishop of Canterbury, Sir John Simon, the editor of *The Times* and many others, and assured us of their sympathy: to the direct question as to whether they could help us they gave evasive answers. Last of all we visited the Chief Secretary.

We were introduced to him by Joe Devlin, the Northern nationalist who had for many years represented Belfast in the Imperial Parliament. Devlin presented us formally. 'Mr Chief Secretary, these are the two barristers whom I spoke to you about – '

But, before he could complete the introduction or even mention MacCabe, who had accompanied us, Greenwood interrupted him jovially. 'Well, Joe,' he said, 'how is the world using you?'

He was a burly red-headed man with a loud laugh; it was easy to see that assumed geniality was one of his most valued weapons. In the present case its object was clear – firstly, to deprive the interview of the serious character which it might be expected to have when the lives of two men were at stake, and, secondly, to isolate us by a show of intimacy with Devlin which left it to be supposed that he, as a 'decent' Nationalist, was in his heart on the side of law and order and against Sinn Féin.

Devlin did not fall into the trap: he resumed the introduction in the most formal manner, stated that he personally had no connection with Sinn Féin, but that when two young Irishmen had been unjustly condemned to death it was his duty to help them regardless of party, and asked the Chief Secretary to hear our account of the cases as well as MacCabe's evidence. Wyse Power went in detail through the testimony given on behalf of Moran, emphasizing the unfair nature of the directions given to the Court by the Judge Advocate, I did the same on behalf of Whelan, MacCabe repeated what he had already told the Court of his meeting with Moran at the time of the shooting. When he had finished, Greenwood asked, 'Is that all, Joe?'

Devlin answered that he could add nothing further: we said goodbye and left the room. 'I hope you will be the first judge in my new Ireland, Mr Power,' said Greenwood politely, referring to the scheme of limited autonomy which Sinn Féin had rejected, and as we were on our way to the door he called after us, 'Mr MacCabe, I hope to see you in the future as a member of the Parliament of Southern Ireland!'

Shortly after our return to Dublin Moran and Whelan were hanged, together with six other young men. Wyse Power received a letter from Devlin telling him that after our departure he had not let the matter drop, but had visited Lloyd George personally to plead the cause of the condemned men: he had been met by the reply that the military authorities in Ireland had been given a free hand to deal with the rebellion and His Majesty's Government did not see its way to overrule their judgment.

The court-martial sat nearly every week to try members of the IRA. It would be hard to imagine a more heartbreaking task than that of defending them. If they had been arrested some days after the committal of the offence with which they were charged, one could at least attempt to prove an alibi; if they had been captured on the scene of action with weapons in their possession, there was nothing to be done. Most of them were young men between twenty and thirty years of age, some even younger; they came from all classes of the community – students, workmen, shop assistants, farm labourers, clerks. Without exception they stood their trials with dignity and courage. I often wondered whether it ever occurred to the officers forming the Court or to the Judge Advocate or the Crown Counsel that such heroism was only possible in men who were actuated by a pure spirit of self-sacrifice. But none of them ever showed by word or sign that they regarded their prisoners as anything but common criminals.

And yet it may have had more influence than we in Ireland dreamed – if not on the military, at least on their civil chiefs in London. Towards the end of the spring of 1921 a new phenomenon became visible: for the first time since the beginning of the conflict we heard of peace feelers from the English side. The Connaught Rangers in India mutinied as a protest against Black-and-Tan outrages in Ireland. The amazement and indignation in England knew no bounds: the man in the street could not believe that soldiers in the service of His Majesty the King could remain faithful to their own country. The leaders were shot, the others sentenced to long terms of imprisonment, but no-one could foresee how far the disaffection among the Irishmen in the British Army might extend in the future or what forms it might take. The mutiny was perhaps the most heroic action in the whole campaign; there can be no doubt that it had a decisive influence on the course of events. When the continued existence of the Irish regiments was at stake, it was worth while making a concession of principle even to the extent of negotiating with the criminal conspiracy of Sinn Féin.

The Australian Bishop Clune had made an attempt to mediate which had been wrecked by Lloyd George's insistence on the surrender of the arms of the IRA before a declaration of truce. Lord Derby was reported to have been a visitor in strict incognito to a prominent Southern Unionist. General Smuts made a tentative speech on the possibility of reconciling Ireland's national ideals with the British Commonwealth. King George in

Belfast gave expression to his regret at the sufferings of my 'my Irish people'. Eamon de Valera returned from the United States of America, where for a year and a half he had engaged in an oratorical campaign in favour of the Irish Republic and a million-dollar loan. He was arrested by an over-zealous policeman and released next day by order of the higher authorities.

Not all were treated with such regard by the English. In the last court-martial at which I appeared, I represented Seán MacEoin, the 'Blacksmith of Ballinalee', later Minister of Defence in the Government of the Republic of Ireland. MacEoin, a man of exceptional physical strength, who held the rank of general in the IRA, was responsible for the death of a District Inspector of the Royal Irish Constabulary, who had come with a large force of police to arrest him. He had escaped for the time being, but two months later he was arrested in the town of Mullingar, handcuffed and led away to the barracks: on the way, despite his manacles, he succeeded in knocking out four of his escort and escaping once more, and only after he had been wounded by a gunshot had it been possible finally to place him under lock and key.

When Noyk and I entered the City Hall, the officers had already taken their seats. Each of them had a loaded revolver lying ostentatiously on the table before him. Instead of the usual spectators, the benches in the back of the room were occupied by soldiers. It was evident that the military had got wind of the proposed rescue: I wondered if it would nevertheless be attempted. But the trial pursued its course without disturbance: the officers were able to lay aside their revolvers, unused.

Even in the matter-of-fact descriptions given by the witnesses for the prosecution MacEoin's fight against overwhelming odds assumed epic dimensions. More than one Auxiliary testified that he had fought chivalrously, making provision for the care of the wounded police and insisting that his men should treat their disarmed prisoners with the regard due to prisoners of war. MacEoin himself in his address to the Court claimed the treatment due to an officer who had been taken prisoner while fighting in defence of his native land. 'I have always acted in accordance with the usages of war,' he said. 'The acts committed by me and the officers under me could stand any test by an impartial tribunal. The prisoners who fell into my hands were treated in a fair way. The treatment I meted out to the Crown forces was different from what I received when wounded in Mullingar. As I was on my way to the barracks, I was beaten with rifles . . .' In view of the evidence of the Crown witnesses, even the members of the Court could scarcely doubt that he was telling the truth.

The Judge Advocate had been giving signs of growing dissatisfaction as the story of MacEoin's exploits was revealed to the Court: whether he feared that its members might hesitate to bring in a verdict of murder or whether his apprehension was directed to the effect on the public, it was clear that he was awaiting the occasion to re-establish the moral guilt of the accused man. At last the opportunity seemed to offer itself: a witness testified that after the wounding of the District Inspector, MacEoin had knelt down by his side and spoken to him before taking flight.

It was the evidence for which the Judge Advocate had been waiting: 'He was so conscious of his guilt', he told the Court, 'that he, the murderer, found himself impelled to ask his victim for forgiveness. If he had been the idealist it has been sought to depict him as, remorse for his crime would not have obliged him to excuse himself.'

'Mr Judge Advocate,' I interrupted him, 'I would like with all respect to call your attention to the fact that you have misunderstood the sense of MacEoin's behaviour. He did not excuse himself to the dying man; what he whispered in his ear was not an expression of remorse for his deed. We Catholics believe that there can be nothing so important to a dying man who is soon to stand before his Creator as repentance for the sins of his life. If he is no longer able to collect his thoughts, another speaks the words of repentance for him, and the dying man, who perhaps cannot even move his lips assents in his heart. That was the Act of Contrition, as it is called by Catholics, which MacEoin whispered to the District Inspector: he considered it so all-important that he did not hesitate for a moment to kneel by the dying man's side and to remain there till he was sure that he had understood his words – even though his own freedom, perhaps his life, was at stake.'

I do not know whether the Judge Advocate appreciated my explanation or not; he only said, 'Very interesting!' in an annoyed voice. Three days later MacEoin was sentenced to death.

But there was a feeling of peace in the air. As a preliminary to negotiations, rumours were circulated that Ireland would be starved out by economic blockade or reduced to submission by the occupation of all railways, post offices and other public buildings by British troops. But at the same time the worst outrages gradually ceased. Blocks of houses were no longer blown up by the military and few creameries burned by the police. Emissaries of the British Government sought contact daily with the Sinn Féin leaders.

We heard that negotiations for a truce were taking place. The political prisoners were to be released – even those condemned to death. The military authorities insisted on their right to hang MacEoin. Sinn Féin rejected the proposal. The offer was repeated – this time with no exception. Sinn Féin accepted it. At twelve o'clock on the 11th of July 1921 hostilities between England and Ireland were suspended. There were some who believed that we were at the end of our troubles.

★ ★ ★

Sinn Féin activities were of course not confined to fighting the British forces. Its aim had always been to set up, so far as the circumstances permitted, a counter-government, and the institution which had most success and enjoyed most popularity was that of the Republican Courts of Law. Sinn Féin set up these with lay judges, assisted in complicated cases by qualified lawyers, whose duty it was to decide on the causes brought before them in the light of commonsense and natural justice. In the majority of cases the courts functioned admirably, and, above all, they could, unlike the British courts, rely on their decrees being carried out.

I have always been glad to remember that I was the first barrister to appear in the Republican Courts. Most of the sittings were held in school-houses or deserted dwellings or presbyteries, but occasionally they achieved a certain picturesqueness. I remember in particular a session of the District Court in a Western county which would have done honour to any stage director.

A colleague at the Bar and I had received briefs in a number of claims made by the tenants and farm labourers against one of the large landlords in the district. We had been mysteriously informed that in order to avoid observation it would be wise to leave the train at a wayside station instead of continuing our journey to the county town. When we emerged from the platform on to the bog-road, we found awaiting us a pre-War Ford car with a driver who saluted us in military fashion and asked us to take our seats.

'Where are we going?' we asked.

But he shook his head with an important air and did not answer, and we made no further inquiries. The car threaded its way through a number of bye-roads and lanes for some fifteen or twenty miles; finally we came to a halt by the side of a hawthorn and privet hedge which a man with a shears was in the act of clipping. As we approached, he laid down his shears and in his turn gave a military salute.

'All clear, Tom?' asked the driver.

'All clear!' replied the man with the shears.

We turned in through a gap in the hedge and drove over a couple of fields; there had been rain some little time before, and the tyres squelched through the mud, but everyone in Ireland knew that Ford cars could be relied on better than any others for cross-country journeys. After crossing the fields we came out on a gravel-covered avenue meandering between ornamental bushes. From behind a rhododendron a man popped up with a bandolier over his shoulder. He too saluted and announced, 'All clear!' It was highly reassuring, and we began to feel that instead of two commonplace barristers come down with the prosaic intention of earning our fees we were playing some romantic role in a patriotic drama.

The Ford turned a corner of the avenue and halted on a broad gravel sweep. Before us stood a typical Irish country house of the eighteenth century. Three broad granite steps led up to a hall-door surmounted by a wrought-iron fanlight. The building itself was overgrown with ivy and Virginia creeper. At the other side of the gravel sweep was a grass lawn: here and there its surface was dotted with small formal flower-beds now nearly trampled out of recognition. The lawn was furrowed by the tracks of heavy motors.

The driver got out of the car and rapped on the hall-door. Immediately it was opened, and a man with a rifle beckoned us to enter. 'I'll wait for you here,' said the driver. We went in, and the door closed behind us. We found ourselves in an enormous bare hall two storeys high; the windows on the ground floor were nailed over with boards, and the only light came from those in the second storey. The ceiling over our heads was badly damaged: much of the plaster had dropped to the floor, but some of the portions that remained were painted pink and white with the figures of buxom eighteenth-century nymphs and shepherdesses. A flight of steps led up to a gallery supported by pillars of imitation marble: the gallery ran all along the rear of the hall.

On the floor of the hall stood at regular intervals plaster casts of Roman emperors and the gods and goddesses of Olympus. Many had lost their heads or arms: nearly all showed traces of burning at some date in the near past. The missing parts lay on the wooden floor where they had fallen or been kicked into a corner. It was clear that an ancestor of the present owner, whoever he might be, had like so many of the Irish gentry in the days of Grattan made the Grand Tour on the continent of Europe, whence he had returned with a cargo of statuary for his country house.

I wondered what else he had brought with him – probably half a dozen landscapes by Canaletto, I thought, of which one might possibly be genuine. And, no doubt, some models in alabaster – St Peter's, for instance, or, if that had been too popish for his taste, the Leaning Tower of Pisa. And almost certainly there had been some Dresden china – not the product of Augustus the Strong's Royal Porcelain Manufacture in Meissen, but the imitations made at a later date by some small firm in Dresden which abound in all Irish country houses. Yes, almost certainly the original furniture had been cleared away into a lumber-room or sold, unless the owner's grandfather had been possessed of singularly good taste for a man of his time –

and I did not think that probable, since he had not thrown out those monstrous plaster casts.

But now I would never know, for he had obviously removed all his furniture at the first hint of approaching danger, and had stored it in Dublin pending the return of better times or even sent it to England to create a new home for himself among people who could be trusted not to indulge in guerrilla warfare. And I did not believe that he would ever restore the house as it had been before, because the cost of restoration would be prohibitive and because we were there in the name of the Irish Republic to hear the claims of his neighbours to his lands and thereby to make the old life which his ancestors had enjoyed before him impossible for him in the future. It was right that we should do so, and that he should be driven out of his position of privilege, because he was no economic asset to the community and contributed nothing to the material well-being of his neighbours, but I could not help being sorry, because the strangeness of the surroundings had lent a grotesque pathos even to the plaster casts and because once an Irish nobleman had taken pride in them and set them up as monuments of culture in a cultureless land.

In the centre of the great hall was a long deal table looking like a kitchen table, and around it deal chairs which were evidently kitchen chairs: either the cost of transport had been greater than their value, or they had been left for the use of some caretaker. Now they were occupied by the Republican Judge, who in private life was the village schoolmaster, and valuers and auctioneers; the Republican police with rifles and bandoliers stood around the walls, and the litigants and witnesses strolled about among the statues, and smoked their pipes and cigarettes and from time to time spat furtively on the floor. My colleague and I took the places reserved for us at the table: we were no less essential a part of the picture than the others. The clerk to the Court rapped on the table for silence. Pipes were knocked out, and cigarette-ends trampled under heel.

'In the name of the Irish Republic . . .'

We were silent, as some four hours later we clattered once more over the country roads to the station. Only in the train that carried us to Dublin did my colleague comment on what lay behind us. 'Today for the first time,' he remarked, 'I see clearly that an era is over and another is dawning. All day long I have been trying to find a suitable symbol for the change, but I only succeeded a few minutes before we left, when I saw our friend Jimmy MacGovern striking a match on the backside of the Apollo Belvedere.'

'I quite admit', I answered, 'that Jimmy MacGovern and his match symbolize the Ireland of the future as many would like to see it. But it doesn't follow that no other Ireland is possible. It's up to us, people like you and me, who pose with a certain amount of justification as men of culture, to see that our ideas prevail against Jimmy MacGovern's. And in any case you can't suggest that Lord Glenkerry's plaster Apollo is the symbol of the future Ireland as we would like to see it.'

'Can't you forget Lord Glenkerry and the plaster and concentrate on the Apollo?' asked my colleague, whom I will call Liam because it is not his name and he will thus be spared all responsibility for the opinions which he held a generation ago. 'The old Anglo-Irish aristocracy of the eighteenth century had a tradition of culture and an ideal of beauty. We are now engaged, you and I and the whole lot of us, in destroying that tradition because it comes from England. It may be right or wrong to destroy it, that is not the question, because, right or wrong, it is inevitable, but I often ask myself what we're going to put in its place. Or are we going to hand over Ireland to the Jimmy MacGoverns with their red faces and codfish eyes?'

'To quote your own words,' I said, 'can't you forget the red face and the codfish eyes and think of Jimmy MacGovern as a man made in God's image as surely as Lord Glenkerry – or at least as the representative of a tradition which is not that of the Anglo-Irish eighteenth century? When he makes use of the Apollo Belvedere as a matchbox, you only see a proof of his blindness to things of the spirit, whereas I prefer to look on it as a deliberate gesture of emancipation from a tradition which is not his own and which has struck no root in the hearts of the Irish people.'

'There may be something in what you say,' Liam admitted. 'In fact, I noticed a sort of shamefaced defiance in his manner which makes me think you're possibly right. But that doesn't get us any further. Emancipation is always negative. It only becomes positive when you know what you're going to do with your newly won freedom. It's all very well to talk about the time when "them that are down will be up and them that are up will be down, and we all change places at the Risin' of the Moon", but it doesn't seem to me to be worth fighting only so that A may take the place of B and B the place of A, unless A can achieve something outside the capacities of B. Have you any idea yourself what we're going to do with our freedom, when we get it?'

'Good God!' I exclaimed. 'Here we are in the middle of a struggle for our national existence, and you sit there and tell me seriously that freedom is a negative thing and ask me what we're going to do with it!'

'The fact that we're in the middle of the fight is the very reason', he pointed out, 'why we ought to know what we're fighting for. When the fight is over, it will be too late. Up to the present we have had something of English culture in Ireland — apart from English culture we have had none at all. We are hoping to liberate ourselves politically from England: does that mean that we want equally to liberate ourselves from English culture?'

'Obviously,' I said. 'If we have no culture of our own, we are not a nation. If our only culture is English culture, we are English, however independent we may be politically.'

'You may be right,' said Liam, 'though personally I'm inclined to think there's an enormous amount that could be said on the other side. But for the moment I'd only like to ask you one question. If we succeed in eradicating English culture, what do you propose that we should put in its place? Can we improvise a new tradition and a new culture on the spur of the moment? And, if so, what source are we going to draw on for the material? Or are we to leave the intellectual development of the country to Jimmy MacGovern and his friends?'

'We must return to the Gaelic tradition,' I said.

He smiled. 'We've been hearing that for so many years,' he complained, 'and I don't see that anyone has returned yet. As a matter of fact, I'm never sure what the Gaelic tradition is. Have you yourself returned to it?'

I shrugged my shoulders and spread out my hands in deprecation. 'Well you see, the life of a busy lawyer doesn't seem to give much opportunity. But my own imperfections don't mean that I'm not right – '

'Precept rather than example?'

'Precisely. I admit that it has nearly died out, but I believe that it still exists and that it appeals to something in the Irish soul which has remained in spite of all outward anglicization. The seed is still there: the duty of any national government will be to enable it to grow. And, if the people shows the same determination in the fight for its soul as in the material fight, we will succeed in forming a new native culture from the ruins of the old Gaelic tradition.'

Liam smiled again. 'That would sound very well in an election speech,' he said, 'but it wouldn't stand a minute's cross-examination in the witness-box. You're like so many of the people who talk about Gaelic culture – you don't know what you mean by it. A mixture, I suppose, of the Abbey Theatre and a street trumpeter playing "Let Erin Remember" and a vague recollection of Fionn MacCumhaill and some of Yeats' earlier poems and the first volume of O'Growney's Irish Grammar?'

'You know me too well,' I said.

'You see, you can't deny it. And of course they're all excellent things in their way: I appreciate them as much as you do. But don't you think them rather meagre as a substitute for the whole of English culture?'

'Of course they are. But they won't remain for ever in the embryo stage. A Gaelic culture will develop like any other.'

'No doubt. But it will take time. And in the meantime what do you propose? Would you admit Shakespeare?'

'Logically, no,' I answered. 'After all, Shakespeare is the supreme representative of English culture. There can obviously be no place for him in a Gaelic state.'

'Yet he is read and acted all over the world without apparently denationalizing other countries.'

'That's different,' I said. 'They have Shakespeare in their own language, we would only have him in English.'

'I thought we'd come to that,' said Liam. 'Then, what you

really mean is that Ireland must become Gaelic-speaking and, so far as possible, forget English?'

'No,' I corrected him, 'not forget it, but keep it for commercial purposes only. Naturally our literature, will be written in Irish.'

'So that our literary men, if we have any, will have to starve or emigrate. Do you really think that it is so important for everyone to speak Irish?'

'I do. I think it's essential if we're to survive as a nation.'

'What do you mean by surviving as a nation?'

'Look here, Liam, I'm not in the witness-box,' I protested.

'There's no compulsion on you to answer. But I'd like to know what you mean.'

'You're quite right, but it's rather hard to explain. We're a small nation of three millions, and of those three millions the overwhelming majority are English-speaking. Only a few hours' distance by sea there are forty millions of English-speakers. On the other side of the Atlantic there are a hundred and twenty millions. Isn't it inevitable that in the course of time we must lose our individuality and become completely assimilated to them?'

'Dublin has been English-speaking for a number of centuries, yet I don't see that it has been so completely assimilated.'

'It was different a hundred years ago,' I pointed out. 'Irishmen only went to England on rare occasions, and then it was a serious journey. Now, it's only a couple of hours till you're in London. We have the English papers every morning at our breakfast-table and English books in our book-shops. In our cinemas we have no chance of seeing any films but in the English language. When the troubles are over, our hotels will be full of English tourists once more. How can we expect to hold out against such a continuous stream of propaganda? Surely, if we haven't a language as a natural bulwark, we are bound in time to succumb to English influence, to become English with a little local colour, just as the Scotch in spite of all their protestations are nothing more than English with a few picturesque local customs.'

'"*Gan teanga gan tír*"', he quoted. 'I know that's the orthodox Gaelic Leaguer's point of view, "no language no nation". But I've never understood why it should be so.

'It isn't mere independence,' said I. 'A language is far more. It is the defence which God has given to small nations so that they may preserve their individuality. It is the wall of insensibility which He has erected around them in order to protect them against the influences of the outside world. It is the weapon which He has given to the weak against the strong. Once it is lost, they are defenceless: the enemy has taken their first line fortification, and is free to direct his attack against the citadel.'

'You're not very hopeful. You seem to think that the Irish people are bound to be anglicized.'

'On the contrary, I believe firmly that they will find their way back to the Gaelic language and Gaelic civilization.'

'Why? Everything you've been saying and all that we can see around us is against it.'

I hesitated for an instant. 'I suppose', I said finally, 'that I'm really like those people who believe in the immortality of the soul because otherwise existence would lose all meaning to them. I believe that the Ireland of the future will be Gaelic, because otherwise the sacrifices of the last five hundred years would have been in vain and the history of Ireland would have lost all its meaning.'

'But that is a possibility,' said Liam.

'I refuse to admit it,' said I.

'A typically romantic and sentimental attitude. I would never have expected it of you.'

'Well,' I said, 'even if it is, I suppose I'm entitled to it as a private luxury, so long as I don't let it interfere with my profession.'

'It's the sort of luxury', said Liam, 'that might easily cost you a great deal in your career.'

'Perhaps,' I agreed. 'That's usually the way with luxuries. But I'm terribly obstinate.'

'There at least I can agree with you,' said Liam.

THREE

In Germany and France

The Armistice had been declared, and no-one doubted that we would come to a settlement with England. A republic, it is true, was out of the question, but Lloyd George was obviously prepared to grant us wide powers of self-government. We could make use of them first to create a national state and later to eliminate the last links which bound us to the British Empire.

I knew that few of my countrymen had any knowledge of or interest in foreign languages, and it occurred to me that here lay my most promising field of activity. I asked the Minister for External Affairs in the Provisional Government whether he would send me as Irish representative to Germany. He told me that there was already a political representative in Berlin, but that, if I wished, I could go there as trade representative. I jumped at the chance, and set out for Germany in November 1921.

The political representative – unaccredited to the German Government, as our status was not yet determined – was one John Chartres. As I had never heard his name in Ireland, I made inquiries about his previous career. I was informed that he had spent many years in the employment of the London *Times* and, incidentally, that he was married to the Italian novelist Annie Vivant, the friend of Gabriele D'Annunzio, but that she continued to live in Italy, meeting her husband for a week every year in Vienna.

There was nothing in this to qualify him as representative of the nascent Irish state, and I inquired further how he had got into touch with the Irish leaders. It appeared that he had been brought to the negotiations with the English in London by Erskine Childers, the son of an English Chancellor of the Exchequer, but Irish through his mother's family and conversion. Chartres' speciality was said to be constitutional law. De Valera, then 'President' of the non-existent Irish Republic, had sanctioned his presence at the negotiations as 'expert': there was no lack of Irish constitutional lawyers, but de Valera has always had greater respect for the capacities of the English. Not, indeed, that Chartres would have admitted to being English: he claimed descent from a County Cork family. I have since verified the accuracy of his claim: the name Chartres appears among the councillors of the town of Bandon at a time when no Irishman or Catholic was allowed to live within its walls.

Events, however, had not gone smoothly in the house in Hans Place where our delegates resided. An unbridgeable gulf had begun to open between those who were determined to put an end to the chaos and destruction in Ireland and those who would accept nothing less than the formal recognition by England of an Irish Republic. Chartres, needless to say, was, like Childers, on the side of the stern unbending Republicans. His convert's zeal had at last so irritated Arthur Griffith, the leader of the delegation and father of Sinn Féin, that it was decided to find a job for him in some quarter of the earth remote from Hans Place. Chartres mentioned that in his youth he had spent some time as student in a German university. Griffith at once sent him as 'envoy' to Berlin, where with his secretary he occupied a suite of rooms in the Eden Hotel.

I walked into the lounge of the Eden to keep our appointment. In an armchair, reading *The Times*, sat a middle-aged man with a monocle attached to a black ribbon, whom I would have taken for an English tourist if I had not known him to be the Irish Republican 'envoy'. I introduced myself.

'Trade representative?' said Chartres. 'Yes, yes! My friend Gavan Duffy wrote me that you would arrive here.'

He spoke with the throaty voice and Oxford accent of the English upper-middle class, while he surveyed me graciously through the monocle.

'I should like to make it plain', he went on, 'that our duties lie entirely apart. I have no connection with trade matters, and I hope you understand that you have no concern with political matters, which are my exclusive responsibility.'

I had not hoped for much assistance from him, but I found my reception slightly disconcerting. However I said meekly that I quite understood that our activities would henceforth lie in different spheres.

'I suppose you didn't see anything of our people in Hans Place?' asked Chartres.

'Oh, yes,' I answered. 'I lunched there every day during my stay in London.'

'Rather weak on the constitutional side,' said Chartres. 'But I daresay Childers will keep them straight.'

He made some further reference to his friendship with the Sinn Féin leaders, then dismissed me with a 'Well, I must be getting back to my duties. My secretary will see you out.'

As we walked towards the hotel door, I remarked, 'I suppose Mr Chartres speaks good German?'

Almost without embarrassment the secretary replied, 'Mr Chartres has a perfect knowledge of the German language, but he doesn't actually speak German.'

Chartres' linguistic deficiencies were, however, atoned for by a nationalism which can seldom have been equalled for fervour and ferocity. He was never tired of denouncing England's misdeeds, and let it be known that he was engaged on the composition of an important work on the British Empire, to which he had given the simple but eloquent title *Bloody England*. To the tourists from Ireland who visited Berlin he was fond of saying in his upper-class English accent that he would never consent to give his hand to an Englishman. As he must during his fifty years in England have shaken hands with members of the detested race on average at least four times a day, one could only admire the strength of character which had enabled him to dissemble his feelings for the greater part of a lifetime.

As there seemed little hope that our diplomatic representative would give me any assistance in the promotion of trade between Ireland and Germany, I next proceeded to a German-Irish Society which had been founded for propaganda purposes during the War. Outside the door of a flat in the Knesebeckstrasse, a cardboard notice indicated that here was the seat of the *Deutsche-Irische Gesellschaft*.

To my surprise, Mrs Grabisch, the lady who received me, was neither of German nor of Irish origin: she was in fact an

American named Bullitt from one of the Southern States, who had come to Berlin as a journalist and married a German. 'Yes,' she said in answer to my unspoken question, 'it *is* rather peculiar my being secretary, but there seemed to be no-one else. And of course I've always been tremendously interested in your fight against England. At the beginning of the War I was helping in the section of the German Foreign Office which deals with English affairs, and so I often used to meet poor Sir Roger. So then, when the German-Irish Society was founded, I wanted to do what I could to help.'

'It was very good of you,' said I. 'And what does the Society do now?'

'It doesn't,' replied Mrs Grabisch with a smile. 'It has never been dissolved, but it has scarcely met in the last two years – and of course there wouldn't be much for it to do, now the War is over. We were very active during the War: here is the review we brought out – ', and she showed me some green-bound magazines with the title *Irische Blätter* containing articles on Irish themes up to the Rebellion of 1916.

'Did the German public take much interest in Ireland?' I asked.

'They have always been interested in Ireland to a certain extent,' she said, 'and they were even more interested because of being at war with the English. And, when you meet Dr Chatterton Hill, he's certain to tell you how the strikers in a munitions factory went back to work after he had addressed them on the subject of English misgovernment in Ireland.'

'Is that so?' I said politely.

'Well, I'm not in a position to contradict him – and he's certainly a very clever man. He and Mr St John Gaffney went to represent Ireland at the Socialist Conference at Stockholm during the War.'

'I saw that in the papers. But they weren't very successful, were they?'

'No, but they couldn't expect to be successful. All the Socialists were for England and against Germany. It was good propaganda, though.'

I thought it well to return to the object of my visit. 'Do you think', I inquired, 'that Dr Chatterton Hill could be of any help in promoting trade relations?'

'He might be,' said Mrs Grabisch in a voice completely devoid of conviction.

'What about Gaffney?'

'He lives in Bavaria writing books about how he retired from being American consul on conscientious grounds when America declared war on Germany. The first one was called *Breaking the Silence* – which seemed rather queer, because no-one believed that Gaffney had ever been silent. His spare time he spends visiting the Kaiser in Doorn.'

'Is there any other member of the German-Irish Society living in Berlin?' I asked.

'Well, there's Professor Pokorny.'

I well knew Julius Pokorny, the Viennese professor of Celtic languages in the Berlin University, by repute; he was of international fame and enjoyed considerable popularity among Irish students. Incidentally he had published a pamphlet proving that the Irish race was ethnically akin to the Eskimos, and had been much impressed on his visits to Ireland by the frequent recurrence of the Eskimo type among the fishermen on our western seaboard.

'I don't suppose he has much influence in industrial circles,' I said.

'I don't suppose he has,' assented Mrs Grabisch.

'And there's no-one else,' she echoed.

So with regret I concluded that the *Deutsche-Irische Gesellschaft* could be of no practical assistance to me in the task of building up trade relations. I took a small office in the Joachimstalerstrasse in Western Berlin, engaged a typist, and studied the German language in the many hours left free by my official duties.

Before setting out for Ireland in a German submarine in the days before Easter 1916, Sir Roger Casement had attempted to form an Irish brigade from the prisoners-of-war of Irish origin in the German camps. The object of the brigade was to be the liberation of Ireland from British rule after German troops had landed in Ireland.

Casement's brigade had not met with the same success as the Czech Legion, the majority of the Irish prisoners having replied to his invitation with the frigid intimation that, though

Irishmen, they had also the honour of being members of His Majesty's Army. It seemed to me a fine dramatic gesture, but too theatrical to be convincing. Accordingly, I made it my business to get into touch with the ex-members of the brigade who still remained in Germany.

One of them, whom I will call Michael Dempsey, was employed as porter in a house in the Handjery Strasse in the Berlin working-class district of Neukölln: he had married a German and had a family. When he heard of my presence in Berlin, he invited me to afternoon coffee in his porter's lodge; it was easy to see that he welcomed the opportunity of confiding in someone who could understand his language and his point of view. I asked him how it was that only a small proportion of the Irish prisoners had joined the brigade.

'They made a balls of the whole thing,' he said. 'They didn't know how to go about it rightly. Poor Casement – God rest his soul! – didn't understand the Irish soldiers, and I needn't tell you the Germans knew damn all about us. The first time he come to our camp, I gave in my name – not because I wanted better grub, but because I wanted to fight for Ireland. But I soon saw that the others that gave in their names were nearly all the greatest blackguards in the camp. They did it for the grub – nothing else. The better class of soldiers wouldn't join the brigade when they saw the class that was joining up. I'd have left myself, only it meant making a bloody show of myself.'

'What could they have done?' I asked.

'What could they have done?' he echoed. 'That's easy, man! They should have chosen their man out of the prisoners – Monteith would have been the best, the same as went over to Ireland with Casement. He'd have got the right men to join and let the rest go to hell! Monteith would have arranged it all right, but it seems it wasn't to be.'

He sighed and took a sip of his coffee. 'What happened to you after Easter Week?' I asked.

'We was sent out to a number of camps all over the country. They had forgotten all about us. We had our uniforms all right, but there was no discipline. We was always having rows. The grub wasn't any too good, and of course we got no parcels from home. You should have heard them chaps cursing! The

Germans treated us well, but they had enough to do looking after themselves. In the end I got fed up. I asked for permission to work as a civvy; I'm a smith by trade, you know. They sent me off to East Prussia, I was working in a village there. I can tell you I was only too glad to get shut of the rest of them.'

'What did you do after the Armistice?' I inquired.

'We all had to come back to Berlin – myself with the wife and kids. At first we thought they'd hand us over to the English, but they didn't do that. Some went to them themselves and asked for a free passage to Ireland. I heard tell that one of them, Quinlisk, was shot by the IRA as a spy.'

'That's right,' I said. 'It was in all the papers. In the County Cork it was they shot him.'

'Poor devil! He was one of the first to join us. He wasn't a bad chap, but he always wanted to show himself off, you see, and anything he got, it slipped through his fingers. God have mercy on him!'

'What did you do yourself?'

'I was in the German Army for a bit. When I was on night sentry duty and the women came and bothered me, I used to curse them in Irish. I could hear them say, "That's a Polack!" I got great sport out of it, I can tell you. But it didn't last long, because German soldiers have to be German, you see. Then one of the gentlemen that had to do with the Irish prisoners got me a job. So between one thing and another I'm here now. But I have a side-line as well.'

He looked knowingly at me. 'What's that?' I asked dutifully.

He got up, opened the door of a cupboard and pointed to a blue uniform with a red collar hanging from a peg. 'Do you see that?' he asked proudly. 'It's the uniform of my fourth army' – he counted them on his fingers – 'the British Army, the Irish brigade, the German Army, and now the Salvation Army. I play the French horn in the band three times a week in the streets around here. They don't pay me much, but I get a lot of sport out of it.'

★ ★ ★

In the first flush of enthusiasm after the signing of the Armistice with England, a World Congress of the Irish Race had been planned. The scene of its deliberations was to be Paris, its aim the demonstration of Irish unity. But before the date of the Congress conditions had changed, and the die-hard Volunteers with the approbation of de Valera were arming themselves for war against the new Irish Government. However the invitations had been sent out and could not be withdrawn without admitting in the face of the world that the hour of our liberation had found us more disunited than ever in the course of our history. I obtained permission to attend the Congress as representative of the Irish citizens resident in Germany.

Its chief organizer was an Irish-American named Thomas Hughes Kelly, its secretary a Canadian journalist of Irish descent called Katherine Hughes. Neither had ever spent more than a few weeks in Ireland; both were enthusiastic supporters of de Valera and opponents of the proposed treaty with England. De Valera and the more prominent members of the minority had without exception communicated their intention of taking part in the proceedings; the Government party was to be represented by the mild Professor Eoin MacNeill, as Griffith and Collins, the natural exponents of the majority programme, were compelled to stay in Dublin and devote themselves to the ungrateful task of getting the new Government on its feet.

Paris was at its gayest; the flower-beds on the Place de la Concorde sparkled joyously in the sun, children raced after coloured balloons in the gardens of the Luxembourg, and around the Café de la Paix the sellers of pornographic postcards hoped to do business with such obvious provincials as the delegates from the Island of Saints and Scholars. But our Congress was not in a mood for gaiety or pornography: the ideas of Free Staters and Republicans alike were directed only to the one end – victory over their opponents in the Congress.

On the evening before its opening, the delegates met in a hall of the Grand Hotel. A friend introduced me to the Countess Markievicz as 'the delegate from Germany'. I was delighted to meet so famous a figure as the Countess who had commanded in Stephen's Green during the Rebellion, whom Yeats had described in one of his most celebrated poems:

That woman's days were spent
In ignorant good-will,
Her nights in argument,
Until her voice grew shrill.
What voice more sweet than hers
When young and beautiful,
She rode to harriers?

The expectations I had formed from the poem were not disappointed: true to type, the Countess, who took me for a German, plunged at once *in medias res*.

'*Vous savez quelque chose de notre guerre?*' she asked me.

I decided to humour her. '*Mais oui, madame,*' I replied. '*J'ai entendu bien des histoires sur les exploits épiques de votre fameux hero Michael Collins.*'

The Countess's face darkened. '*Michael Collins a fait rien du tout!*' she exclaimed. '*Rien du tout!*'

The bystanders were beginning to laugh, so I thought it better to break off the conversation. Two days later, when it fell to me to address the Congress, I saw the Countess in the front row. I had not spoken ten words before she rose up in outraged majesty and left the Congress hall.

The Congress opened in the Hotel Continental under the honorary presidency of the Duke of Tetuan, as head of the historic family of O'Donnell. He took but little part in the proceedings, as he understood neither Irish nor English, but with a stoutness of heart worthy of his lineage he was present at nearly every sitting, smoking one cigar after another and restoring his energies from time to time by a brief nap. I never heard what impressions he formed of the countrymen of his ancestors.

The resolutions before the Congress were (in the circumstances, inevitably) highflown and general – which did not prevent the speakers on each side from delivering tirades with the object of proving that their party also could claim to embody Ireland's secular traditions. Miss Mary MacSwiney, in particular, the sister of Terence MacSwiney, the Mayor of Cork who had died after seventy-four days hunger-strike in Brixton Gaol, made a speech which lasted three hours on Ireland's right to freedom and the impossibility of restricting her independence by a treaty dictated by weakness and cowardice.

Her arguments, though completely out of touch with the realities, were lucid, logical and well-delivered; her obvious sincerity and depth of feeling made a powerful impression. One could see that for her it was genuinely a matter of life and death for the nation: however widely my views might differ from hers, I could not help admiring her passionate earnestness. I made a remark in this sense to my neighbour, but he only answered, 'It's easy to see you're listening to her for the first time. If you'd heard those arguments as often as I have, you'd have something else to say about them!' He was right: next day Miss MacSwiney made practically the same speech. After the first half-hour Osmonde Esmonde whispered to me, 'We've heard that before. What about adjourning for a drink?'

We found seats in the bar; a group of press photographers called across the room, 'How long will it last?'

'Only a few hours more,' said Esmonde consolingly. The photographers groaned and ordered another round of whiskeys-and-soda.

'Have you seen them taking the groups for the morning papers?' Esmonde asked me.

'No,' I said. 'Why?'

'Wait here till they come out. It's worth your while.'

We sat on: at last we heard the noise of chairs being pushed back and the buzz of talk. Immediately, the photographers leaped to their feet and took up a favourable position at the end of the corridor. Two ladies issued from the Congress hall, hurried down the corridor and placed themselves directly in front of the cameras. A group gathered around them, but they maintained their places in the centre of the picture. The audience streamed out, amongst them de Valera with a supporter. De Valera cast a rapid glance in the direction of the cameras; then with long swift strides he advanced towards the group, as if he had some urgent business which happened to lie in their direction. The group sundered as he approached, like the waves of the Red Sea; the two ladies moved apart and de Valera took the place left vacant and looked with satisfaction at the camera-men. One of the ladies called out, 'All right! You can start now!'

Events in Ireland were going from bad to worse.

Our delegates in London had signed a treaty with the British Government. We had not obtained the Republic, but the status of a dominion for Ireland without the six Northern Counties. We had full economic freedom and the right to an army and a fleet. Members of the Dáil were obliged to take an oath of allegiance to the King of England. It was not everything we could have wished but it was far better than we could have hoped to obtain at the beginning of the struggle, and there was nothing which we could not alter, once the executive power was in our hands.

But de Valera was dissatisfied: he denied the competence of the delegates to sign the Treaty without further consultation with himself and announced that he would oppose its ratification. The IRA was split: some of its leaders said that we were not in a position to continue the fight, others maintained that we had never been so strong. I was more than ever convinced of the necessity of a compromise: it was only through the unity of the country that we had advanced so far, and now that unity had been broken and further fighting was impossible.

The debate on the Treaty took place in the Mansion House and was conducted with unexampled violence: on the 7th of January 1922 it was ratified by sixty-four votes to fifty-seven. De Valera after a passionate speech against all compromise resigned his position as President; Griffith was elected his successor. The excitement on both sides was intense; each party accused the other of sacrificing Ireland's future to personal and party interest. The hatred between Free Staters and Republicans appeared to be as strong as that which had formerly existed between IRA and Black-and-Tans. One could only hope that de Valera, who never tired in his speeches of singing the praises of democracy, would now bow to the will of the majority.

New elections were held in June 1922, in which the Government obtained a majority of ninety-three to thirty-five. But de Valera refused to accept the result of the polls: amid the applause of his supporters he declared, 'When I want to know the will of the Irish people, I need only look in my own heart.' It was a convenient theory of democratic statesmanship, to which he has always remained faithful. In another speech he warned the Government of the danger that the Irish people would wade in blood as a consequence of their treason: in a later explanation he complained of the wrong done to him by interpreting his well-meant warning as a threat of bloodshed. In the circumstances, civil war was inevitable: in a short time a guerrilla war was raging in the four provinces of Ireland, in which the 'Irregulars' applied against the Free State Army the same tactics and methods as the IRA had formerly employed against English military and police.

Chartres, needless to say, rejected all compromise with England and blamed the delegation for not availing itself of his advice. The Government sent its foreign representatives precise instructions on their attitude to the civil war: in all communications to the press or public, emphasis was to be laid on the fact that the conflict was not to be regarded as an outbreak of hostilities between two contending political parties, but as the revolt of a disloyal minority against the lawful government of the country, which had been elected by an overwhelming majority.

Chartres had been in the habit of issuing monthly an *Irish Bulletin:* he composed it in English, and his secretary translated it into what she hoped was German. Now, a number was published dealing with the civil war: it contained short, neutral notices of the careers of the leaders of the Government Arthur Griffith and Michael Collins, lengthy and eulogistic biographies of de Valera and the most prominent Irregulars and a comment on the 'contest between the parties in Ireland'.

As the Government was paying for Chartres' services and for the issue of the *Irish Bulletin,* I thought it had a right to be informed in more detail about the value it was getting for its money. Without comment I sent the Minister a copy of the *Bulletin* with translation. Chartres much to his indignation was recalled to Dublin and given a subordinate post in one of the Ministries. His life-work *Bloody England* still awaits publication.

The civil war continued to rage in Ireland. Griffith died suddenly of heart failure, Collins was shot in an ambush. The Government arrested Childers and executed him for being in possession of a revolver which Collins had given him in the time of the Black-

and-Tans. The Irregulars published lists of functionaries to be assassinated for 'treason to the Republic'. A Government deputy was shot in the street in Dublin; as a reprisal, the Government executed four Republican prisoners without trial. The English Parliament did not conceal its delight: a Minister told the House of Commons that it was a matter for satisfaction that the Irish were shooting each other instead of England being compelled to restore order. Childers' death, in particular, was greeted with exultation: Churchill spoke of the 'traitor and renegade' who had met the fate he deserved.

There was no longer any suggestion of making use of our present status to advance farther on the road to freedom. Griffith's successor Cosgrave failed to realize that the very intransigence of the minority was his trump card in negotiations with England: he could only think of the danger of coming between two fires. Till the enemy on the left was eliminated, he had no wish to conjure up another on the right. The negotiations in London implementing the Treaty were carried out in a spirit of the utmost friendliness; it might have been thought that the settlement of 1921 was destined to last for all time.

The Government had forgotten its project of accrediting our representatives abroad as ministers or even as consuls. Not even a new passport system had been introduced; we had to travel with English passports, and in the event of difficulties with the authorities we would have had to apply for protection to the British consul.

No doubt many excuses could be made for the inaction of the Government; its hands were full with the civil war forced upon it by de Valera and his Irregulars. But I came to the conclusion that nothing was to be gained by my remaining any longer in Germany as the unaccredited representative of a half-independent state.

In the spring of 1923 I resigned my post and returned to Ireland to resume my interrupted career as a barrister.

FOUR

The Law of Ireland

It did not seem to me on my return to Ireland that much had changed during the two years of my absence. True, the vermilion letter-boxes in the streets had become green. On our stamps the King's head had given place to the Celtic cross, the map of Ireland and the legendary Sword of Light. From our coinage His Majesty had equally been banished: for some reason which still remains to me a mystery he was replaced, not by Ireland's saints and heroes, but by a number of the birds, beasts and fishes bred within our boundaries and adapted to culinary or sporting purposes. The designs were made by a young English artist and corrected where it was considered necessary by the veterinary experts of the Department of Agriculture.

But, in spite of the green letter-boxes and zoological coinage, in spite even of the many genuinely beneficent reforms introduced by the Government, there was among the people a sense of disillusionment. I shared it myself, though I did not ascribe much importance to my own feelings, being fully aware of my temperamental impatience and of my tendency to expect a short cut to the Earthly Paradise. But the discouragement of the man in the street could not so simply be explained away: it was in part the reaction after two years of unparalleled strain, but it went deeper than mere reaction. The civil war, in particular, had been a moral shock to the country: many seemed to have lost faith in themselves and the justice of their cause – one even heard doubts whether we were capable of self-government. I heard a working-man exclaim as he read the news, 'And that's what they call the Island of Saints and Scholars!'

The Republican Courts with their lay judges and their decisions by the light of commonsense undimmed by legal pedantries had been abolished, and our new judges carried on like their predecessors according to the precedents in the English law reports. If the people had felt under British rule that the administration of justice was an alien system which they were entitled to frustrate by every means in their power, there was little in the present procedures to convert them to another opinion. The Attorney-General Hugh Kennedy shared my view. In face of the apathy of Government and people he could do little to reform the system, but he determined at least to revolutionize the outward trappings of the law. In a memorandum addressed to the Government he emphasized the fact that the wigs and gowns worn by judges and barristers were relics of one of the most corrupt periods of English history, that so far from having any connection with Irish tradition they were regarded by the people of Ireland as a symbol of alien oppression, and that greater respect for the administration of justice could best be attained by substituting for them a modern adaptation of the robes worn by the old Irish *ollamhs* or Brehon judges. To this end he had obtained from Mr Charles Shannon RA series of designs for the robes of the judges of the different courts.

The designs were in themselves extremely artistic. The worst that could be said of them was that they were possibly too reminiscent of a scene in the Russian ballet to be entirely suitable to the prosaic atmosphere of a Dublin courthouse. The *ollamh* was according to tradition entitled to add a colour to his costume for every augmentation of rank, so that a judge of the Supreme Court would presumably have worn robes of four or five different hues; but in practice the exuberance of Mr Shannon's fancy would have been toned down to suit the exigencies of everyday life. The Government considered and sanctioned Kennedy's proposal, which was then submitted to the benchers of the King's Inns, as the official representatives of Bench and Bar.

But the benchers were less enamoured than Kennedy of the proposed change. They were largely taken from the Unionist minority, which until recently had furnished a majority of the legal profession; but, to do them justice, I do not believe that they were actuated by political motives so much as by the fear of looking ridiculous in Mr Shannon's rainbow-hued creations, when by large majority they rejected the resolution. The reason assigned for their decision was the unwarranted financial burden on junior members of the Bar who had already been put to the expense of purchasing wigs and gowns. The Government accepted their decision with indifference, and the project was dropped. Only Kennedy, who had in the meantime been appointed Chief Justice, announced that he would never wear the wig on the bench. In fact it was several years before he consented to conform to the prevailing custom.

★ ★ ★

And, on the positive side, what had we got that would justify the struggle and the sufferings of the past three years?

There was first of all the Constitution, which had been proclaimed by the Government with a certain pomp as the corner-stone of the new State. It contained in its numerous articles traces of most of the democratic constitutions of the world: the United States of America, France, Czechoslovakia, even Republican Germany had contributed their part. The result was an admirable document, which guaranteed to the individual every conceivable kind of liberty – liberty of speech, liberty of public meeting, liberty of propaganda; it only forgot that every law must of necessity be a restriction of the liberty of the individual and, while guaranteeing every liberty to the individual, it omitted to make provision for a government unhampered by the technical obstacles put in its way by the individual. And, if the members of the Government had any misgivings with regard to the progress they had made, no such misgivings ever entered the minds of the permanent civil servants on whom ministers must necessarily depend for guidance and counsel. The majority of these had gained their experience in the service of the British Government; while in some cases highly competent, they had been trained entirely in a tradition which, however admirable for an Empire which had lasted three hundred years, was scarcely the ideal one in a small state which had barely come into existence. They would undoubtedly have carried out any policy adopted by the ministers, but unfortunately the ministers, being of necessity devoid of technical experience, depended on the advice of their permanent officials, who in the desire of avoiding a responsibility which should never had been thrust upon them never failed to recommend a policy of *laisser faire*. It was an ideal policy for all parties concerned: the permanent officials could not be called to account for the decisions of the Department, since every decision was nominally taken by the minister, while the minister in his turn could protect himself against critics by the plea that he had acted on the advice of his technical advisers. Only the country suffered by their inaction.

The Department of Finance, for example, was directed by officials who had gained their experience in English ministries. It was an admirable training, but their powers of assimilation seemed to have atrophied about the year 1906, and for them the doctrines of free trade, unrestricted competition, open markets and no interference with the laws of supply and demand were a gospel which it would have been a blasphemy to doubt. It did not apparently occur to them that in Great Britain itself conditions had changed during the War and that Free Trade was no longer even in its birthplace the infallible dogma that it once had been – still less, that if we were to develop industries in the future we must at least protect them against foreign dumping by tariffs or subsidies in their infancy.

The result was deplorable in the national interest, but our officials maintained undisturbed their Olympian tranquillity: conscious that they had acted throughout in accordance with the rules of political economy which they had learned in their student days, they could not imagine that the result would be in the best interest of the country. It was a curious and pedantic misunderstanding of the actual practice in Great Britain, where, as in any other state with political experience, little importance is ascribed to the observance of the dogmas of the professors, provided the outcome be favourable.

I quickly gave up any idea I might have had of entering politics, and devoted myself to the recovery of the legal practice which had passed into other hands during my two years' absence. My friend John O' Byrne succeeded Hugh Kennedy as Attorney-General: by his direction I received briefs in civil and criminal proceedings on behalf of the State, and in little more than a year I had as much work as I could cope with. To him and his successor John A. Costello, later head of the first Government of the Irish Republic, I owe a deep debt of gratitude for the help they gave me. It is a pleasure to me to put on record, after the lapse of so many years, my memory of their kindness.

★ ★ ★

One of the first tasks of the Government was the compensation of those who had suffered in the struggle of the years 1919-21. It was no light problem, for the losses in human lives and property had been enormous, and after the lapse of four years it was not easy to test the accuracy of the claims.

The local courts were scarcely able to cope with the applications which flowed in from every county in the Free State. Every class of society was represented – from the factory-owner whose buildings had been reduced to a heap of smoking ruins to the village shopkeeper whose stock had been looted by drunken Black-and-Tans. In addition, provision had to be made for the dependants of those who had fallen in the fight: it seemed an irony to talk of compensation in pounds, shillings and pence for the loss of human lives, but it was the duty of the judges to assess as best they could the financial loss suffered by the widows and children of our soldiers of freedom. It speaks volumes for the inherent honesty of the Irish people that out of the thousands of claims against the State only a minute percentage were fraudulent or even deliberately exaggerated.

I had returned to my practice in the Western counties; a large part of the time was occupied by the applications for compensation for loss of life and property. Among the monotonous routine of assessors and valuers and the wearisome calculations of the experts of the Department of Finance one case stands out clearly in my memory.

The court was being held in a Connemara village; it was a grey autumn day with rain driving in from the Atlantic. Wisps of wandering mist drifted over the soaked fields, while here and there one could see the ghostly outline of some thorn tree bent double by the winter gales. To the West, grey, lowly clouds merged imperceptibly into the grey sea; there was no horizon, and heaven and earth seemed wrapped in a grey coverlet of mist. On the bog stood, dark and dripping, the stacks of newly cut turf; in all the landscape the eye could discover no living creature.

The judge took his seat in the village courthouse, an assessor from the Department of Finance was in attendance. The little courtroom was crowded by the people; the water dropped from their Connemara frieze coats over their heavy boots and made puddles on the muddy floor. The women were draped in their heavy black shawls; from the drenched clothing of men and women clouds of vapour steamed into the air. A smell of wet earth mingled with that of turf-smoke. The fine misty rain of the West of Ireland ran down the dim panes of the small windows. Through the open door one caught from time to time a glimpse of the desolate and rain-swept street.

A little old woman in her late sixties climbed into the witness-box. She was wearing the red flannel petticoat and narrow white cap that all countrywomen in the West of Ireland used formerly to wear. Equally traditional was her greeting, '*Go mbeannuighe Dia dhibh!*' she said. 'May the blessing of God be with ye!'

'*Go mbeannuighe Dia's Muire dhuit!*' answered the clerk of the Court. 'What are you claiming?'

'I lost my boneens,' she said, 'ten good healthy boneens. I'm looking for their price.'

The words sounded perhaps a little comic, but no-one was inclined to laugh. The judge said, 'Tell me what happened.'

'It was in the spring before the Truce,' she said. 'We had had word they'd be coming our way that night. My son had been out with the boys; they were looking for him to shoot him wherever they'd find him. I said to himself – he died since, God rest his soul! – "You must go away out of this. If they don't find Paddy, they'll shoot you in his place." He wouldn't go at first, but in the end I got him to go. So I stopped there alone to look after the house.

'It was late when they came – between two and three in the morning it could be. They were on a lorry, eleven or twelve of them. I opened the door. "Where is the murderer?" they asked me. "I know no murderer," I said. "You know well who we mean," they said, "your son the murderer." "My son is no murderer," said I, "he's not here, he's gone away." "Where is he?" they asked me. "I don't know where he is," I said. "And your husband?" they said. "He's gone too," I said. "We don't believe you," they said, "we'll look in the house to see if we can find him." Then two of them went and stood at the back door, the others came into the house.'

'How big is the house?' asked the judge.

'Two rooms, your Honour. It would be hard for one to be hiding in it. They took out the mattresses from the bed and stuck their bayonets in them. They knocked down the holy pictures from the wall and broke them on the floor. They broke up the crockery that was standing on the dresser. In the end they saw there was no man in the house, and they went out of the door. I thought to myself they were done with it and I could clear up after them. Then one of them that was standing outside said, "There's a pigsty out there." We had a sow with ten boneens, she had littered three weeks before, your Honour. They went across to the sty and one of them opened the gate. The sow was waiting for them, she came rushing out between them and got away in the dark. Then one of them gave a call, and another brought two tins from the lorry. He took one of the tins and poured the petrol on them, and when the first tin was empty he emptied out the second on them. Then he struck a match and threw it down on them.

'It was terrible to see the poor innocent creatures, one of them taking fire from another and all of them crying the way you'd think they were children. Then one of them opened the gate of the sty, and they were all out running over the fields. You could see them running by the flames that were rising up out of them.'

'What did the men do then?'

'They got on their lorry and drove away.'

'Did you find any of the boneens again?'

'I went out to look for them that morning, your Honour. I found them all, one had breath in it still.'

★ ★ ★

It might have been expected that the officials of the British Government in Ireland would be transferred to equivalent posts in England or the colonies. But our delegates had made a bad bargain in 1921, and Ireland was saddled with the payment of compensation to the English civil servants who chose a life of leisure. The amount of compensation was fixed in a test case by the Irish Supreme Court: it was liberal enough in all conscience, but two Englishmen named Wigg and Cochrane declared themselves dissatisfied and lodged an appeal to the Judicial Committee of the Privy Council, which had the right to decide in the last instance on all actions brought before Irish or dominion courts.

Obviously the reservation of the ultimate decision in all cases of importance for the tribunal of a (now) foreign state is an anomaly which could only be justified by very exceptional circumstances. English juristic writers find that justification in the necessity of protecting the rights of minorities in the various parts of the Empire – or, in other words, in the incapacity of any but English courts to do justice to minorities. In Ireland, conscious that our Government had treated the racial and religious minority with scrupulous justice, the suggestion that any class of the community needed the protection of a British tribunal was intensely resented.

But the right of appeal to the Privy Council was embodied in the Treaty, and we could do nothing but submit. A preliminary application for leave to appeal was made on behalf of the civil servants. With John Costello, then Attorney-General, I crossed to London and duly made my appearance at Number 11 Downing Street. I must frankly admit that the solemn character of the surroundings, the knowledge that next door to us stood the Prime Minister's residence where so many decisions had been taken which had altered the history of the world, the majestic and silent servitors, the combined air of learning and tradition which seemed to invest the building – that all this taken together was not without an intimidatory effect on me. I could not entirely suppress the illogical fear that their Lordships would approach the case from some angle undreamed of by us or produce from the stores of their accumulated legal knowledge some precedent which we had overlooked.

Their Lordships took their seats, we were called in, the arguments began. What impressed me, however, more than the argumentation was the fact that the highest judicial authorities of the British Empire obviously knew very little of the Pensions Acts and nothing whatever of the various laws and orders governing the relations between Great Britain and Ireland, and that they had not taken the trouble to familiarize themselves with them before the hearing. The questions which they addressed to counsel did not betray a high degree of legal acumen; from time to time one or the other would make an amiable little joke. One had the impression that the whole affair was to them of supreme unimportance.

When the hearing was over, I walked down Whitehall with Costello. 'Do you know the average age of the judges?' he asked me.

'They must be pretty old,' I said, 'but I haven't looked up their exact ages.'

'I have, though,' said Costello, 'in *Who's Who*. The youngest is seventy-one, the oldest eighty-seven. Their average age is seventy-five.'

'I suppose that explains the fact that after the first half-hour there was never a moment when all five were awake together.'

'Anyway,' said Costello, 'now that I know what the Privy Council is like, I've made up my mind that it must go. It's a scandal that such a court should have the final decision in the Irish cases.'

Leave to appeal was duly granted: a little later the appeal itself was heard. The proceedings took practically the same course as before. At intervals one of their Lordships would address an inquiry to counsel in the languid and slightly bored voice which is the prerogative of the English upper class and has so exasperating an effect on the rest of the world. A month after our return to Dublin we received a copy of their decision: the Privy Council had decided against us, though in its judgment it did not once mention the section of the Act on which the whole case turned. Costello was ready with his next move. At his suggestion the Irish Government addressed a note to the Dominions Office stating that in view of the unsatisfactory nature of the judgment of the Privy Council it did not consider itself bound by it.

For the British Government the situation was no doubt a painful one. Lord Cave, who had presided over the court, had before his death some weeks earlier expressed doubt of the correctness of the decision, and the English Law Officers had given their advice in the same sense. In the course of time a reply was delivered: it admitted that the proceedings before the Privy Council had not in all respects been satisfactory, and suggested the constitution of a special tribunal to retry the appeal. The Irish Government agreed to the proposal, and some weeks later we arrived once more in London.

The special tribunal consisted of four English Law Lords with the addition of a judge of the Canadian Supreme Court. We delivered our arguments, which were listened to courteously, though the new court did not any more than the old show signs of having mastered the intricacies of the Pensions Acts or the provisions regulating the relations between Great Britain and Ireland. The English Attorney-General expressed his complete agreement with us and explained to the Court that he did not wish to rely on the judgment of its predecessor which for various reasons he characterized as unsatisfactory. Knowing that the new tribunal had been constituted for the express purpose of setting right the erroneous decision of the Privy Council, we had little misgiving about the result. All the greater, therefore, was our amazement when the special tribunal gave judgment in the same sense as its predecessor, deciding that the Irish Government was bound to pay the pensions on the scale demanded by the claimants.

It is easy now to see the motives which induced them to so strange a decision. The Judicial Committee of the Privy Council, as supreme tribunal of the British Empire, enjoyed a reputation of quasi-infallibility; its pronouncements were regarded with reverence by the courts of every dominion and colony; throughout its long history no voice had ever been raised to question its authority. And now, to set right some trifling question of the amount of pension payable to a couple of civil servants, the Law Lords, sitting in special tribunal, were asked to declare that it had committed a gross error. Such a declaration might have had far-reaching results: in more than one dominion the abolition of the right of appeal to the Privy Council had already been suggested by opposition parties, and an official admission that it had failed to do justice to the claim of a Dominion Government could not fail to give food to such agitation in the future. The judges of the special tribunal took the view that the prestige of the Privy Council must at all costs be upheld.

I do not know whether the British authorities expected that our Government would tamely accept the decision of the special tribunal; if they cherished such a hope, they did not know Costello. On his advice a second note was handed to the Dominions Office, stating that the Irish Department of Finance would pay the pensions at the rate fixed by the Irish Supreme Court but no more. In the end, the supplements declared to be payable by the Privy Council were paid to Messrs Wigg and Cochrane by the British Treasury.

It was some years before the right of appeal was formally abolished, but in fact no decision of the Irish Supreme Court was ever reversed by it after the case of Wigg and Cochrane.

FIVE

Minister in Rome, 1929

My wish came true at last: I was appointed Minister to the Holy See. In July 1929 I started in Rome in the company of Joseph Walshe, the Secretary of the Department of External Affairs.

I had known Walshe for many years, but he had always been somewhat of an enigma to me. He had during the troubled times been secretary to our unaccredited 'envoy' in Paris before the Treaty, in which capacity he had insisted, unsolicited, on taking an oath of loyalty to the Republic. At the Congress of the Irish Race in January 1922, however, his Republican faith had begun to waver, and he had asked me what I thought of the prospects in the coming election.

'There will certainly be a majority for the Free State and against the extremists,' I answered. 'The people are tired of fighting.'

Walshe sighed and observed, 'It's terribly difficult to know what to do.' However, a little later he had declared himself in favour of the Free State, of which he was now an enthusiastic supporter.

On the morning after our arrival in London he said to me, 'We have an appointment in the Dominions Office at eleven o'clock.'

'Whatever for?' I inquired.

'I want to introduce you to the officials there. You must always remember that the Minister's policy is to collaborate as closely as possible with the British.'

It was the first indication of the policy of the Minister which I had received; no instructions of any kind had been given me before leaving Dublin. I wondered for a moment why the Minister should not have informed me of his wishes in person. In my simplicity, it did not occur to me that Ministers sometimes shrink from formulating their policy even to themselves and leave the task of explaining it to others in the hands of their permanent officials, who have no responsibility except that of interpreting the desires of their superiors.

We were received by one of the Under-Secretaries. 'Well, Mr Walshe,' he said blandly, 'what can we do for you today?'

'Oh, thank you, Sir Hubert,' said Walshe with a deferential smile, 'I only want to introduce our new Minister to the Holy See. We hope, Sir Hubert, that the relations between your Legation and ours will always be most cordial.' He beamed through his spectacles on the Under-Secretary, who assured him with perfect courtesy, though without visible enthusiasm, that he too hoped to see the best relations established between the two Legations. It was now my turn: I expressed my determination to do all that lay in my power to promote cordial relations between the British Legation and my own.

A silence followed. Then the Under-Secretary said, 'Is that everything, Mr Walshe?'

'Yes, thank you, Sir Hubert! And thanks for your kindness in receiving us, Sir Hubert!' In his gratitude for Sir Hubert's amiability he shifted perpetually from one foot to the other: I could not help thinking of an overgrown puppy frisking around its master.

We took our leave; as we drove away, he explained to me, 'It's very important to be on good terms with the English officials. They can be of great use to us. Whenever I have difficulties of any kind, I only need write them a couple of lines, and they give me their advice. I don't know what we'd do without them.'

I made no comment: the methods of diplomacy were for me a closed book, and I was still prepared to assume that the Minister for External Affairs knew his business without assistance from me. Next day we continued our journey to Rome.

The Irish colony in Rome is out of all proportion to our small population. Apart from the Irish College for the secular clergy, the Irish members of the Franciscan, Augustinian and Dominican Orders have their Houses. The Irish Franciscans possess the Church of S. Isidoro in the neighbourhood of the Via Vittorio Veneto; in the seventeenth century one of their members, Luke Wadding, had been the last representative of Ireland to the Holy See. The Irish Dominicans are in possession of the historic basilica of S. Clemente with its famous crypt and Mithras temple. The Irish Christian Brothers conduct a school for Italian boys between the ages of seven and seventeen. In addition, there were many members of the Irish clergy in the international foundations. I suggested to Walshe that I should start a round of visits.

He assented, and added, 'It's very important that you should visit the British Minister to the Holy See and the Ambassador to the Quirinal. You can make your other diplomatic visits later, after you've presented your credentials.'

It was a highly embarrassing situation. The Irish clergy in Rome could not fail to interpret my promptness in visiting the British as a political demonstration. Moreover, before I had left Dublin, my friend Con Curran, brother of the Vice-Rector of the Irish College, had expressly warned me that any preference given to the British would be strongly resented by the Irish clergy. I told Walshe of the warning, but he only exclaimed, 'Curran thinks he knows our job better than we do!' In spite of my misgivings we paid a formal visit to the British Ambassador, and three days later to Monsignore Hagan, the Rector of the Irish College.

Monsignore Hagan was well known to be a convinced Republican; he had been bitterly opposed to the acceptance of the Treaty, and had not yet resumed his social relations with the English College which he had broken off in 1920. He had rendered the Irish cause precious service at the Vatican; he was, in addition, a prelate of very great distinction and an exceptionally strong personality. It was in any event questionable whether he would recognize the validity of my appointment, and the fact that I had called on Sir Ronald Graham, the British Ambassador to a state to which I was not accredited, before I visited the Irish College, was not likely to conciliate him.

The Monsignore received us with complete correctness, if not with cordiality: after not more than five minutes' delay he entered the waiting-room into which we had been shown.

After a formal greeting he said politely, 'I hope you are enjoying your stay in Rome.'

I assured him that we were.

'Is it your first visit?' asked Monsignore Hagan.

'I was once here for a week,' I said.

'You will find much to interest you.'

The conversation continued on similar lines for ten minutes: when we left he expressed no hope of seeing either of us again. Once we were outside the door, Walshe said, 'Did you notice that he treated us as tourists – that he made no reference to my position or yours?'

'It would have been hard not to notice it,' I replied.

'Outrageous!' exclaimed Walshe.

I assented, but in my inmost heart I could not help recognizing that there was, given his political tenets, every justification for the Monsignore's attitude. I resolved to put matters on a better footing at our next meeting, but to my sincere regret the opportunity was not vouchsafed me. Monsignore Hagan left his card at my hotel, but did not return the visit and declined all invitations to social functions at which I was likely to be present. I never saw him again up to the date of his death two years later.

Walshe left Rome, I presented my credentials at the Vatican, life settled down into the normal routine of the representative of a small state. And at this point it may be well to recall that the functions of the diplomatic representatives of the small states – Ireland, Bolivia, Monaco – are, not only in degree but in kind, different from those of the representatives of the Great Powers.

A Great Power has its interests throughout the world; no event of importance in any one of the five continents can leave it entirely unconcerned; it plays an active part in the drama of world history. Consequently, an adequate information service is to it of the utmost importance in order to safeguard it against surprise moves on the diplomatic chessboard. Its foreign missions are collectors of information for their government: they have their confidential agents, their financial resources, their special funds.

A small state is in an entirely different situation: the majority of the events which take place in the world do not directly affect its interests and even when those interests are touched, it cannot hope except in very rare circumstances to play any but a passive role. Special information has for it no particular importance: if it has allies, they will ascertain the facts without its assistance; if it has no allies, it is doomed to suffer, and the best information service in the world will bring it no profit.

I remember a conversation which took place many years later between members of the Berlin Diplomatic Corps after Hitler's reoccupation of the Rhineland.

'I heard about it at ten in the morning from a man whom I have always found reliable,' said the Czechoslovak Minister with a hint of triumph in his voice.

'I got the news at half-past eight,' said the French Ambassador with the tranquillity of one who regards it as a matter of course that his organization should be the most efficient.

'I don't remember when I heard about it,' said the Norwegian Minister, 'even if it had been late in the evening or on the next morning, it would not have made the slightest difference to my Government. A little country like mine can only look on at international politics.'

And another Norwegian Minister in Rome, on being asked what were the major diplomatic questions between Italy and Norway, replied laconically, '*Baccalá*' – *baccalá* being the Italian name for the dried haddock which forms one of the chief Norwegian exports.

But with *baccalá* – or, in other words, with commercial relations – I was not concerned; the Vatican state with its few hundred inhabitants could scarcely hope to become an important importer of Irish products. On the other hand, there was a reason for my existence and that of the other Irish missions which did not apply to the other small states.

At the present day the world is used to the spectacle of Ambassadors or Ministers of the British dominions. But in 1929 Canada and South Africa had appointed their first Ministers to foreign capitals, while Australia and New Zealand still looked on a separate diplomacy as a mark of disloyalty to the Empire. No wonder, then, that to the majority of foreign observers the idea of 'British colonies' with independent Legations seemed a paradox and that I was frequently asked whether I made my reports to the British Embassy to the Quirinal or to the British Legation to the Holy See.

I considered it my first and most important duty to make clear our independent status. But the situation was highly embarrassing – both to me and to the British. It was not unnatural that they should regard us – the South African Pienaar and myself – as amateurs; it spoke entirely of the kindness of their hearts that they were always willing to help us with their counsel, while it also corresponded with their conception of the British hen sheltering the dominion chickens under her wings. But this was exactly the conception which we were determined to destroy: the 'Commonwealth' consisted at least nominally of 'free and equal nations', and we would not accept a patronage animated by the most amiable of intentions.

No doubt it would have been simpler for the British to abandon us to our own devices, but such abandonment would have implied an acknowledgment in the face of the world of our independence. Hence they felt themselves obliged continually to make advances to us, which we for similar tactical reasons felt ourselves forced to decline. It was not always easy: for instance, I never succeeded in finding a solution of the problem of my behaviour when a member of the British Embassy referred to me in public as '*our* Irish Minister'.

Pienaar would possibly have been better able to cope with the situation, as he had come to Rome a few months before me as Minister to the Quirinal. On his arrival Sir Ronald Graham had written him a letter inviting him to the British Embassy and offering him help and advice if they should be needed. 'And what do you think the damned fellow did?' the British Secretary who was telling me the story asked dramatically.

'No idea!' said I, scenting a first-class scandal. 'What did he do?'

'He wrote back', said the Secretary solemnly, 'that he would do himself the honour of calling on the Ambassador when he had presented his credentials and visited the Nuncio as doyen of the Diplomatic Corps. And the incredible part of it was that he wrote to the Ambassador in French! These people from the dominions are really impossible!'

'Thanks for your good opinion of us!' I said.

'Oh, you're quite different,' said the Secretary handsomely.

I do not know whether he was referring to my English education or to my visit to the Ambassador or to the fact that I sometimes rode with him in the Giardino Borghese; perhaps he was only trying to get out of an awkward situation. But even if his good opinion of me was sincere, it was not long till, through no fault of my own, I became definitely *persona ingrata* in the eyes of the English colony.

★ ★ ★

Despite its inactivity, the Cosgrave Government remained in power. It had lost its popularity in the country, but none of its confidence that no other party could take its place. De Valera had refused 'on conscientious grounds' to enter Dáil Éireann on account of the oath of allegiance to the English king required of deputies, and defeat in a parliamentary division was inconceivable in the absence of an opposition.

But the Government had failed to reckon with de Valera's mentality. Faced with the prospect of permanent exclusion from parliamentary life and moved by the natural desire of playing a part on the political stage, he decided to enter the 'colonial parliament' which for years he had denounced as illegal. There remained the obstacle of the oath of allegiance: de Valera ransacked Ireland for a theological authority who would tell him not only that an oath taken under compulsion is not binding on the conscience, but also that the oath of allegiance could be considered to have been taken under compulsion. Whether the authority was forthcoming or not must remain a mystery but de Valera regarded himself as justified in subscribing his declaration of loyalty to King George. Later, he explained that it should be regarded as an 'empty formula', and stated in all apparent seriousness that he had turned away his head while affixing his name to the declaration.

The men of the IRA, who had fought a bloody civil war in protest against the 'colonial parliament' and the oath of allegiance, were not entirely convinced that the validity of an oath depends on the position of the head of the person taking it, but the majority of the politicians opposed to the Government were delighted to be able to re-enter public life without excessive loss of face. A parliamentary republican party was formed with the high-sounding name *Fianna Fáil,* the Hosts of Destiny: the Government was for the first time threatened with an embittered opposition in parliament.

At last it awoke to the precariousness of its position. But even now it could not believe that any other body of men could take its place. Ministers proclaimed that, even if by some extraordinary chance de Valera obtained a parliamentary majority at the next election, his incompetence as head of the Government would soon provoke so powerful a reaction among the people that Cosgrave and his party would be sure of returning to power with an overwhelming majority at the next election but one. A few years later the German Social Democrats fell into the same error: if Hitler ever came into power, he would soon be swept away by the force of public opinion. The world is still paying the penalty for their blindness.

Only one serious effort was made to meet the attacks of the Opposition. The head of the Civic Guard General Eoin O'Duffy drafted a report on the activities of the IRA and in particular of an association closely connected with it entitled *Saor Eire* (Free Ireland): special emphasis was placed on their relations with international Communism. Copies of the report were sent to the Nuncio and the Bishops: if they accepted O'Duffy's conclusions, they might reasonably be expected to condemn *Saor Eire* and the IRA as Communist organizations. And, if the IRA was condemned by the Bishops, de Valera's chances in the forthcoming election would be gravely affected.

But the Bishops, who had sources of information at least as reliable as those available to O'Duffy, declined to accept his conclusions. They renewed in their pastorals the condemnation of Communism and Communist organizations which they had already more than once pronounced, but scrupulously refrained from any reference to the IRA or *Saor Eire*. It was a bitter disappointment to Government circles; the pastorals could be interpreted almost as an acquittal of the IRA from any suspicion of Communism.

I happened to be in Dublin on leave and reported in the usual way to the Secretary of the Department of External Affairs.

'We hoped the Bishops would come out strong,' said Walshe, 'but they have no courage. The only hope is that the Nuncio will make them see reason.'

'What does he think about it all?' I asked.

'I was three hours with him yesterday,' said Walshe, 'explaining the world situation. I suppose you'll be going to see him?'

'Yes,' I said, 'he's asked me to lunch tomorrow.'

'Try to make it clear to him', said Walshe, 'that the Communists really are a danger to Ireland. Perhaps he'll come out against them.'

It goes without saying that I had no intention of carrying out the mission entrusted to me. I knew that Monsignore Robinson had far too acute an intelligence and too highly developed a sense of justice to let himself be made use of in a conflict between Irish political parties. It is possible that after his prolonged interview with Walshe he had some inkling of the instructions likely to have been given me, for he took an early opportunity of remarking, 'Seán MacBride was here with me yesterday. A nice young fellow.'

Seán MacBride, later Minister for External Affairs, was the son of Major MacBride who had led the Irish Brigade in the Boer War, and of Maud Gonne who had hung out a skull and crossbones over Queen Victoria's entry into Dublin. He was now one of the most important members and certainly by far the ablest leader of the IRA: he was perpetually looked for by the police, though there was nothing against him but his political views. He had been one of de Valera's secretaries at the Congress of the Irish Race in Paris nine years earlier, but had severed all connection with his old chief since the entry of Fianna Fáil into the Dáil. Both political parties looked on him as a dangerous character; the Nuncio in receiving him had given proof of breadth of view and insight into the essentials of Irish politics.

'Your Excellency didn't find him a dangerous Communist?' I asked.

The Nuncio smiled in reply. 'No,' he said, 'I didn't notice it.'

I reported to Walshe that I did not believe that the Nuncio would condemn the IRA as a Communist organization. He made a despairing gesture, as if the burden of responsibility which rested on his shoulders was too great to be borne. I returned to Rome on the conclusion of my leave. Nothing more was heard of the danger to State and Church of Communism in Ireland.

It was the last despairing effort of the Government to find a slogan for the election; after its failure the Ministers let events take their course. There could be no doubt of the result. De Valera and his Hosts of Destiny won a smashing victory. Cosgrave resigned, and de Valera formed the new government.

It is popularly believed that 'new brooms sweep clean'. De Valera in 1931 was a living proof of the contrary.

There were members of the pro-English minority in Dublin who looked on his accession to power as something like the Last Judgment: as they believed that the role of the Damned would infallibly be allotted to themselves, they packed their belongings, took the first steamer to England and rented small villas in Kent or Devonshire. But they were few, and consisted mainly of elderly couples with a steady income in War Loan: the majority of the ex-Unionists accepted the situation less tragically. They did not at least for the moment expect any sensational development in Irish politics, and comforted themselves with the reflection that, even if the worst should unexpectedly happen, their money was already invested in England, where their British passports would enable them to rejoin it whenever they wished.

The Republicans did not at first declare themselves: in spite of the abolition of the oath they declined to enter the parliament of a British dominion. Like de Valera, they aimed at the freedom and unity of the nation, but only on the basis of the already existing Republic: if the Government put in the front of its programme the resumption of the fight for complete independence, it could count on their unconditional support. But the Government was not prepared to take so drastic a step. No official pronouncement was made, but in Government circles it was pointed out that de Valera would not be justified in so radically altering our status without having first obtained a mandate from the people. His relations with the IRA became cooler; its military evolutions continued. Its leaders reserved to themselves the right of opposing the new Government, if it should betray their hopes, with the same active methods which they had employed against its predecessor.

Meanwhile the International Eucharistic Congress had been fixed to take place in Dublin in the summer of 1932. Cardinal Lauri was appointed Papal Legate. It was an event which captured the hearts and the imaginations of the whole of Catholic Ireland: even politics were for the moment forgotten.

I made my visit of congratulation to the Cardinal. As I was coming out a Monsignore in attendance took me aside and asked me, 'What decoration does your government intend to offer the Cardinal Legate?'

In some embarrassment I answered, 'We have no decorations in Ireland, Monsignore. I don't know whether it will be possible to offer him any decoration.'

'That is of no consequence,' said the Monsignore. 'It could institute an order specially for the Eucharistic Congress and ask the Cardinal to accept the first Grand Cross. I have been looking into the question: on a similar occasion some years ago in one of the South American Republics which had no decorations, the Government decided that it would be wrong not to pay any honour to the representative of His Holiness the Pope, so it introduced a new order and conferred the first Grand Cross on the Legate.'

It was clear that the matter was regarded as having some importance: I promised that I would at once report to the Government and do what I could to persuade them to institute an order. Some ten days later I received the answer: the Cabinet had carefully considered the question, but had with regret come to the unanimous conclusion that it would be impossible to offer a decoration to the Cardinal, as the democratic feeling of the Irish people was opposed to the conferring of decorations.

The painful duty devolved upon me of informing the Monsignore of their decision. When I had conveyed my message, he remarked, 'I cannot believe that the Irish people would be opposed to the conferring of any honour on the representative of the Pope.' I said nothing: I could not contradict him, and it would have been difficult to explain that the Government – in the highest interests of the country – held it to be its duty to do nothing which would possibly involve a loss of votes in the constituencies.

The Congress took place in Dublin amid scenes of the utmost enthusiasm. After the Cardinal's return I met one of his suite and asked him his impressions. He said, 'We were all delighted. I have attended two other Congresses but we have never had such a reception as in Dublin. Even the poorest had hung out flags and decorated their houses. One could see that the people had no other wish than to do honour to the Holy Father.'

'And official Ireland?' I inquired. 'I'm sure it showed the same enthusiasm as the people.'

'Oh, yes,' he said, 'the Government received us with the utmost courtesy.'

I fancied I could distinguish an undertone of reserve in his voice. I waited for him to continue.

'There were just a few things that we didn't quite understand,' he went on. 'For instance, when our steamer entered the harbour of Dublin, we saw the Nuncio with the Diplomatic Corps, the Bishops, an enormous crowd. We wondered if it was possible that the Government was not present. Then a group of men in dark coats and soft hats whom we had taken for detectives came up to us. They were the Ministers.'

I could say nothing. How could I explain to him that de Valera and his friends, when they were in opposition, had in the name of democracy attacked Cosgrave's Ministers for the wearing of top hats and morning coats on official occasions? How could I tell him that they were the slaves of their own demagogic propaganda, that they did not dare to appear before the people in a headgear that only a year before they had denounced as the badge of English Imperialism?

During the Congress the presence of the Governor General had been a thorn in the flesh to de Valera. The fact that James

McNeill was an old adherent of Sinn Féin and had been nominated by Cosgrave's Government did not mollify his sentiments: he found it intolerable that the representative of the King should have precedence over himself, and did all that was possible to avoid being present at the same functions as his rival. The one-sided contest reached its climax shortly after the conclusion of the Congress. The occasion was a ball in the French Legation. The guests were assembled, among them a number of Ministers, though not de Valera himself. The Governor General was announced; the orchestra struck up our national anthem 'The Soldier's Song'. But at the sound of the first line –

Soldiers are we, whose lives are pledged to Ireland,

the soldiers of Ireland who had attained ministerial rank took to instantaneous flight and did not appear again. No-one could come to any other conclusion but that they were acting under instructions. Possibly it had not occurred to the deviser of the plan that their gesture might be embarrassing not only to the Governor General, but also to the French Minister.

On the following day those who had had the good fortune to be present had to retail twenty times in the course of the morning the details – whether the Ministers had seemed embarrassed, whether they had said good-bye to their host before leaving, how long the other guests had remained, how McNeill had behaved in the painful circumstances. Only the Government made no pronouncement: it appeared to think that the episode might be regarded as a normal occurrence in social life.

Its view was not widely shared: even in Rome de Valera's latest political move was the subject of unfavourable comment. On the following Friday morning, as we waited our turn for admission to the Cardinal Secretary of State, the Belgian Ambassador remarked to a colleague in an undertone possibly intended for my ears, '*Mais ce sont des paysans!* They are peasants!' I could only pretend to have heard nothing: it would have been useless to tell him that there could be nothing more alien to the nature of even the humblest Irish peasant than deliberate discourtesy to the host whose hospitality he was enjoying.

McNeill had preserved silence, but gradually the rumour went round that he had addressed a letter to the Head of the Government, in which he enumerated the various slights to which he had been subjected, and demanded an apology. No-one knew what answer he had received; it seemed strange that not a word had appeared in the press. But it was not long till the mystery was cleared up. McNeill had sent copies of the correspondence to the Irish papers but the Government had threatened the editors with the penalties prescribed by the Official Secrets Act if they published official documents whose divulgence to the public might bring the State into danger. McNeill did not appeal to the article of the Constitution guaranteeing freedom of speech; he took the simpler course of sending copies of the letters to an English paper with a wide circulation in Ireland. The Irish press was thus enabled to print as quotations from the English paper the same documents whose publication in the first instance would have endangered the interests of the State.

The Governor General received no apology: on the contrary, he was made responsible for the friction between himself and the Government. In answer to his complaint that the behaviour of the Ministers made it impossible for him to carry out the duties of his office, he was advised to draw the logical conclusion and resign. McNeill, who was seriously ill and had no desire to expose himself further to public affronts, followed the advice and retired into private life. The Irish public, while averse on principle to the existence of a Governor General, asked itself whether the same result could not have been attained by other methods.

A new Governor General was appointed – a personal friend of de Valera. In order to conceal the fact that constitutionally nothing had been changed, he was called by the Gaelic title of Seanascal. He received a quarter of the salary of his predecessor, lived in a villa in a Dublin suburb, and undertook not to appear in public without the express consent of the Government. De Valera needed no longer to fear that he would not have the first place in all official ceremonies.

A new election was announced. Shortly before the date fixed I was once more in Dublin and called on Walshe who had remained permanent Secretary to the Department of External Affairs.

'How do you find the new Minister?' I asked him.

'Dev is far and away the best Minister we've ever had,' he answered. 'You'll be delighted with him when you meet him.'

'What do you think of the prospects at the election?' I asked him.

'It's as good as certain that we'll have a bigger majority this time.'

'And what about the Republic? Will he make up his mind at last to take the decisive step?'

Walshe giggled, as was his habit when pleased with himself and the world. 'I think we've got him off the idea of a Republic,' he said.

He was right: the election took place without an appeal to the people for a mandate to declare the Republic. The Government succeeded in slightly improving its position.

De Valera had announced his intention of visiting Rome in the month of May 1933. The rumour had been circulated by persons hostile to Ireland that he was a dangerous revolutionary and Bolshevist, and that the Pope would refuse to receive him. It was a more than favourable opportunity of making the standpoint of Irish nationalism better known in the Vatican and of demonstrating once and for all that we had nothing in common with the Communists of Eastern Europe: I felt that in making the necessary arrangements for his ten days' stay I was doing useful work for the country. But de Valera himself seemed to annex greater importance to a problem which, I admit, had not occurred to me. The Department of External Affairs sent me an urgent inquiry as to whether it would be necessary for him to wear a top hat on his way to his audience with the Pope, or whether it would excite unfavourable comment if he went bareheaded to the Vatican.

The inquiry would have surprised me even more if I had not known that our Ministers' democratic principles had prevented them from wearing top hats at the Eucharistic Congress. And now the same principles were being transplanted to Rome, and a precedent was being set for such Irish Ministers as should in the future visit foreign states. All depended on my giving my approval.

I racked my brains for an argument sufficiently cogent to coerce de Valera into wearing the clothes prescribed by the protocol and to prevent him from making not only himself but the country ridiculous in the eyes of the world. Finally I informed the Department that strictly speaking protocol had laid down that those who possessed no diplomatic or military uniform should wear evening dress and a top hat, but that I was certain that, if there were urgent reasons against doing so, the Vatican authorities would show themselves indulgent. At the same time I considered it my duty to point out that Mahatma Gandhi had recently visited Rome, but had not been received by the Pope: popular rumour had circulated the ridiculous story that he had refused to go to the Vatican without his goat and spinning-wheel. The story was obviously pure invention, but I feared that the Roman populace, whose sense of humour was as highly developed as it was scurrilous, might seize the occasion to make unsuitable comparisons. I received a curt communication that the Prime Minister would wear a top hat.

And in fact de Valera submitted to the exigencies of protocol, dutifully wearing his top hat whenever no photographers were about. He was received by the Pope and the Cardinal Secretary of State, by the King of Italy and Mussolini; Victor Emmanuel as a fluent speaker of English gained his special commendation. The Holy See conferred on him the Grand Cross of the Order of Pius; he accepted it without feeling himself bound to any return in kind.

Two minor episodes of diplomatic activity or non-activity, occurred whilst the Prime Minister was in Rome. I had accompanied de Valera and his secretaries to a ceremony in St Peter's: after we had left the Basilica, we were led by the Papal master of ceremonies to a balcony from which we could assist at the Pope's benediction *urbi et orbi*. By chance the former King of Spain was present on the same balcony; de Valera was introduced to him by the *Cerimoniere*. Without wasting time on superfluous courtesy King Alfonso said, 'Mr de Valera, I should like to tell you that I consider your policy towards England wrong and foolish.' A painful silence followed, which was broken only by the cheers of the Roman crowd at the appearance of the Holy Father. It would not have been difficult to find an appropriate answer; the success of King Alfonso's statesmanship in Spain scarcely justified him in giving gratuitous advice to the leaders of other states of whose circumstances he was supremely ignorant; but de Valera's silence was more dignified. Moreover, I had already noticed that he was never offended by the accusation of exaggerated nationalism: only the suggestion that he had been false to the ideals of Sinn Féin never failed to provoke his indignation. It was an unfortunate circumstance that this charge too was brought against him before the end of his journey.

Since the beginning of the First World War Professor Donal Hales had been settled in Genoa. He was a member of a well-known County Cork family which had taken a prominent part in the Sinn Féin campaign. In 1921 he had been appointed consul of the Republic without *exequatur*, as I had been in Berlin. On his taking the side of the Irregulars in 1923 he had been dismissed by the Cosgrave Government. He had disapproved of the entry of Fianna Fáil into the Dáil, and had thenceforth avoided all contact with de Valera's Government.

In the hope of winning over the recalcitrant Republicans, de Valera determined to make a conciliatory gesture. He wrote to Hales, proposing a meeting at Genoa. But Hales, despite the obvious personal advantages of the friendship of the authorities, was not to be conciliated; he intimated that he saw no object in a meeting, and de Valera returned to Ireland without having spoken to him.

I mention the episode because it was one of his last attempts at reconciliation with the extremists: its failure went a long way to convince him that further efforts would be in vain. From this date onwards his policy underwent a change of orientation: his ultimate aims remained the same, but the enemy was henceforward on the left.

SIX

'We in Berlin'

I had been four years in Rome when the Government decided to transfer me to another post. We had not many foreign missions, and those in England and America were reserved for candidates who had no knowledge of any other language than English. Accordingly, I applied for the post of Minister to Germany; the former Minister, moved by an equal dislike of Hitler and de Valera, had sent in his resignation after the accession to power of the National Socialists and the Hosts of Destiny. There was no competition for the post and in summer of 1933 I set out for Berlin.

With the double object of impressing foreign opinion and of conciliating the Puritan element always strong in Germany, the National Socialist administration had undertaken the moral regeneration of the capital. As I walked one evening shortly after my arrival down the Kurfürstendamm, I could scarcely believe that so great a change had been effected in so short a space of time. In place of the hordes of women who had badgered the passer-by at every footstep, not a prostitute was to be seen – or at any rate not one who ventured to ply her trade openly. No placards tempted the tourist with the attractions of the *Nacktballett* of Celly de Rheidt or Lola Bach. From the newspaper kiosks the countless reviews propagating nudism with appropriate photographs had disappeared; one would have asked in vain for a copy of Professor Magnus Hirschfeld's *Freundschaftsblatt,* whose pretensions to a purely scientific treatment of the homosexual problem were belied by the advertisements of elderly gentlemen seeking the company of good-looking young men between twenty and thirty years of age. The shabbily elegant touts no longer whispered the address of gaming-dens in the Kleistsrassse; in the deserted side-streets no ragged form emerged from the darkness to exhibit his packet of pornographic photos under the meagre light of a gas-lamp. In the Renaissance-Theater the 'proletarian' dramas, which in the absence of wit or humour had relied for their effect on such popular expressions as *'Scheisse'* and *'Arschloch'*, had made place for a classic repertory of Goethe and Schiller. I passed down the Motzstrasse in front of the much advertised Eldorado, where young men (former officers according to the management) with rows of imitation pearls in the *décolletés* of their white silk dresses had been willing for a consideration to dance with the stranger in search of a sensation: now it was closed, and thick planks were nailed across its multicoloured glass windows.

Undoubtedly the Nazi broom had swept away many of the scandals which had earned for Berlin the fame of the most immoral city in Europe; it was evident that the licence of the last ten years had given way to an iron discipline. I asked myself how long the Puritan aspects of the National Socialist revolution would last: it was difficult to believe that Röhm's moral sentiments would be shocked by the homosexuals of the Eldorado or that Goebbels would shrink in horror from the spectacle of naked dancers. I mentioned the changed aspect of the city to a German acquaintance: in the exasperating manner to which I was soon to grow accustomed, he gave me in reply the stock Nazi cliché which one read every day in the *Völkischer Beobachter*.

'Yes,' he said, 'the Führer has put an end to this morass of Czech-Jewish corruption.'

He was of course only repeating like a parrot the phrase that was daily dinned into the heads of the German people. He knew as well as I did that innumerable persons concerned in the vice traffic were neither Czechs nor Jews, but for the moment it suited the authorities to pretend that the immoralities which had grown up in the years succeeding Germany's defeat had been forced on the German race by the ethnically inferior Slavs and Semites.

At the end of September President Hindenburg returned from his estate at Neudeck in East Prussia, and a day was fixed for the newly arrived Ministers to present their credentials. The

'WE IN BERLIN'

President was standing to receive me in the enormous reception-room of the Präsidentenpalais in the Wilhelmstrasse – a colossal over-lifesize figure in his old-fashioned frock-coat, reminding me irresistibly of the 'Iron Hindenburg' into which the German people had hammered its patriotic nails during the War. In spite of his more than eighty years he was as erect as a wooden statue; his head was densely covered by wiry grey hair; he used no spectacles – a remarkable feat for one of his age even if his speech was written for him in letters an inch high.

Before my admission to his presence one of the Foreign Office officials had asked me what military service I had seen.

'None,' I said. 'There has never been conscription in Ireland. Why?'

'Do you go in for shooting?' he continued.

'No,' I said. 'I have shot an occasional rabbit, but nothing more.'

My interlocutor seemed slightly worried. 'Do you ride?' he asked.

'Oh, yes,' I said. 'I used to hunt in Ireland. I have always been fond of riding.'

The look of preoccupation on his face gave way to one of relief.

'That's all right, then,' he said, as he hurried off.

The object of his questioning became clear to me when after the conclusion of the formal proceedings we had taken our places in the armchairs of the reception-room and the President began, 'When I was a young man, I had an Irish mare. She carried me well for many years – '

I felt that there were many advantages in German *Gründlichkeit:* owing to the thoroughness of the Foreign Office I had been spared a possibly embarrassing moment. On military service or big game shooting I would have been hopelessly at sea, but on horses I could hold my own.

On the next day the heads of all foreign missions had been invited to the *Parteitag* at Nürnberg. It was, strictly speaking, not a state function, but the annual congress of the NSDAP, the National Socialist German Workers' Party. In consequence, the Ambassadors of the United States, England, France and the

USSR, and the Ministers of Holland and Roumania, had declined the invitation, but the other Governments, regarding more the substance than the form and considering that for practical purposes the Party was the State, had instructed their representatives to attend.

Apart from its political significance it was a pleasant enough week. In view of the unimaginable overcrowding in the town, we remained in our special train at a siding in the outskirts of Nürnberg; each Ambassador had two sleeping-car compartments from which the communication-door had been removed, an SS man as his personal attendant, and a car at his disposal. On the platform there were bathrooms and a hairdresser; ample provision had been made for every personal need. Our days were occupied by speeches, demonstrations, and again speeches; we saw the Army, the Air Force, the SA, the SS, the Hitler Youth, the Labour Service; nothing was omitted which could make the forces of the Party imposing in our eyes. If bands and banners and searchlights could have made proselytes to National Socialism, not one of us would have remained outside the fold.

But the German mentality is not adapted to make converts outside its own race; some of the methods adopted had the opposite effect to that intended. It was, for instance, scarcely likely to conciliate the Ministers of such neutral states as Switzerland or the Scandinavian kingdoms that the deputations of their fellow-citizens in shirts of various colours should be the Party's guests of honour. In Ireland we had no corresponding movement, but the Chief of Protocol announced to me with an air of importance, 'Mrs Guinness is here!'

'Who is Mrs Guinness?' I asked without excessive interest – I had in 1933 never heard of the later notorious Mitford sisters.

'She has great influence in the British Fascist Party.'

'Really?' I said.

'The Fascist Party in England is making great progress. Don't you think so?'

Slightly annoyed that he should apparently connect me with English political parties, I replied, 'I don't really know much about it. I thought it was more of the nature of a Society game.'

My sally had no success: it was obviously tactless to jest on such subjects as authoritarian parties, even in foreign countries. I had little doubt that my remark would be repeated further, and resolved for the future to abstain from all frivolous comment.

One day in the week was set apart for an excursion of the Diplomatic Corps: on the night before, our train left Nürnberg for the Black Forest or the Bavarian Highlands; we were met on the following morning by a fleet of some fifty Mercedes and Porsche cars which carried us through the most picturesque German landscapes with frequent stops for meals, civic receptions, the inspection of waterfalls and the like. A triumph of organization: as it recurred annually we noticed that it invariably coincided with the declarations of policy which might be considered least adapted for profane ears. Thus, in 1935, we were absent from the announcement of the *Nürnberger Gesetze,* the racial laws which deprived 'non-Aryans' of their rights of citizenship. We could read the proceedings in the *Völkischer Beobachter* next morning, but the written page has never the same effect as the spoken word – and in any case the speeches were always rigidly censored before they were handed to the press. Not that at times we did not hear pronouncements unlikely to enhance National Socialism in our eyes. Hitler delivered an address every year on Nazi culture: on one occasion he occupied himself with the problems of modern art. Problems, that is to say, for the decadent democratic artists; to the Führer they presented no difficulty. 'The duty of the painter', he thundered, 'is to paint the sky blue and the grass green. There are so-called modern artists who paint them in other colours and say in their defence that they see them in some peculiar way different from ordinary humanity. One of two things: either they see them as we do and paint them in other colours for self-advertisement. In that case, they are dishonest and must be forbidden to paint. Or they really see them in some abnormal way. In that case, they are suffering from schizophrenia and should be sterilized.'

After enunciating this profound truth, Hitler bestowed a self-satisfied smirk on his audience; the crowd burst into a roar of applause. I caught the eye of the Argentine Ambassador: I could see his lips silently forming the words, '*C'est incroyable*! It's incredible!' I too imagined that nowhere outside the atmosphere of the *Nürnberger Parteitag* could such complete incomprehension of the elementary principles of art be hailed as inspired truth, until many years later I read of the condemnation by official Communism of the totality of modern non-realistic art and of the facetious commentaries of Kruschev – which would undoubtedly have been hailed with enthusiasm by the Nazis assembled in Nürnberg.

It was the triumph of ignorance and lack of culture, but it was accepted throughout Germany as dogma. Alfred Rosenberg wrote in the *Völkischer Beobachter* that the artist had but one duty – to paint 'heroically'. His meaning was not clear to me until I visited the annual exhibition of official German art in Munich: here I found that the places of honour had been reserved for pictures of life-sized Aryans in Nazi uniform hurling hand-grenades at a presumably non-Aryan and Communist foe. The German painters of merit, Nolde, Hofer, Heckel and the rest, were either forbidden to exhibit or ceased of their own volition to inflict their pictures on a hostile public. My friend the Berlin art-dealer Carl Nierendorff, who later transferred his business to New York, told me that he had with difficulty obtained permission to hold an exhibition of landscapes: in spite of the official sanction he had found after the private view scrawled in large letters across one of the exhibits, 'We want no Bolshevist art in Germany!' I could only suppose that the sky was not blue or the grass sufficiently green.

But in 1933 National Socialism was still to most of us an unknown quantity, and the *Parteitag* had not yet assumed the militaristic character of subsequent years. Even the SS had not yet won its later notoriety, and the members in attendance on us, picked for their knowledge of languages (I was informed that mine spoke Gaelic, but had no opportunity of verifying it), could not have shown us greater attention. One of our evenings was spent in their camp at Himmler's invitation: after a supper of beef and sausages they sang *Volkslieder* and marching songs, *Volk, ans Gewehr!* and *Ich hatt' einen Kameraden* and the inevitable *Horst Wessel Lied*. Under the stars by the flickering torchlight it produced, as it was intended to do, an idyllic effect: it would have been hard in 1933 to imagine anything sinister in the obliging young men in their well-cut black uniforms or in their friendly chief who went round clinking glasses with his guests.

Such influences, however, were subsidiary: the best propaganda of the Party was the obvious enthusiasm of the rank and file. It is possible that in later years participation in the ceremonies of Nürnberg became a matter of routine; in 1933 there cannot be a shadow of doubt that the average SA man could imagine no higher honour than to be selected to represent his comrades at the *Parteitag*. It was no bed of roses: they came, often by forced marches, from all parts of Germany; the nights on their straw couches were short; the days of parading or standing guard under a blazing sun or in streaming rain were long; but every privation was accepted as an honourable sacrifice in the cause of the Fatherland. There was little enthusiasm for or comprehension of the peculiar doctrines of National Socialism, but there was a tremendous conviction that after the humiliations of the last fifteen years Germany had been reborn, and a fanatical devotion to Adolf Hitler as the man who had accomplished the miracle and would give the Fatherland its place in the sun and the German workman his beer and *Schnapps* and freedom from the nightmare of unemployment.

For a foreigner it was impossible to understand the feelings of the rank and file of the SA for Hitler. We could only see a commonplace figure mouthing commonplace sentiments with the self-sufficiency of the half-educated. There was not one of us who was not convinced that in his own country such a man could never have risen to power. But there was equally not one of us who did not recognize that with all his banality and lack of charm he must possess some quality, beyond the scope of our perception, which appealed to the German soul. When at a night meeting in the Luitpoldfeld, surrounded by banners and searchlights, he assumed the Messianic air of Germany's predestined saviour, we could see nothing but pretentious theatricality. But a glance at the faces around us was enough to show that for his audience he was genuinely the Messiah foreordained by Providence to redeem his people and the world.

We were of course aware that our presence at Nürnberg was being exploited to convince the man in the street that the Third Reich had won the approval of our respective states. It was an embarrassing situation, but there was nothing we could do to obviate it. The crowds cheered us incessantly, when our cortège of motors passed along the streets; we could only respond by lifting our hats. Finally, the Ministers of China and Haiti, whom the order of precedence had placed in the same car, responded by extending their hands in the 'German salute'. They were scarcely ideal representatives of the Nordic race, but they earned considerable momentary popularity.

★ ★ ★

The *Nürnberger Parteitag* came to an end, and we returned to the everyday life of Berlin. To the foreign observer it was of intense interest to see the strata into which German society was divided, the watertight compartments which existed side by side with no points of contact. Only in the Embassies and Legations did they meet, but even there they preserved an armed neutrality and so far as possible ignored each other's existence.

There was in the first place the old aristocratic and military caste, which had seen its best days before 1914 and, impoverished by the inflation of the post-War years, had retired from all participation in public affairs. There were the surviving members of the ruling class under the Republic of Weimar – the business-men and bankers, in part Jewish, who had flourished under Wirth and Brüning and had done so much to place Germany on the way to material recovery. And, finally, there was the new class of Nazi functionaries who were determined to profit to the full by the occasions of power and riches opened to them by Hitler.

With these last we came into contact at official entertainments; for the most part they were far from sure of themselves and painfully anxious to make a good impression and to convince us of the necessity of National Socialism if Europe was to be saved from Communism. For myself I needed no argument to convince me that National Socialism, whatever might be its defects, should be upheld by the Western Powers as the strongest, perhaps the only, force which could prevent the spread of the Communist Empire over half Europe – and subsequent events have more than sufficiently confirmed my view. But I need not say that my admiration for Hitler's régime as a bulwark against the East did not imply an unquestioning acceptance of all its practices. Most vivid in my memory is a *Sturmführer* Schmid, whom I met at an evening party given by the Chief of Protocol. He had told me of the persecution of Nazis under the 'red' Government of Weimar; in particular, he complained that the Communists who had murdered SA men had been either acquitted by the courts of law or condemned to some trifling period of imprisonment.

I knew that what he said was correct: nothing had created more bad blood than the discrimination against the SA by the law courts. But what was the use of discussing the past? 'There's nothing to be done about it now,' I observed.

But he was far from agreeing. 'It would be contrary to justice', he retorted, 'if a man like Ali Hoehler who murdered our Horst Wessel was to get off with the five years' imprisonment that the judges gave him.'

'Do you propose to bring him to trial again?' I asked.

'No,' he replied. 'Ali Hoehler will never be brought to trial. He is dead.'

'How did he die?' I inquired.

'I shot him,' said *Sturmführer* Schmid calmly. 'It would have been unjust that he should not pay the penalty for his crime, so as Governor of the prison it was my duty to put an end to him.'

In spite of my amazement I could see that he was entirely satisfied of the correctness of his action – indeed, if he had not been convinced that any impartial person must approve of it, he would scarcely have made such a confidence to me. He must have noticed my consternation, for he went on, 'For us National Socialists the important thing is justice, not mere paragraphs.' It was another of the stock sayings of the Party: Hitler, Goebbels and Rosenberg repeated it perpetually in their speeches; one could read it daily in the *Völkischer Beobachter:* the man in the street had taken it over and delivered it with the air of one who has discovered a profound verity.

I looked around me; it was a typical scene of bourgeois comfort. Diplomats and Foreign Office officials in black coats and striped trousers were sitting in well-upholstered armchairs, eating *belegte Brötchen* and drinking beer; the bookshelves were filled with leather-bound editions of the German classics; upon the wall there hung a reproduction of Boecklin's 'Island of the Dead'. And in this everyday atmosphere a mild-looking man with the expressionless china-blue eyes of the north German had told me in casual conversation that he had shot a prisoner in cold blood, because he had believed it to be in the interests of justice. I wondered how far our host and the other members of the *Auswärtiges Amt* would approve his action.

'Of course he was a common criminal,' *Sturmführer* Schmid continued, 'not a political offender. You mustn't believe that there is any foundation for the lies of the foreign press about our maltreatment of political opponents.'

'What do you do with them?' I asked.

'We have camps for them. We can't leave them free to work against the interests of the country, but they're well treated so long as they behave themselves.'

'Who have you got in the camps?'

'A number of Communists and Social Democrats,' he said vaguely. 'There's the son of President Ebert for instance. He's a bad type. He got a beating the other day. But if they behave themselves well, nobody interferes with them. Would you like to visit a camp? Here's my address and telephone number. Ring me up, and we can fix a day. Bring anyone you like with you.'

But on considering his offer I decided not to ring him up. In spite of his apparent frankness, I did not believe for a moment that a visit to the camp would have revealed anything but what the authorities wanted me to know nor that I would have obtained any information from the prisoners on their real conditions of life. I was not even certain whether to believe that he had really shot Ali Hoehler: his boast might merely have been intended to make himself important in my eyes. But, true or false, it was significant that he should have considered it a subject for boasting.

I never met *Sturmführer* Schmid again: if his indiscretions came to the ears of his superiors, they must unquestionably have debarred him for the future from all contacts with the Diplomatic Corps. Nor was I ever again made the recipient of similar confidences; even the most fanatical member of the Party soon recognized that many of their exploits were best kept secret from even the friendliest of foreign ears.

The new official class had no relations of any kind with the representatives of the previous régime: it was strictly forbidden for any person in the service of the Government to associate even casually with a member of the Jewish race. A distinguished general on arriving for dinner in a foreign Embassy, found that the place allotted to him at table was next to a Jewish lady; he sent his excuses to the Ambassador by the footman and left the house. No doubt he felt the ungraciousness of the gesture, but any other course might have cost him his career.

Many of the Jews left Germany in 1933, but the majority, sometimes from the desire to save their material interests, more often from genuine affection for the land in which they and their ancestors had lived for centuries, preferred to remain. Until 1935 they continued, in spite of daily affronts, and the prospects of worse to come, to lead a fairly normal life. Frau Friedländer Fould continued to entertain in her palace on the Pariserplatz; Stresemann's widow was an honoured guest in the Legations; Herbert Guttmann, despite his expulsion from the Wannsee Golf Club which he had founded and financed and of which he was President, was still one of the figures of Berlin Society; Baron von Schwabach, banker and friend of the Kaiser, received his guests in the well-known apartment in the Matthäikirchstrasse with the Lenbachs and Menzels on the walls and the table-services of eighteenth-century Meissen and Fürstenberg.

But it was their last desperate effort to defy the forces determined on their destruction. Frau Friedländer Fould left Germany with her Dutch passport; Käthe Stresemann took refuge in Switzerland; but Schwabach's fate was more tragic. His son had died suddenly of infantile paralysis; under the *Nürnberger Gesetze* he himself was threatened with the confiscation of his property. His death was announced in the press: few doubted that he had taken his life in order that his non-Jewish wife might inherit free from the fear of confiscation.

The survivors of the Kaiser's Germany, the so-called 'Potsdam Excellencies', were a class by themselves, who disliked with equal intensity the Republic of 1919 and the Third Reich of 1933, though as their families were traditionally destined for a military career they had never formed an overt opposition. Through Gräfin Koenigsmarck, originally an O'Nolan from County Wexford, I learned to know them well and to make many friends among them. The weekends spent with the Koenigsmarcks in Schloss Plaue on the Havel near Brandenburg or in the other castles in the neighbourhood of Berlin are among the most pleasant memories of my life in Germany.

They had certain attributes in common with the corresponding class of country gentlemen in England, for which country most of them nourished an unreasoning admiration dating from the time of Queen Victoria and German influences at the Court of St James'. For Ireland I soon found in spite of their friendship for myself that they had not the slightest sympathy, regarding it as the same disturbing element in the British Empire as Alsace-Lorraine had been in the German Reich. It would be an exaggeration to say that they were anti-Semites; they were genuinely horrified at the racial laws and the official discrimination against members of the Jewish race; but, like their fathers before them, they refused to associate with persons of Jewish blood and considered marriage with a Jew sufficient to place the offender irrevocably outside the pale.

With the exception of a few families from Silesia or the Rheinland, they were Lutheran, but their Lutheranism was of the unthinking, traditional kind. When the Evangelical Church in Germany split in two – the *Deutsche Christen Bekenntniskirche,* the Confessional Church, of which Pastor Niemöller was a protagonist – the majority proclaimed themselves members of the latter, but, so far as I could judge, for purely political and personal reasons. Some told me that they could not adhere to a Church which supported Hitler, others (quite incorrectly) that the *Reichsbischof* was always drunk; but, when I asked if there was any difference of doctrine between the two bodies, I could never obtain a definite answer.

Once a year the Kaiser's second wife, the 'Kaiserin Hermine', spent a fortnight in Berlin. She occupied a small flat in the former Crown Prince's palace, whose upper floors had been adapted as a gallery of modern art. I was a frequent guest at dinner where the Kaiserin Hermine enjoyed the opportunity of airing her English. She never spoke directly of the actual régime. Only once, when I asked her if she had gone to a recent performance of the *Rosenkavalier*, she said, 'No, I never go to the opera now. I don't want to see those people sitting in the Imperial box. I know that his sons go, but I myself will not. It is the least I can do for the poor old man!'

Except for Ulrich Stang, the Counsellor to the Norwegian Legation, I was the only foreigner admitted to the circle of the Potsdam Excellencies. From 1914 onwards foreign travel had been difficult for Germans, and most of them had forgotten whatever French or English they had learned in their schooldays so that the only diplomats whom they invited to their homes were those whose foreign nationality they could forget in the course of conversation.

They were typical representatives of a Germany which is too little known outside its own borders – neither the intellectual Germany of the *'Dichter Denker'*, nor the international Germany of the post-War democracy, still less the demagogic Germany of the new rulers. Their interests were confined to their class, their estates, the incidents of their daily lives. They were, if you will, restricted in their outlook; in the modern world they were certainly survivals of a previous age. But they had in compensation the virtues of their class – patriotism, loyalty to their ideals even when these were as clearly lost as the Hohenzollern monarchy, a sense of honour limited perhaps in its objects, but within those limits of a punctiliousness which I have seldom seen equalled, a determination to do their duty as they saw it which admitted of no compromise.

Now, as a class they have ceased to exist. The Kaiserin Hermine died in the utmost misery in a common lodging-house in Frankfurt on the Oder. Those who did not perish in the bombardments or in the famine of the post-War years survived as best they could by the sale of the valuables which they managed to carry with them on their flight before the Russians. Norah Koenigsmarck spent her last years acting as interpreter and giving lessons in German to the American officials in Bad Kissingen. And, lest any trace of reaction should survive, their homes, Schloss Plaue and Fredersdorf and Bendeleben and hundreds more, have been levelled to the ground by order of the Russian military command or converted into institutions for the propagating of Communism.

★ ★ ★

Princess Hohenlohe had been born Stefanie or 'Steffi' Richter in humble circumstances in Vienna. Being blessed with more than her share of Viennese charm together with an exceptionally keen intelligence, it was not long before her name began to be known outside her native district of Ottakring, and in the years after the first war she reached what was for the moment the apex of her ambition by marrying a member of the Hungarian branch of the princely family of Hohenlohe.

The marriage was presumably not an undiluted success from the sentimental point of view, for it was closely followed by a divorce, and the young princess set out for Biarritz in search of a wider outlet for her talents. Her title was sufficient to guarantee her entry into the best, or at least the smartest Society; if any difficulties arose, they were swiftly swept away by her new acquaintance King Alfonso of Spain, to whom a princess was a princess, whatever her origin – especially if she was as charming as Steffi. In the Twenties she was recognized leader of the international set in Paris; in the refrain of a song in one of Rip's *revues* on the *métèques de Paris,* the first name mentioned in the long list of distinguished foreign ladies was '*la Princesse "O' enloh"*'.

But Steffi's interests were not confined to Society; politics had their attractions for one so intelligent. Her Hungarian title brought her into contact with Lord Rothermere, who at the time was fascinated by the idea of ascending the throne of Hungary and leaving a dynasty of Harmsworths to take its place in the annals of European monarchy on an equal footing with Bourbons, Habsburgs and Bonapartes; she became his private secretary at a salary of £5000 a year.

The dream of succession to the crown of St Stephen vanished into thin air like so many other mirages of the post-

War years, but the Princess retained her post. To the insular British business man with ambitions to play, if not a royal, at least a principal role in European politics, she was the ideal assistant – fascinating, familiar with the latest and most fashionable movements in art and literature, speaking fluently all the main and some of the minor European languages, with connections in the Society of every European capital. Lord Rothermere made her the bearer of confidential communications to Hitler, Horthy, the Austrian leader Starhemberg and a number of other prominent personalities on the European political stage: she subjugated all whom she met and was able to carry the best of news on her return to her principal.

I first met her in the years before the outbreak of the Second World War. It was a Sunday afternoon in summer, and we had been invited by the Chef de Protocol Vicco von Bülow-Schwante to his castle some forty miles from Berlin. As we strolled about the lawn before supper, a motor drove up from which there descended Frau von Dirksen and Frau von Manteuffel, two pillars of the Prussian military aristocracy, and an exotic-looking personage, no longer in her first youth, dressed in the height of fashion which to my inexperienced eyes seemed Parisian rather than Teutonic, and wearing pinned to the front of her dress the unmistakable *goldenes Parteiabzeichen*, the emblem of the National Socialist party in gold. This was only conferred by the Führer personally for particular services rendered.

'Who in Heaven's name is that?' I asked a German fellow-guest.

'That's Princess Hohenlohe,' he replied. 'The Hungarian branch of the family.'

'And her gold *Hakenkreuz*? It doesn't seem to go with the cast of her features.'

'No, of course she isn't purely Aryan. But what does that matter?'

'To me, nothing. But I thought it might matter to Hitler.'

'Our Führer is very good at shutting his eyes when there is something he prefers not to see. Or, to put it in another way, he decides who is Aryan and who is not.'

'And he has given her an Aryan genealogical tree?'

'Better than that – he has given her a photo with the inscription "To the most faithful of Germans – Adolf Hitler."'

'And what is she doing here?'

'Who knows? She is living at Schloss Leopoldskron near Salzburg, which belonged to Max Reinhardt until the Anschluss.'

'And who pays for it all?' I asked.

'I don't know,' he said discreetly, 'but of course she couldn't live in Schloss Leopoldskron without the consent of the German Government.'

The Princess was my neighbour at supper: our conversation was conducted exclusively in German, from which I inferred that her first allegiance of the time being was to Hitler and not to Lord Rothermere. We discussed modern art: she did not carry her allegiance to the point of condemning Picasso and Matisse, Kandinsky and Barlach and Klee as degenerate. It was a different type of talk from any to which I was accustomed in Berlin.

Not everyone received the Princess Hohenlohe with enthusiasm, but I met her often during the round of receptions, official and non-official. 'You haven't invited me yet to see your pictures,' she remarked.

'No,' I admitted.

'What day would you like me to come to lunch?'

'Next Friday,' I said, and gathered a small company to meet her.

The Princess came, admired my Utrillos and Signacs, and graciously invited the whole party to visit her at Schloss Leopoldskron. After the departure of the guests the butler asked me according to his usual routine whether everything had been in order.

'In perfect order,' I said.

'I think', he remarked pensively, 'that the Princess must be a very religious lady.'

'For God's sake!' I said. 'Have you been discussing questions of theology with her?'

'When I was serving her Highness,' he said, 'she took only vegetables, and when I said, "May I call your Highness' attention to the roast chicken?" she said, "Don't you know that I as a Catholic eat no chicken on Friday?"'

Not long afterwards she left Berlin; it was rumoured that

Hitler had lost confidence in the 'most faithful' of his Germans. For some time nothing more was heard of her; international relations became increasingly strained, social ties were broken and many familiar faces disappeared. And then, suddenly, I read of her once again in the English press. Lord Rothermere had decided to dispense with the services of his private secretary and as a natural consequence to cease the payment of her salary.

★ ★ ★

Almost alone of the old aristocracy in openly proclaiming her devotion to the Führer was Viktoria von Dirksen, the 'grandmother of the National Socialist Revolution', a lady of portly presence and bluff manners who delighted in playing the role of the bull in the political china-shop. By family and tradition monarchist, she had grasped at an early stage the fact that in Germany there was no conceivable chance of a restoration of the Hohenzollerns and had transferred her allegiance to Hitler's rising star. Hitler was not unmindful of the importance of one in touch with the Prussian *Adelstand,* with the military caste, with the members of the Imperial family: the Dirksen house in the Margaretenstrasse was one of the few private residences which he honoured with a visit. It was the only common ground on which one was likely to meet the Crown Princess and Dr Goebbels, the Nazi Chief of Police Graf Helldorf and the Empress Hermine.

Frau von Dirksen was not backward in her comments on the members of her class who remained loyal to the old order. 'I have no patience with them,' she told me. 'They don't see how ridiculous they are when they refuse to recognize that the only hope for Germany is our Führer.' They in return regarded her as an intriguer and a traitor to the dynasty, and referred to the alleged fact that her mother had been a cook. But she cared little for their opinion, and continued with a certain success her pro-gramme of bringing together the old and the new dispensations.

With the members of the Diplomatic Corps she was on the best of terms, although she had the habit of astonishing them by her outspoken comments on international affairs. After the annexation of the Sudetenland and the destruction of Czechoslovakia I met her one day by chance. She greeted me with a broad grin and said, 'I'm afraid I've just put my foot in it with the Polish Ambassador.'

'What have you been saying now?' I asked.

'I said that everything was settled but the question of the Corridor, but that it wouldn't take long till we got back what belonged to us there. I shouldn't have said it, but it slipped out. You should have seen Lipski's face.'

I wondered whether her *gaffes* were really so spontaneous as she pretended: at any rate they afforded her great amusement in observing the reactions which they caused. To me she said in the course of the War, 'I suppose you expect that the Führer will come to the help of Ireland?'

'Not in the least,' I said. 'He has never shown the least interest in us.'

'It's just as well you realize that,' said she. 'He would make a separate peace with England tomorrow if he could. He has never wanted to destroy England.'

But even if her bluffness of manner was deliberately affected and behind her intentional blunders there was a shrewd and calculating mind, her devotion to Hitler as a man and as the redeemer of Germany was beyond all doubt sincere.

He owed her much, and it was a shock to her and to all who knew her when in the last year of the War she was arrested on some trifling charge. She managed to send a message to him from prison. But Hitler only replied, 'The woman does not interest me.'

She was released shortly afterwards, but died almost immediately. I asked one of her friends the cause of her death.

'*Ich denke, sie ist vor Gram gestorben,*' he replied. "I think she died of a broken heart.'

Among the younger generation of the nobility there were of course some, though not many, who either from conviction or in the hope of a career proclaimed themselves in favour of National Socialism or even joined the Party. Goering, in particular, delighted to create for himself an aristocratic background, took pains to secure their services for his entourage. By their own class they were looked upon with regret and a certain distrust: it was felt that they had lowered the banner which their ancestors had carried in honour.

I was introduced to Prince Eberwyn of Bentheim and Steinfurt. His ancestors had reigned over the minute principality of Bentheim and Steinfurt near the Dutch frontier until its absorption into the Reich; he himself had resigned his hereditary rights as head of the family on contracting what turned out to be the first of a series of extremely morganatic marriages. Now, he was wearing the brown uniform of the SA.

'For me,' he began with the air of one making a memorable pronouncement, 'there are three great men in history – Jesus Christ, Martin Luther and Adolf Hitler.'

'My dear Prince,' I replied, 'you can't expect me as a Catholic to be so enthusiastic as you are for . . .'

I paused, and there was a tense silence among the listeners.

'. . . Martin Luther,' I concluded.

★ ★ ★

By far the most brilliant member of the Diplomatic Corps in Berlin was the French Ambassador. André François-Poncet knew Germany as few foreigners know it: he had published works on German literature, and was a perfect master of the language – indeed his occasional speeches, made as Doyen of the Diplomatic Corps on the frequent occasions when the Nuncio was unable or unwilling to be present, were a model in form and content. What, however, gave them particular piquancy was the contrast between the perfection of the phraseology and the pronounced French accent in which they were delivered – so pronounced that I often wondered whether the Ambassador was not purposely exaggerating it.

Be that as it may, François-Poncet was considered by the majority in Berlin as one of Germany's truest friends; it is incidentally remarkable that for almost all Germans a thorough knowledge of their language is accepted unquestioningly as a proof of sympathy with Germany's political aims. Hitler, it was reported, held the same view; if he could be considered to have a liking for anyone, it appeared to be for the French Ambassador, whose method of speech he imitated in moments of relaxation among his intimates. Many in Berlin, with the layman's habitual overestimation of the value of personalities in international affairs, regarded his presence in Germany as a guarantee that there would be no war between Germany and France, and deplored his substitution in 1938 by Coulondre as a blow to the cause of peace.

François-Poncet was only incidentally friendly to Germany or unfriendly to National Socialism. He was in the first place a genuine lover of peace, who desired nothing more than to see a prosperous Germany take her place in the family of European nations, but he was also a patriotic Frenchman, who refused, in spite of any sympathy he might feel for the German people, to close his eyes to the dangers threatening his country. It was, unfortunately, an attitude of mind which the leaders of the Third Reich were unable to understand.

Mastný, the Czechoslovak Minister, had been transferred from Rome to Berlin in 1932. It was the most arduous, the most ungrateful and the most exposed post to which a Czech diplomat could be appointed: throughout the existence of the Third Reich Czechoslovakia never ceased to be the target of the Party press, and Mastný's private correspondence consisted largely of anonymous letters in which that peculiar term of vituperation *Monokelhengst* (monocled stallion) was the most frequent, if not the most violent, mode of address.

Yet Mastný never let his personal feelings deflect him from the policy which he had been sent to Berlin to carry out; he knew from the start that his country's fate hung in the balance and that an ill-considered action on his part might suffice to bring about the disaster which he feared. His influence was always used to counsel moderation to both governments, though it was barely heeded. Only once, after the Anschluss of Austria, did he succeed in obtaining a definite undertaking from Germany that it had no designs on the independence of Czechoslovakia: he had asked Goering for the assurance that no such *coup* was being prepared against the Government of Prague and had been told in return that it was unthinkable, since the Czechs were a non-Germanic people, whereas the Germans of Austria had of their own accord declared themselves in favour of unity with the Motherland.

'Do you think he was in good faith?' I asked him.

'For the moment, yes,' said Mastný, 'but who knows how long it will last? I never wake in the morning without wondering whether I will hear that the German *Luftwaffe* has wiped out Prague.'

The justification for his scepticism was demonstrated less than a year later, when Hitler under threat of war and with the connivance of the Western Powers occupied the territory of the *Sudetendeutsche*. But even then Mastný did not lose hope of preserving the independence of his country. The Czech Government had given a pledge that it would grant complete autonomy to the Slovaks and treat the other racial minorities, Poles, Magyars and Ruthenians, with due regard to their national aspirations: it was not long till the same stories of oppression of minorities began once more to be printed in the German press as had appeared during the Sudeten crisis.

His pessimistic predictions were realized to the full: when the Third Reich decided to create an independent state of Slovakia and to reduce Bohemia and Moravia to a Protectorate, it fell to his lot to accompany the Czech President Hacha to Hitler. Hacha had arrived from Prague at midnight and had proceeded at once to the *Reichskanzlei*. A rumour was in circulation he had been drugged before the interview: I asked Mastný if it was true.

'No,' he said, 'not in that sense – it wasn't necessary. He had to sign anything they put before him in order to prevent the country from being wiped out. The truth is that when Hacha arrived, he was in a state of collapse. As we were waiting in the ante-room, Hitler's doctor came and asked whether he would like to have the stimulant which Hitler always takes when he is overworked. Hacha agreed, and it did him some good for the moment. But he would have signed in exactly the same way without an injection.'

After the incorporation of Bohemia and Moravia in 'Greater Germany', Mastný returned to Prague, where he lived in retirement during the War. After Prague had been taken by the Allies, he was imprisoned by the newly installed Government of Beneš: the treatment given him by his jailers was such that he died shortly after his release. I can only say of him that I have seldom met a more single-minded servant of his country – nor one who received a more unworthy return from those whom he served.

Sir Nevile Henderson's advent in Berlin was awaited with more interest than usually attends the coming of an ambassador. In the first place, his predecessor Sir Eric Phipps had made little secret of his distaste for Germany and the Germans; he made a point of telling all and sundry that he had passed half his life in France, that his first wife had been French, and that he considered himself almost as much French as English. It was a harmless vanity, but one hardly calculated to enhance his prestige or that of his country in the Third Reich. He was transferred to Paris, and Henderson was sent to take his place with the avowed object of carrying out the British Government's policy of appeasement of National Socialism.

There was, however, for the Ministers of the smaller countries another reason for looking forward with curiosity to his arrival. A series of obviously inspired paragraphs had appeared in the press to the effect that he attached no importance to so-called social life, but had made it his practice to associate only with the most important personalities of the capitals in which he had been accredited. For those of us who could not possibly flatter ourselves that we belonged to the most important personalities in Berlin it was a matter of conjecture whether he would recognize our existence at all. It soon revealed itself that our doubts were more than justified: Henderson was invariably stricken with blindness when he met the representatives of the smaller states, or so deeply sunk in thought that he overlooked their presence. For the countries which belonged peculiarly to the British sphere of influence he appeared to have an especial contempt. To an inquiry whether he proposed to attend the reception given to the Egyptian Legation on the King of Egypt's birthday, he replied, "No, why should I go to their reception? Egypt is only a colony." It was in no sense a confidential utterance; all Berlin knew of it the same evening, the Eyptian Minister next morning.

Henderson's absence of mind was, however, intermittent, and his memory for faces was at times as good as that of anyone else. The wife of the Swiss Minister was fond of relating to her friends how he invariably failed to recognize her, though they had been three times introduced. 'Only once', she recounted, 'was I more fortunate. I was sitting and talking to Princess X. The British Ambassador happened to come in; he looked around him and at once came over to me. *"Chère Madame,"* he said, "I'm delighted to see you again. Would you be so kind as to introduce me to the Princess?" But when I met him next day he had forgotten my face again.'

Another of Henderson's peculiarities was his habit of wearing in and out of season a red woollen pullover. On finding himself, clad in plus-fours and the inevitable pullover, at a theatrical performance given by the Diplomatic Corps at which the rest of the company were in evening dress, he exclaimed irritably, 'If these people think I've time to change my clothes for their shows, I can only say they're greatly mistaken!'

But want of time alone did not account for his eccentricities of costume. The German authorities always indicated on the invitation-cards for any State function what dress they considered appropriate for the occasion: for the *Heldengedenktag* we were requested to appear in black coats. It caused therefore a mild sensation when Sir Nevile Henderson turned up in an elegant grey morning-coat and grey top hat with a carnation in his buttonhole, as if he were about to start for the Royal Enclosure at Ascot.

Not less significant was my own experience with Henderson; our relations were slight and came to an abrupt end, but they are not without interest. Mindful of the delicacy of my position towards the British Ambassador and anxious to give no pretext to any suggestion of discourtesy, I took the first opportunity after his arrival to ask when I might have the honour of calling on him: an hour was fixed, and I proceeded to the yellow and white Embassy in the Wilhelmstrasse. I was shown into a waiting-room, until such time as Sir Nevile should be free to receive me. I heard afterwards that he had evolved a highly personal system of receiving callers: the time which they spent in the waiting-room was graduated according to their importance. It is unnecessary to add that I was not at once admitted to the presence of the British Ambassador.

On a table in the waiting-room stood a framed photograph of Queen Victoria. I remembered having seen similar photographs in other British Embassies; the Queen had in some mysterious way become a symbol of the Empire as none of her successors had ever done. I wondered whether it was due to an unconscious but unerring instinct that the sixty-five years of the old Queen's reign had represented a golden age in England's history, an age that had passed and could never return.

In such meditations I was interrupted by a footman who informed me that His Excellency was now free to receive me. I followed him to the Ambassador's study; after greeting me formally, he cleared his throat and said, 'I see no reason why our relations should not be perfectly friendly.'

I hastened to assure him that I hoped for my part that our relations would always be maintained on a friendly basis, and Henderson continued, 'The last time that I had to do with Ireland was in the year 1913, when I helped my brother-in-law Leitrim to bring in guns for the Loyalists in Ulster.'

Without doubt he meant it kindly: he only intended to show me that he was not entirely ignorant of the recent history of Ireland. Possibly he had not even adverted to the fact that the guns had been smuggled into Northern Ireland for the purpose of shooting down the people whom I represented. It was on the tip of my tongue to say, 'I didn't enter politics quite so early: it was only in the autumn of 1914 that I started speaking against recruiting for the British Army on the Sinn Féin platform.' But I felt that nothing was to be gained by a sharp answer, and continued to give him credit for good intentions. My visit lasted the prescribed ten minutes: on their expiration I took my leave and made my way between the heavy mahogany tables and cabinets of the Victorian age to the door of the Embassy. Was it my fancy, or was the air of the Wilhelmstrasse really so fresh and stimulating after the atmosphere of the past from which I was emerging?

It was Henderson's misfortune to be born a century too late: in the days of Castlereagh or Palmerston, when sword-rattling was one of the duties of British diplomacy, he would have been

'WE IN BERLIN'

in his true element. The qualities which the French describe as *morgue* and *spleen* would have been in keeping with the tradition of the English *milord,* and no-one would have resented the eccentricities which went to make up that most picturesque of figures. But fate had decreed that he should have to deal with a Hitler, not a Talleyrand nor a Metternich, and to conduct his diplomatic mission against methods which were not in existence at the time of the Congress of Vienna. It was a world against which he was in revolt and in which he felt himself a survivor from a better and brighter past.

For Henderson it was a law of nature that world affairs should be administered by a small and privileged class of representatives of the Great Powers; they might have their own conflicts on questions of interest, but at least they would always by tacit consent and under England's leadership be prepared to unite in suppressing the aspirations of small insurgent nationalities and the claims of the unprivileged classes to take a part in the government of their own states. Equally abhorrent in his eyes were the idea of a Labour government in his own country and that of the right to self-determination of small nations which Great Britain had placed in the front of her war programme in 1914: it was a never-ending source of mortification to him that Irish and Egyptians and a horde of 'lesser breeds without the law' should be placed at least theoretically on the same level as himself. He did his best to ignore their existence, and their opinion of him was a matter of less than no importance in his eyes. In spite of his general unpopularity, I could never dislike him as a man; he was a perfect specimen of his type, and that type was too remote from modern life, one might almost say too grotesque, to be judged by ordinary standards.

★ ★ ★

Whenever I met the American Ambassador in Berlin, I found myself involuntarily thinking of a book which I had read in my youth. It was the story of an Irish middle-class family which through some freak of fortune was called on to play a part on the international stage. Its author was Charles Lever: he had given his novel, which had no doubt solaced the tedium of my great-grandparents' journeys on the first Irish railways, the name of *The Dodd Family Abroad*. I cannot help regretting that the title has already been used: it would otherwise have been so eminently suitable to the literary works of the Ambassador and his daughter.

The humour of the novel consisted in the attempts of the Dodd family to apply to a world of statesmen, generals and diplomats the standards which they had at home regarded as absolute, in the misunderstandings which arose from their ignorance of foreign habits and foreign languages, in the righteous indignation with which they condemned all that they did not understand, and in the involuntary pride which they felt at finding themselves, if only for a passing moment, entitled to rub shoulders on terms of equality with brilliant and aristocratic sinners.

The modern Dodd family remained true in every respect to the traditions of its predecessor. All who knew them in Berlin had the impression that they judged diplomatic life in a European capital by the standards of the Middle West. Ambassador Dodd was in the words of his friend and biographer Charles A. Beard, 'a Baptist of the Roger Williams tradition with Jeffersonian leanings'. The exact significance of the definition may seem obscure to those unversed in the finer shades of Baptist theology, but it would perhaps not be going too far to say that the teachings of Williams and Jefferson neither sufficed as qualifications for a man who was to represent the United States of America in Germany in the critical years 1933-38 nor enabled him to form an objective opinion on the European situation.

For Dodd, the test of every movement and every individual was democracy, which for some reason not at once obvious he identified with primitive Christianity: on the occasion of a memorial service for Marshal Pilsudski in the Hedwigskirche, the Catholic cathedral of Berlin, he writes in his diary:

> To me it was all half absurd. There was probably not one follower of Jesus in the whole congregation. Now neither the Catholics nor the Protestants believe in, nor practise, Christian or democratic principle.

'WE IN BERLIN'

But, apart from its religious character, it would be difficult to say what he meant by the term 'democracy'; that it had little to do with the will of the people was evident from the fact that he intensely resented the opposition to Roosevelt by the American Senate, although to the impartial observer the Senate appeared no less a democratic institution and no less qualified to express the popular will than the President.

It was clear that to Dodd what he understood by 'democracy' was an end in itself irrespective of its results. Once only I ventured to suggest to him that not every so-called democratic government was perfect. He had spoken of England, and I objected, 'But, Mr Ambassador, it has been the democratic governments from Cromwell to Lloyd George which have been responsible for all our troubles.'

Dodd looked at me joylessly and without enthusiasm: it was evident that my point of view did not fit in with his scheme of things. He had in any event no great opinion of the Irish – possibly because they could not be reckoned among the Baptists of the Roger Williams persuasion. He broke off the conversation: clearly he saw no object in talking on political subjects with persons whom he regarded as Fascists. That his idea of Fascism was an elastic one, is shown by the entry made, apparently in perfect seriousness, in his diary in the year 1937: 'I believe that the British Ambassador is almost a Fascist, as I think are Baldwin and Eden.'

Diplomatic dinners seem not only for the Ambassador, but for the whole Dodd family, to have represented the height of dissipation in the sinful city of Berlin. In her book *Through Embassy Eyes,* his daughter Martha describes in moving terms her nervousness when she saw the rows of knives, forks and spoons lying on the table before her and asked herself in despair how she was to cope with them. It is a touching picture – the modest prairie rose wilting amid the decadent splendours of Europe's gilded saloons: the vision of such innocence must have warmed many a heart among the Baptists of the Roger Williams tradition in the Middle West. One would have to be a confirmed cynic to inquire whether knives and forks are a luxury so entirely unknown in the house of an American professor.

Dodd's distaste for diplomatic life was not, however, confined to its meals. He found in his colleagues no comprehension of the spirit of democracy as he understood it, and suspected many others besides Sir Nevile Henderson of sympathy with Fascism. There chanced to be a celebration of the fourth centenary of Martin Luther during his term of office in Berlin, and he spent much of his time in giving addresses on *Luther and Democracy* in the various German cities. In consequence, he was highly dissatisfied at having to spend on the duties of his office as Ambassador the hours which he would have preferred to devote to his self-imposed mission. Once he asked me, 'Do you know what my Government has written me?'

'No, Mr Ambassador,' I said humbly.

'It has written that it wants me to make weekly reports on the political situation.'

I observed mildly that the American Government was possibly not alone in requiring reports from its foreign representatives.

The Ambassador dug me in the ribs with his elbow, as was his custom when he had something of importance to communicate, and pursued, 'Do you know what I answered them?'

'No, Mr Ambassador,' I said again.

'I wrote back that they should read the newspapers. Our reporters are very smart young chaps who know far more about it than I do.'

Such naïvety may sometimes have its own charm, but in Dodd it was marred by a self-complacency which led him to regard all that he could not understand as sinful or childish. He could not or would not see that things which lay outside the bounds of his personal experience were not necessarily to be condemned. I met him once at the Berlin Horse Show; a French team was competing against the Germans. Dodd, who was attending as a matter of duty, suddenly leaned forward and asked me 'Did you know that horses could jump?'

'Yes, Mr Ambassador,' I said, 'jumping is a speciality of our Irish horses.'

Dodd and his family lived in the spiritual atmosphere of Main Street. They saw the world through the spectacles of Babbitt. They were living examples of the old tag –

coelum non animum mutant qui trans mare currunh.

'WE IN BERLIN'

Neither the Germans nor the Ambassadors of Great Britain and France nor even the members of his own Embassy took him seriously. Finally, during his temporary absence from Berlin, the *chargé d'affaires* received instructions from Washington to follow the example of the British and French Ambassadors and attend the *Nürnberger Parteitag* of 1938. Dodd regarded the attitude of the American Government as a personal slight and resigned his position. His place was taken by a career diplomat Hugh Wilson.

It may be that, if Wilson had taken Dodd's place five years earlier, something might genuinely have been accomplished in the cause of peace by making clear from the start to Hitler and Ribbentrop through the mouth of a serious diplomat for whom they could have felt respect that the patience of America was not unlimited. It may be, on the other hand, that Hitler had already decided upon war, and that the fatal course of history could not have been stayed. But, whatever conjectures one may make on the missed opportunities of averting the catastrophe, it can only be a matter for regret that, at a time when the fate of Europe hung in the balance, the greatest material and moral power in the world should have been represented in the country of its potential adversary by an unworldly amateur who had no more idea of diplomacy than to expect Fieldmarshal Hindenburg to disavow the German Government in the casual conversation of a dinner-party, and whose personal activities did not reach beyond the delivery of homilies on Martin Luther in the conventicles of German provincial towns.

★ ★ ★

I had not been long in Berlin before I received an invitation from Röhm, the Chief of Staff of the SA and Minister of the Reich without portfolio. Characteristically he invited the newly arrived Ambassadors and Ministers to a *Herrenabend,* an evening without the company of ladies, in his Headquarters in the Bendlerstrasse; when I arrived, I found my colleagues together with the Chief of Protocol and a handful of Secretaries of State immersed in a crowd of higher officials of the SA. Among these latter were two well known to me by name and reputation – Ernst and Heines.

Ernst, the former liftboy, had become a protégé of Röhm and now held the post of *Gruppenführer* of the SA for Berlin and Brandenburg: he was fond of boasting that he had under his command a greater force than Napoleon had commanded at his age. In fact, he was still very young and callow, with blue eyes set in a chubby face; probably he had been an industrious and obliging liftboy. Too obliging to Röhm, who had removed him from a milieu in which he could have earned an honest living! Unlike Napoleon, he was not always completely sober when he reviewed his troops, and on one occasion he had fallen from his horse before the eyes of his 100,000 SA men. In spite of his deficiencies he was a pathetic and not altogether unsympathetic little figure.

Heines, the Gauleiter of Silesia, was a very different type: his appearance was in itself a confirmation of the reports which everyone had heard of his brutalities in the province over which he possessed powers of life and death. I found myself placed next to him at Röhm's party; as he addressed no remark either to me or to his other neighbour, I at first ignored him then, thinking that he might be ignorant of English and French, I made some observation to him in German. As he still made no reply, I looked at him more closely: it was not difficult to see that he had long since reached that stage of intoxication at which hilarity gives way to coma. After dinner he disappeared, and I saw him no more.

I mention Röhm's *Herrenabend,* because three months later in July 1934 I found by chance the printed list of the order at table. On comparing it with the list of those executed after the 30th of June, I found that with the exception of the Kaiser's son Prince August Wilhelm of Hohenzollern, the 'Nazi prince', not one of the SA officers present had survived. Ernst, whose recent marriage Hitler had attended, was arrested in Bremen on his way to embark on a cruise in the West Indies: he was brought to Berlin and shot in the Lichterfelde barracks. His last words were '*Heil, Hitler!*' Heines, like Röhm, was arrested at Wiessee in Bavaria: Goebbels delivered on the wireless a tirade on the immorality of his life and described in a voice trembling with virtuous indignation how the Führer on his midnight visit had found him in bed with a male prostitute. The facts were correct, but the proclivities of Röhm and Heines and their friends had been well known to Hitler and Goebbels, as they were to the whole of Germany, when Röhm had been appointed Chief of Staff and Minister and Heines appointed Gauleiter.

Some time later I happened to be in Breslau, the Silesian capital, and came into conversation with my taxi-driver. 'It's a good job', he said, 'that Adolf Hitler put an end to all that clique. You can't imagine what it was like here with Heines and Fräulein Schmidt!'

'Who was Fräulein Schmidt?' I asked.

We were drinking beer together in a night café; the taxi-driver looked round him cautiously before he replied, 'He was a boy from here – we always called him Fräulein Schmidt. His mother was a respectable women. He used to go round the shops ordering suits of clothes and silk shirts and anything he took a fancy to. When they asked him to pay, he told them to send the bill to Gauleiter Heines.'

'Did Heines pay?' I inquired.

'*Ach wo!* What do you think?' said the taxi-driver with contempt. 'Once Fräulein Schmidt took my taxi. I drove him all round the town. When I told him the fare, he took out his revolver and told me to go to the devil. Of course I could do nothing.'

'I suppose not,' I agreed. 'Is that the same boy who was found in bed with Heines at Wiessee?'

'The same,' said the taxi-driver. 'Heines used to take him round everywhere with him. Another beer?'

'Thanks!' said I. 'And what happened to him afterwards?'

'To Fräulein Schmidt? He came back here after the 30th of June. He had nowhere else to go.'

'And then?'

'When the people knew he was here, they went out after him, and when they got him, they tore him in pieces,' said the taxi-driver. 'Well, *prosit!*'

'*Prosit!*' said I.

Dr Robert Ley did not enjoy the favour of the Diplomatic Corps. His unpopularity may have in part been due to the chequered nature of his career, which had led him from a public-house brawl in Paderborn, in which he shot dead a couple of Rhenish separatists, to the leadership of the *Arbeitsfront* and one of the most influential posts in the Third Reich; but I imagine it arose equally from the fact that we never succeeded in establishing any kind of contact with him. When it fell to his lot to sit next to a diplomat at an official function, he replied in monosyllables to the conversation addressed to him, breathing heavily, but otherwise breaking the silence only by an occasional embarrassed snort. It was little wonder that, when I asked the Argentine Ambassador at the annual lunch given by Rudolf Hess at the *Nürnberger Parteitag* what member of the Nazi hierarchy had fallen to his lot, he answered gloomily, '*J'ai la mort dans le coeur!* I have death in my heart! I'm sitting next to Doctor Ley.'

Yet Ley could not have arrived at his position without positive qualities and in fact he possessed many of the attributes likely to appeal to the crowd. He was an excellent mob-orator in an illiterate style; he was endowed with a crude faculty of repartee; above all, he was able to talk to the working-man in his own language. If Hitler gave himself the airs of a demigod, Goebbels those of an intellectual condescending to the masses, and Rosenberg those of a professor, it must have been a relief to the man in the factory to find in Ley one with the same weaknesses as himself.

Even in his drinking he was democratic. The illustrated papers might publish photos of Goering in one of his brilliant uniforms raising his glass of champagne to the chief of a foreign state, but Dr Ley could be seen after his public meeting in the plain brown shirt of the SA drinking *Schnapps* in the nearest public-house with the *Parteigenossen*, the comrades from the factories. His colleagues considered that a *Reichsleiter* should display more personal dignity, and Hitler even administered a mild rebuke. Dr Ley, no whit abashed, referred to it in his next oration.

'I used to be a consumer of alcohol,' he informed his audience with a wink, 'but the Führer pointed out to me that there was nothing to be gained by consuming wines and spirits. I saw at once that he was right, and since that day not one drop of alcohol has passed my lips.'

On his accession to power and riches, Dr Ley divorced his elderly wife and married a ballerina from Leipzig of less than half his age. Many stories were told of the couple; some were even true. Before the wedding they visited Paris, where they were entertained at lunch in the German Embassy. The Ambassador did the honours in a manner befitting guests of such eminence; amongst other courtesies he exhibited the historic bed in which Marie Antoinette was reported to have slept. Entirely unimpressed by its regal associations, Ley nudged his fiancée.

'*Das wäre was für uns, Häschen!*' he remarked. Which may be approximately translated, 'Just the thing for us, honey!'

After the birth of a son and heir, he made his appearance at a reception to which the Diplomatic Corps was invited. The Spanish Ambassadress, knowing of the recent happy event, presented her congratulations to the proud father.

'Yes, Excellency,' replied Dr Ley, 'it was smart work. Engaged, married, and the first child – and all in six months!'

My first conversation with Alfred Rosenberg took place at a dinner in the Czechoslovak Legation. I had often seen him before, as every second Thursday evening under his presidency lectures on the doctrines of National Socialism were given in the Adlon Hotel to the accompaniment of beer and sandwiches. As spiritual and cultural leader of the movement, he reserved for himself themes of such importance as the *Rassenfrage*.

It might have been imagined a somewhat delicate theme on which to address the representatives of some fifty nations drawn from every continent. But such considerations did not trouble Rosenberg: in his harsh Baltic accent he developed the well-known thesis that all progress in the history of man, all good in morals or statesmanship or art, came from men of Germanic stock. The great figures of the past, Pericles and Michelangelo and Dante, belonged without exception to the same Nordic race, or at least had a Germanic strain. The same Germanic strain had made France great in the past, but in the Napoleonic

Wars the Nordic Frenchmen, notoriously the most courageous and therefore the first to volunteer in war, had been wiped out, and the Mediterranean majority had brought about the decadence of France.

And so on, and so on. I had heard it all before, and my attention began to wander. On the wall hung a map on which the Germanic countries, Germany, England, Holland, the Scandinavian States, were depicted bright blue, Slavs and Latins had their own colours, and the small nations on the periphery, Ireland and Greece and Portugal, were tinted a muddy brown.

'We don't seem to belong to the chosen peoples,' I whispered to the Greek press attaché Mademoiselle Perra, who chanced to be sitting next to me.

'No,' she whispered back, 'I noticed that. But I'm afraid it's too late to do anything about it.'

My attention strayed again: Rosenberg's dissertation reminded me of his book *The Myth of the Twentieth Century*, which I had made a vain attempt to wade through. Few had in fact succeeded in reading it, but it was assured of a circulation of hundreds of thousands, being together with *Mein Kampf* an almost obligatory portion of the equipment of every *Parteigenosse*. Its tendency was unquestionably deplorable; the Catholic Church and the Jews were made responsible for all the evils of humanity. On the other hand, its dullness was the best antidote to whatever influence it might have had. I had been fascinated by Rosenberg's proof of the superior ethos of the Germanic to that of the Semitic races: the inscriptions in Latin found by archaeologists, it seemed, rarely if ever transgressed the bounds of decency, whereas those discovered in the Etruscan language were nothing but a farrago of obscenities.

I thought of Martial and of the wall decorations of Pompeii, which I presumed Rosenberg had never seen, but most of all I wondered how he had succeeded in deciphering the inscriptions of the Etruscans which had defied the study of generations of etymologists. It was only when I read the official reply of the Catholic Episcopate of Germany to *The Myth* that I ascertained the solution: a German professor had in fact announced at an international congress his discovery of the clue to the characters found in the Etruscan tombs and had startled his colleagues by his revelations of their exclusively pornographic nature. But Rosenberg had not known, or at least had not referred to, the fact that immediately after his address the professor had been certified as insane and that his discovery was no more than one of the delusions of his madness.

Rosenberg was a perfect example of the inferiority complex masking itself under intellectual aggressiveness. His Estonian origin, his former Russian citizenship, his foreign accent made him determined to outdo the Germans of the Reich in *furor teutonicus*. He was that most dangerous of types, the weak man pretending to be strong. And so, in the Czechoslovak Legation, I met him personally. He had shortly before visited London, where the wreath which he had laid on the Cenotaph had been removed and thrown into the Thames. In his unaccustomed evening dress with the sleeves which stopped short three inches above his wrists and his general air of a fish out of water, he was a forlorn enough figure. Our host led me to his side, said 'I'm sure you'd like to talk to the *Reichsleiter*,' and hastened away. It occurred to me that in the circumstances it might be tactful not to speak of his English visit, but my tact was superfluous: Rosenberg desired nothing better than to talk about England. The incident which another might have resented as an example of boorishness obviously impressed him as a proof of the superiority of the Anglo-Saxon race.

'The English have always been a great people,' he informed me. 'In times of danger they always find the leader whom they need.'

'Yes,' I said dubiously, 'but I don't see anyone at the present time of the stature of the English statesmen of the nineteenth century or even of Lloyd George.'

'For the moment, perhaps not,' he agreed, 'but when the necessity arises they will find him.'

'Perhaps you're thinking of Mosley,' I suggested. 'I don't know much about him, but, judging by the few occasions when I met him, he doesn't strike me as having the qualities of a great leader.'

'Oh, no!' said Rosenberg. 'I don't mean Mosley. He has changed his party too often for the people to follow him.'

'Then who do you mean?' I asked.

'I don't know who it will be, but I believe firmly that when Great Britain is in danger, she will find the man needed to save her.'

'Against belief,' I said, 'no argument can prevail.'

The myth of the Führer's perfection had to be kept up: it would not do to let the public know of his human weaknesses. For the same reason not a word appeared in print of any personal relations which might be suspected of a tinge of sentiment. Thus, at a time when the English press contained daily references to Miss Unity Mitford, not one in a thousand Germans had ever heard her name. As for Eva Braun, no-one outside the inner circles of the Party and SS knew of her until the last year of the War. I had been told in confidence by a colleague that there was a woman living in the Bergeshof who often accompanied Hitler on his journeys, but he did not know her name, and I must confess that I had inclined to the belief that her function was more than anything else to demonstrate to the Führer's immediate *entourage* that he was not sexually abnormal.

We were at dinner. At its end the company adjourned to drink coffee. A small smoking-room had been provided, but nine-tenths of the guests were obliged to remain in the enormous reception-room, in which the Führer had ordered that there should be no smoking, as he disliked the smell of tobacco. It was amusing to see much-decorated dignitaries look timidly up from their cigars in the hope that Hitler's glance was turned in another direction and ladies in the latest creations of Dior and Paquin conceal their cigarettes in the palms of their hands, like schoolboys afraid of discovery. Perhaps on this account the Diplomatic Corps usually departed at an early hour, leaving the German guests to another hour of tobaccoless enjoyment. Hitler took advantage of their absence to call the assembly around him and impart to it his impressions of the evening.

'I cannot understand', he began, 'why our German ladies should not be as elegant as the foreign ladies who represent their countries here. I have been considering the subject this evening, and to my regret I have come to the conclusion that a higher standard of elegance could and should be reached.'

A stifled murmur of indignation went round the female portion of his audience: there was no limit to their devotion to the Führer, but it deserved a better return.

'Look at the ladies who were present tonight,' Hitler went on unperturbed. 'Without wishing to be invidious, I desire to point out to you three in particular whom you might well take as examples – the Italian Ambassadress, the Roumanian Ministress and the Ministress of Irak. Is there any reason why all ladies should not equal them in elegance?'

The Führer had clearly an eye for feminine beauty and *chic:* the three ladies mentioned were without question the best-dressed and most attractive of those present. But a man's eyes seldom get more than a general impression and Hitler, it must be assumed, had no personal knowledge of the cost of the feminine toilette. The wife of a *Reichsleiter* plucked up courage to go to the heart of the matter.

'My Führer,' she said, 'we would most willingly carry out your instructions, but first you must tell our husbands to increase our dress-allowances.'

Hitler laughed and dropped the subject: it was not the only time in his career that he embarked on a programme without having counted its cost.

All these trivialities – and many more like them – combined to make Berlin a delightful and entertaining residence, but they were far from being the reason why I loved it more than any other city I have known – and, indeed, even now I find it hard to give the cause of my affection.

It was not for its beauty: Rome and Paris and Vienna and Stockholm are a hundred times more beautiful. Berlin's modern architecture was for the most part pretentious, ugly, almost vulgar. The caryatides which supported the façades of the villas in the Tiergartenstrasse indicated plainly the years after the Franco-Prussian War, when Germany – the *nouvelle riche* of the nations – resolved that the capital of the Reich should, regardless of cost, take its place among the great cities of the world. Yet Unter den Linden had not the spaciousness or the nobility of the Champs Elysées; the Friedrichstrasse could not for a moment compare for elegance or distinction with the rue de la Paix.

But the charm of a city like that of a person does not depend on beauty alone. For myself I can only say that neither the Place Vendôme nor the Piazza della Signoria have ever inspired in me the personal affection which, contrary to all reason, I felt for the entirely unaesthetic Alexanderplatz with its plump granite Berolina or the shabby Belle Alliance Platz, where the column commemorating Waterloo rose in the centre of a circle of greengrocers' shops and dubious cafés. Even the proletarian districts of Wedding and Neukölln, the slums of the Ackerstrasse or the Grenadierstrasse, had for me something congenial, friendly, inviting.

It was of course due to the character of the people, Berliners of the 'golden heart' and the rough tongue. On the rainy morning of my first arrival at the Friedrichstrasse station in 1921 I took an instant like to them; subsequent experience has only confirmed and strengthened that first superficial impression.

Unlike the inhabitants of other great cities, the Berliner has always found time to interest himself in the affairs of his neighbour. The Londoner or Parisian goes about his business and expects others to do the same; the Münchener wishes only to be left in peace to his beer. To the Berliner on the other hand everything which concerns his fellow man is his concern. But his is a kindly interest: he is proud of his origin, but he does not look down on those who do not share his privilege. One need only observe his conduct when a stranger asks him the way in the street: he is ready to abandon without a moment's hesitation whatever may be his occupation and accompany him to his destination, asking in return only such scraps of information as his interlocutor might offer on his residence, his way of life, his age and and his conjugal or extra-conjugal relations. Like the Athenian of apostolic times, he is ever 'avid of new things', and even the catastrophe of war and defeat had never quite lost for him its spectacular element.

Unlike the inhabitants of most capital cities, the Berliner is endowed with a robust, ironical and frequently coprological sense of humour – the *schnoddriger Witz* for which he is famed in all German-speaking countries. His dialect helps to heighten its effect: onto the primitive German of the Marches of Brandenburg have been grafted the words and phrases imported by successive waves of immigration. The Huguenots who found refuge in Berlin have left their trace, as has the Gallicized German favoured by Frederick the Great, the friend of Voltaire. The Polish labourers from West Prussia have left their mark; the Jewish traders and pedlars from Alsace or Galicia have made their contribution. It is a linguistic League of Nations, in which no element seeks the exclusion of another; it is homelier and wittier and richer in comic effects than Parisian *argot* or the Cockney of Whitechapel.

And, above all, the Berliner is courageous. The world recognizes the courage with which he faced the Russians when the War was drawing to its end: it was even more evident during the endless months when life had become a nightmare under the destruction wrought by Allied bombs. Much has been written of the heroism of the populations of such cities as Rotterdam, London, Leningrad; while giving them whatever credit they may merit, I cannot think that their sufferings were comparable either for duration or for intensity with those of Berlin, and I am sure that they cannot have endured them with greater fortitude.

I have know Berlin for two generations. I first saw it in the days of inflation, when the economic basis of existence seemed to have slipped from under the people's feet. I saw it repeatedly during the days of the Weimar Republic, when civil war seemed imminent and a Communist insurrection might daily be expected. I came to live in it once more after Hitler's accession to power, and witnessed the gradual consolidation of his autocracy and the growth of material prosperity which culminated in the Olympic Games of 1936. I was present during the year of crisis – 1939 – and during the precarious triumphs of the first War years. And I visited Berlin yet again in its agony in the summer months of 1944 when all hope was lost and only Hitler from his lair in the *Reichskanzl* insisted on prolonging the useless slaughter. I have often been shocked by the incompetence, the irresponsibility, the lack of conscience of many German leaders. But never once have I wavered in my admiration for the German people, and above all the people of Berlin, which through no fault of its own suffered, and still suffers, a so-tragic fate.

SEVEN

Eamon de Valera

In Ireland the people's thoughts were turned in another direction. Few realized the danger which overhung the world, and even those who began to regard a European war as probable still thought of it as something remote from us which would scarcely affect our individual destinies. For Ireland, the only political issue was the declaration of a republic and the severance of the final link with England.

In the first years after de Valera's accession to power it had seemed inevitable. He had always declared himself a republican, he had allowed his Ministers after the election of 1932 to style themselves 'Republican Ministers', it only remained for him to crown his life's work by taking the decisive step. The people would without a shadow of doubt have given him a direct mandate if he had placed it in his programme. The Opposition, temporarily demoralized by their defeat, presented no danger to his Government. Pearse and his comrades had proclaimed the Republic of Ireland in 1916; their proclamation had been solemnly ratified by the first Dáil in 1919; de Valera had always professed to be bound by that proclamation and that ratification.

An opportunity was offered him such as had never been offered to any Irish leader; not only had he a sure parliamentary majority, but the youth of the country, even those who had voted against him, would have been solidly behind him in the struggle. There would, it is true, have been opposition from Great Britain, but not one-hundredth part of the opposition which there had been in 1916 and 1919 – and de Valera had shown throughout his career that he was not lacking in tenacity. Moreover, even the British Government could not have insisted for long in its opposition, when its own parliament by the Statute of Westminster had formally acknowledged the right of the dominions to secede from the Empire. Why, then, with everything in his favour did he leave it to others to carry out the policy which he had made peculiarly his own?

Let me say at once that I reject the widely held theory that his failure was due to egoistic or material motives. Such an explanation errs at once by over-simplification and by a misreading of de Valera's character. Although he is no more insensible than any other human being to the amenities of office, such considerations have never held the foremost place in his scheme of life. Ascetic and ambitious, there is no-one who would be more capable than he of renouncing office and emoluments in favour of the leadership of a forlorn hope; in fact, he did so in 1921, when he rejected the post of Prime Minister of the Irish Free State and initiated a struggle against the forces of the state with no prospect of success except in a remote future. Why, then, when the prospects had immeasurably brightened, did he shrink from a renewal of the struggle?

But, as Antaeus lost his strength when he lost physical contact with the earth, so de Valera loses his force when he is compelled to abandon the world of party politics and take his place upon a larger stage. From his little realm he looks out on the great world with the bewildered gaze of a child admiring the activities of the 'grown-ups' without the slightest comprehension of the motives which lie behind them. When he is obliged to speak of international affairs, he displays a complete want of appreciation of the realities of life together with an exceptional naïvety. Even in private conversation he never gets beyond the *cliché,* the *phrase faite,* which he delivers with the half-timid complacency of a schoolboy who has acquired a difficult word without fully understanding its meaning. He is well aware that the inhabitants of the world which lies outside his realm are actuated by other ideas than his own, but he has never succeeded in establishing genuine contact with them. He remains the prisoner of his milieu, of his limited experience, of the little world which he has created for himself: he never crosses the boundary of the magic circle in which he is enclosed.

Since he is endowed with an acute intelligence, he is perfectly conscious of his spiritual limitations without, however, being able to reconcile himself with them. His dissatisfaction has developed, as the representatives of the foreign states accredited in Dublin have not failed to realize, into an inferiority complex, which finds its expression in the rejection of everything with which he is not familiar from his youth. Hence his aversion to the top hat, as the symbol of the formalities and ceremonies of an order of society which he feels in the depths of his being as alien and hostile. Hence, also, his distrust of all who through the accident of birth or education have had another training and experience than his own: neither Robert Barton nor Gavan Duffy nor Art O'Briain ever held a post in his Government, although all three had performed conspicuous services in the national movement. The experience of the world, the knowledge of other countries and other languages, in a word the qualities which would have been of inestimable value to Ireland, were the contrary of a qualification for office in de Valera's eyes. With those who have led a different life from his he can never feel at ease: he cannot rid himself of the unjustifiable suspicion that they look down on him.

His ideal outside Ireland is the United States of America: if he knows little of American life in general, at least he is intimately acquainted with the Irish-American political machine. He feels at home in a country without titles or decorations or uniforms: he admires it for its repudiation of the European traditions which he too repudiates. Its technical triumphs, its wealth, its world position are to him matters of minor importance, its culture he ignores. The only America which he knows is the primitive country which ceased to exist one hundred years ago, the America of the songs of his boyhood –

> *the Land of the Free,*
> *Where the mighty Missouri rolls down to the sea.*

in which the shirt-sleeved sons of toil have swept away the tawdry tinsel of European courts and palaces.

His dearest memories are of the year which he spent in America launching the Irish Republican Loan: the storms of jubilation which accompanied his triumphal journeys were scarcely disturbed by the hostility of Irish-American veterans like Devoy and Cohalan. It was in all probability the happiest time of his life: he could play his part before the eyes of the world without the feeling of embarrassment that overcomes him in Geneva and Rome and Paris when he hears his neighbours exchange ideas in tongues which he does not understand. In New York he discovered with relief that a mastery of foreign languages was not necessary to one who would play a role on the international stage.

The identity of language and a certain similarity of ideology, aided by the sense of inferiority already referred to, have brought de Valera, especially in recent years, very near to England: he has come to the view that Great Britain and Ireland have far more in common than he would have admitted in his youth. English politicians on their side have known how to appeal to his goodwill: he has always been extremely susceptible to well-sounding generalities, and a profession of democracy, even from the most unlikely source, has never failed to win his unconditional sympathy.

Thus, in 1921 he made a loan of $20,000 from the amount collected for the Irish cause in America to Litvinoff and the Bolshevist delegation; in return he received a portion of the Russian Crown jewels, which had recently been stolen by Litvinoff's principals after the murder of the Czar and the Russian imperial family. Neither the American citizens who had contributed the money for the cause of Irish liberty nor the Irish people would have regarded the transaction with anything but horror if they had been allowed to know of it. De Valera took another view: for him the protestations of democracy which the Communists, then as now, were never weary of repeating, outweighed such trifles as robbery and murder, and his Catholic conscience put no difficulties in the way of financing the party whose avowed aim was the abolition of all belief in God. Needless to say, the whole transaction was kept secret from the people of Ireland until 1948, when it was revealed by a political opponent.

It must be admitted that de Valera showed exceptional ingenuity and a profound comprehension of the political naïvety of his fellow-countrymen. He was helped, it is true, by outward circumstances, but no other leader, compromised by his

Republican past, could have profited by those circumstances in such a way as to make his course acceptable to the nation. The slogan which he adopted may be summed up in one word – Democracy.

In the past, whatever the politicians of today may say, the Irish people had cared little for democracy – or, to put it more accurately, it had always subordinated its democratic instincts to the pursuit of national independence. Its leaders, whether Eoghan Ruadh O'Neill, Lord Edward Fitzgerald, Charles Stewart Parnell or Padraig Pearse, had dedicated their lives to the cause of Ireland without giving thought to political systems. The separatist movement had through the centuries sought help abroad, whether in monarchist Spain or in revolutionary France or in imperial Germany, without asking questions on the ideology of its allies. In other words, the gaining of national freedom had been regarded as a preliminary condition to the liberty of the individual: the independence of the nation had always been the ideal, the form of its future government a detail which would automatically regulate itself in an independent Irish state.

Under de Valera everything was changed. Less was heard of national independence, and more of the liberty of the individual – or, rather, the two concepts were used interchangeably, as if they were identical or at least inseparable. Thence it was but a short step to the conclusion that the enemies of individual liberty in their own countries must necessarily be the enemies of our national independence, and that the exponents of parliamentary democracy at home could not be opposed to the rights of others to national self-government. It was a conclusion without justification in history, for while a democracy aims at carrying out the will of the majority of its citizens and a totalitarian state only at what it considers to be in the interests of the state, neither one nor the other necessarily considers the interests of other peoples or states.

It seemed at first doubtful whether even de Valera would succeed in inducing the Irish people to accept his thesis, but he was helped by events in contemporary Europe. Hitler made it plain that the authoritarian government of the Third Reich would not respect the rights of small nations abroad, and though the converse proposition, that a democratic government would aim at international justice, was far from being proved, the average Irishman was totally incapable of making so fine a distinction and readily accepted de Valera's propaganda. And it was only logical under the circumstances that the *Irish Press,* the official organ of the governmental party, should write with indignation in a leading article of the continental powers which dared to write 'twist the British Lion's tail'.

It was something new in Irish nationalist journalism: formerly we ourselves had been taxed with the very procedure which we now so loftily condemned. I ventured to ask de Valera whether the *Irish Press* was not going too far in its enthusiasm for British policy, pointing out that it was hard to convince the world that we had a policy of our own when the Government organ consistently upheld every move which England made on the international chessboard. The same protest had already been made by others. De Valera listened to me attentively, and then he said, 'Yes, I know that there are disadvantages and that our position can easily be misunderstood.' He paused, and then continued, 'I would have the power to interfere in the running of the paper, but I don't intend to do so. The important thing is to leave the press its freedom.'

'But', I remonstrated, 'the paper's policy has to be decided on by someone. I don't see why it should be a limitation of the freedom of the press if the Government, which is in possession of the facts and determines the policy of the country, makes its voice heard in also determining the policy of the *Irish Press,* whereas it is apparently quite permissible for an editor who cannot have the same information at his disposal, to decide for himself more or less irresponsibly what line it is to take in international problems.'

De Valera answered vaguely, 'The important thing is to have a real live paper.'

Much time had to elapse before I understood that 'freedom of the press' gave de Valera the possibility of putting forward in his organ views for which he did not wish to be held personally responsible. Incidentally his desire to see a 'real live paper' did not prevent him from suppressing the small Republican newssheets which ventured to attack the Government. Accordingly, our policy at Geneva under de Valera was one of unconditional support of the policy of Great Britain. The question of Irish interest was never allowed to arise. De Valera, whether from timidity in the face of his foreign audience or from the fear of offending the British Government, to whom he owed his position, did nothing whatever in the League of Nations to advance our national cause, even though his office of President gave him the inestimable advantage of a platform from which his words would have been heard in every country of the world.

To quote the most obvious example, he took no step to have the partition of Ireland and the continued occupation by Great Britain of the Six Counties of Ulster brought to discussion. At the annual meeting of the Fianna Fáil Party the widow of Tom Clarke, the executed leader of the 1916 Rebellion, put the direct question to him why the League of Nations had been inactive in securing the restitution of our lost territory or at least in protecting the interests of the nationalist minority. De Valera's reply was that the question of Northern Ireland was not included in the agenda. The idea that as President he might have it placed on the agenda did not apparently occur to him: he showed the same satisfaction at having found a plausible pretext for doing nothing as another might have derived from the consciousness of having accomplished something for his country. It is hard to say what he would have replied if any delegate had further inquired what Ireland was doing at Geneva at all, seeing that the only question directly regarding its interests was precluded from discussion.

★ ★ ★

Numerous other problems arose from time to time in the League of Nations on which, if the interests of the Irish people were not directly concerned, at least it held definite and vigorous opinions in a sense opposed to the policy of Great Britain. It will suffice to mention a few of the most important in order to show that de Valera's idea of 'democracy' bore no relation to the wishes of those whom he represented.

The vast majority in Ireland, including the Catholic Episcopate and the entire clergy, desired the success of Franco in the

Spanish Civil War against those whom it considered the enemies of religion. De Valera, on the other hand, appeared to ascribe little importance to the fact that the self-styled Spanish 'democrats' were responsible for the wholesale burning of churches, the massacre of priests and nuns and the persecution of the Catholic Church. He had from the start supported the British policy of 'non-intervention'; he had formally prohibited the departure for Spain of a body of volunteers under General O'Duffy; the *Irish Press* habitually referred to the Red Government as the 'legal government of Spain' and to Franco's forces as the 'rebel generals', the Irish wireless spoke of the 'regular Army' as opposed to the 'Insurgents'. Frequent protests were raised by the sympathizers with Franco, but de Valera met them with the assurance that, while his personal sympathies were, like theirs, on the side of the 'Insurgents', his responsibility as Head of the Government compelled him to preserve a position of strictest neutrality. Nor did any doubts enter his mind on the justice of non-intervention, even when the League of Nations set up a blockade of the Spanish coasts, but left the Pyrennean frontier of Spain free for the influx of Communist 'volunteers' from the 'peoples' democracies'.

So far, it could be maintained that everything was at least formally *en règle,* and his opponents could at the most only deplore that the head of a Christian government who never lost an opportunity of proclaiming his devotion to the Catholic religion could find no word of sympathy or encouragement for those who were resisting the forces of atheistic Communism. But, as time went on, the situation changed: the Holy See broke off relations with the Spanish Republican régime, various South American states recognized Franco's Government, and an Irish governess in the north of Spain was murdered by the soldiers of the Spanish Republic on the ground that she and the family by whom she was employed professed the Catholic faith. Irish public opinion was seriously troubled, and parliamentary interpellations and debates followed each other on the continued recognition by the Irish Free State of the anticlericals of Valencia. De Valera assured the Dáil in reply that St Jean de Luz, the French watering-place where the Irish Minister had taken refuge together with the other diplomats accredited to the Republican

Government, was physically nearer to Franco's headquarters at Burgos than to Valencia, the seat of the 'legal government'.

De Valera's plea was naturally not accepted by the Opposition; and he fell back on his third line of defence. He told the parliament that in matters where religion was involved he considered himself bound to follow the example of the Holy See: the Holy See had not up to the present recognized Franco's Government as the legal goverment of Spain, and therefore he did not advert to the fact that the Holy See had long since withdrawn the Nuncio accredited to the Spanish Republic, but let it be supposed that the withdrawal of a Minister accredited to the one government and his accrediting to the other were one and the same procedure. The Opposition, ignorant of foreign affairs and unfamiliar with diplomatic procedure, failed to point out the distinction. So, in spite of his professed resolution to follow in the footsteps of the Holy See, the Irish Minister remained accredited to the Communist Government which the Holy See had long since ceased to recognize.

What was one to think of such arguments and of such a Minister? Was he deliberately insulting the parliament by advancing theories in which he did not himself believe? Or did he really believe in the stupidities which he put forward as arguments? One is unwilling to believe either the one or the other. Perhaps the best explanation is that, having no answer to the plea of the Opposition and at the same time hindered by his loyalty to Great Britain from giving effect to it, he blurted out the first excuse which came to his head, hoping that it would tide him over an awkward situation. But, whatever the explanation, what a humiliation to the country to be ruled by such ignoble subterfuges!

Only in February 1939, when the intention of the British Government to transfer its representative from the Republican Government of Spain to that of Franco was generally known, did de Valera venture on the same course. The fact that his action preceded that of the British Government by some ten days was claimed by his supporters as a proof of his political independence. One of the Opposition deputies, Mr Fitzgerald Kenney, recalled the old Irish folk-tale of the birds who had resolved to elect as their king that one of their number who could fly the highest from the earth: when the eagle had surpassed all his rivals and reached the limit of his force, the wren emerged from its hiding-place under his wing and, flying a few yards higher, proclaimed proudly, 'I am King of the Birds!' At the subsequent Thanksgiving Service in the Dublin Cathedral for the defeat of Communism in Spain, in spite of the presence of the Nuncio, de Valera and his Government were not represented.

A similar dilemma arose in the debates in Geneva on the admission of Soviet Russia to the League of Nations. France and England with an eye on a future ally against the Third Reich supported its candidature; the Swiss Bundesrat Motta had protested energetically against its admission, and various states, such as Holland and Portugal, had announced their intention of voting against it or abstaining from the vote. Public opinion in Ireland, with the exception of a small minority of the Labour Party, was violently opposed. It was a painful situation for de Valera, who knew that the eyes of Catholic Ireland were fixed upon him, but at the same time could not afford to offend the British Government by a contrary vote. But, once more, he found a way out: in his speech he deplored the hostile treatment of Catholics by the Soviet Government, expressed the pious hope that the Russian Bolshevists would turn over a new leaf in the future, and announced his intention of voting for their admission.

The problems of sanctions against Italy following its invasion of Abyssinia, was not one in which the interests of religion were directly involved, but opinion in Ireland was once more divided. Many resented the attack of authoritarian Fascism on a weak native state, others saw in Italy the champion of Christianity and the protector of Catholic missions in Africa. Both tendencies sought to make their opinions prevail with de Valera, who however, influenced by the literature of the League of Nations supplied him by Walshe, spoke and voted for the application of sanctions. The Argentine Ambassador in Berlin had represented his country in Geneva; on his return he gave me his impressions of the debate.

'We could look at the whole question with a certain objectivity,' he said, 'as it did not affect South America in any way. We heard the speeches of the French and English; there was nothing in them that we had not already read in the press. When it was de Valera's turn to speak, we expected to hear another point of view from the Irish. You can imagine our surprise when your Prime Minister showed himself more English than the English themselves.'

Never before had I realized the value of de Valera to Great Britain, and never had I understood why the British Government had always treated him with indulgence in spite of the patriotic speeches which he delivered for the benefit of the Irish voter. I saw that nothing I could say would change his programme by a hair's breadth, but I still felt it my duty to report to him such portions of the Ambassador's observations as I judged would not wound him too deeply. When I had finished, he said, 'I would perhaps give Italy the preference over England, and I would perhaps give Abyssinia the preference over Italy.' I waited for him to continue, but it soon became evident that he had nothing to add.

On the rare occasions when a deputy expressed doubts on the advisability of the course adopted by the Government, de Valera assumed the air of a painfully surprised idealist and reminded the objector that the Irish Government was acting in close collaboration with the democratic forces assembled in Geneva – a reply which never failed to reduce the recalcitrant deputy to silence. To the reproach that his close co-operation with Great Britain was damaging Ireland in the eyes of the world he answered with carefully assumed homeliness of language, 'If I am on my way to heaven, I won't turn back because I don't like the company of my fellow-travellers.' It probably did not occur to him that, having regard to the past records of some at least of his fellow-travellers, it might have been wise to assure himself that he was not *en route* for another destination.

For the same reason no representative of his Government in a foreign state ever received instructions on the policy towards such problems as might from time to time arise. Ministers in foreign capitals were not allowed to see each other's reports and were given no opportunity of meeting and exchanging information. When I pointed out to Walshe that the Swiss Government held a yearly conference of its foreign representatives and asked whether it might not be a valuable precedent for our Government, he replied, 'If they were to meet, they would probably combine against Headquarters.'

It was of course a jest, but one which threw an interesting light on the spirit animating the Department of External Affairs and the mistrust which de Valera entertained for all who did not fit into his scheme of life. Just as the Nazi chiefs suspected German diplomats of succumbing to the infectious atmosphere of Geneva, just as the high officials in Moscow are haunted by the dread that their foreign representatives will be corrupted by the material allurements of capitalism, so de Valera has never been able to rid himself of the thought that those who by the exigencies of their mission are obliged to pass their lives in surroundings other than those to which he is accustomed will infallibly lose their faith in democracy and in himself. Like Ambassador Dodd, he disapproves with all his heart and soul of the pomps and vanities of this wicked world, and, if he were compelled to take part in them even for an evening, he would be capable, like the American Ambassador, after their termination of eating a stewed peach and drinking a glass of milk as a protest against a way of life which is not his.

It is a strange contrast – the autocracy with which he has always ruled his own party and, during his tenure of office, the members of his Cabinet and the Irish people, and the diffidence which he has shown whenever the larger issues of statesmanship were concerned. From his countrymen de Valera demands respect, deference, adulation: it had never displeased him to be addressed as 'Chief' in the style of the Tammany boss. Those who, like Collins and Griffith in the past, declined to place him on a pedestal he regarded with dislike and distrust; later he looked with the same hostility on MacBride, the man who has done more than anyone in Ireland to explode the myth of his superhumanity. The idea of collaborating on terms of equality with his colleagues has never entered his head, any more than it entered the head of Hitler. It is not enough for him to be *primus inter pares:* like all others who are dictators by temperament if not in theory, he is not disposed to tolerate any potential rival.

When he came to power, there were those who prophesied disaster as a result of his imperious methods, there were those who saw in him the heaven-sent leader who would march at the head of his people into the Promised Land of freedom. What no-one, whether friend or foe, expected was an ineffective policy of compromise which in seeking to please all satisfied none. But few in Ireland had realized the peculiar combination of inordinate ambition with the consciousness of his own limitations and the consequent feeling of inferiority which has always been de Valera's bane – which has resulted in his accepting blindly in Geneva, where he knew himself safe from the observation of his country, the condescending patronage of those to whom Ireland was no more than an unimportant geographical entity, while rejecting at home the co-operation even of the members of his own party whose capacities would have been of inestimable use to the common cause.

It would be absurd to deny de Valera's undoubted qualities, his political adroitness, his tenacity in furthering his aims, his genuine belief in himself as the man indispensable to his country; it would be even more absurd to ignore his deficiencies. If it is sought to sum up the man with all his qualities and all his defects in one phrase, then to him, as to countless others in the course of history, may be applied the old classical quotation

capax imperii nisi imperasset.

* * *

King Edward VIII had abdicated in 1936, and the British Empire was left without a head. Parliament lost no time in appointing the Duke of York as his successor for Great Britain and the Crown colonies; the dominions immediately followed its example. De Valera hesitated: it would have seemed an anomaly to the Irish people if the 'republican' leader of the past had taken the initiative in declaring George VI to be King of Ireland.

But, once again, he could not afford to defy his British patrons or jeopardize his standing at Geneva. A way out must be found which would convince Ireland of his independence and England of his loyalty. The draughtsmen to the Irish parliament were set to work day and night on the task of squaring the circle. And at last a magic formula was devised which de Valera hoped would satisfy separatists and loyalists alike. A law was passed declaring that Edward VIII had ceased to be King of Ireland and that 'the king should henceforth be the person who, if His Majesty had died unmarried on the 10th day of December 1936, would be his successor under the law of the Irish Free State'. It was a painfully transparent piece of sophism, which deluded few in Ireland. And in the same spirit he introduced in the following year a new Constitution, in which he proclaimed proudly that the name of the King did not appear once.

But the problem still remained how Great Britain was to be conciliated. Once again, an elaborate paraphrase was employed. Article 29 provided that:

For the purpose of the exercise of any executive function of Eire in or in connection with its external relations, the Government may to such extent and subject to such conditions, if any, as may be determined by law, avail (sic) of or adopt any organ, instrument or method of procedure used or adopted for the like purpose by any group or league of nations with which Eire is or becomes associated for the purpose of international co-operation in matters of common concern.

The only group or leagues of nations with which we were associated was the British Commonwealth — apart from the League of Nations. And, lest there should be any doubt about the position of His Majesty King George VI, de Valera expressly refrained from conferring the former powers of the sovereign on the Irish Executive Council where these had already been conferred on 'some other person' by the legislation of 1936.

Such was the constitutional position: the Irish government could neither sign a treaty nor appoint an ambassador except through the medium of the King, and George VI for foreign states was still Head of the Irish State. But it was still possible for the Irish Government to treat these reserved powers as a mere formality, to regard His Majesty, in the words of a former Irish minister, as a 'rubber stamp' useful only for registering the decisions of a native government.

It had been arranged that the King and Queen of England should make an official visit to Paris in the summer of 1938: its purpose was to be the demonstration of the unity of the British Empire at the side of its French ally. And without the co-operation of the Irish Free State that unity would not be complete.

Our Minister in Paris was Art O'Briain, formerly President of the Gaelic League in London and in fact head of the Sinn Féin movement in Great Britain. A man of wide culture and education, he had not had the fortune to find favour in the eyes of de Valera, even though he had been a convinced opponent of the Treaty and had always supported the Hosts of Destiny. De Valera had appointed him Minister in deference to the expostulations of his friends, but at the same time made it plain that the appointment was not one of his choosing by treating O'Briain with marked hostility and consistently refusing on his frequent official transits through Paris to set foot in the Legation. No doubt he failed to realize that such a slight was hardly calculated to enhance the prestige of O'Briain himself or of the country which he represented in the eyes of the French Government.

Some weeks before the date fixed for the arrival of Their Majesties in Paris, O'Briain received invitations from the King's Private Secretary Sir Alexander Hardinge and the British Ambassador Sir Eric Phipps to be present at their arrival at the Bois de Boulogne Station and at the various functions organized in their honour. The Ambassador further suggested that the Irish Minister should send him a list of such of the Irish community as he thought worthy to be included in the number of British residents in Paris for the invitation to a garden-party.

The Irish Government had some time before sent instructions to all its foreign representatives that official invitations from British authorities should not be accepted unless the members of foreign missions outside the British Empire would be present. Accordingly, as only the representatives of the dominions had been invited to meet their Majesties, O'Briain sent a formal refusal regretting his inability to attend; he also declined to avail himself of the offer to include selected members of the Irish colony.

The matter appeared to be settled in accordance with the instructions previously given by the Department, but a week before the date fixed for the royal visit O'Briain received a telephone call from Walshe, who was still Secretary to the Department of External Affairs, in the course of which the latter instructed him to leave Paris before the arrival of their Majesties and to give notice to the French Foreign Office that the Secretary to the Legation would act as *chargé d'affaires* during his absence. At the same time the Secretary was instructed to accept the invitations declined by the Minister on the ground that it might seem 'singular and discourteous' if he did not participate in the procession from the railway station to the Quai d'Orsay.

O'Briain protested at the 'departure from a traditional national precedent' and stated his apprehension of 'action being taken which would be very harmful to our national prestige and dignity', but his plea fell on deaf ears. He further asked for written confirmation of the telephonic instructions in conformance with the usual practice, but received in reply only a telegram directing him to leave Paris immediately 'for health reasons'. In order that no later misunderstandings should arise on the nature of the verbal communication made to him, he also took the precaution of embodying the substance of the telephone conversation in a memorandum for the Department. As no objection to its contents was ever raised by the Department, it may be assumed to be a correct statement of the facts.

A couple of days later he carried out his instructions by leaving Paris; the *chargé d'affaires* attended the reception of their Majesties at the station and the various banquets given in their honour. His presence was recorded in the French and English press, as well as in the *Irish Times* of the first two days of the visit, but the *Irish Press* made no mention whatever of his attendance. A few days later, however, it published a 'message from Paris' to the effect that O'Briain 'was to retire shortly', adding that he had not been in good health for some years. O'Briain wrote a letter which was published in another Dublin paper, stating that the intimation in the *Irish Press* was the first notice to have reached him either of his bad health or of his retirement.

Let me at this point, even at the risk of wearying my readers, interrupt the narrative by an objective analysis of the situation. My excuse for doing so is twofold: in the first place, the facts which I have recounted have remained unknown to the vast majority of the Irish public, although they denoted, as O'Briain pointed out, a complete break with our national tradition; secondly, they had a determining influence on my own career.

De Valera, it must be assumed, knew from the first that a large section of his supporters would be strongly opposed to the official attendance of the Irish representative at the festivities in honour of the King and Queen of England and might even vote against him at the next election as a protest. He therefore did not instruct the Irish Minister to accept invitations from the British Embassy or the Private Secretary to His Majesty and gave him no reason to suppose that he should not abide by the general prohibition applying to such a case. O'Briain had in fact some time before asked for permission to go on leave for a period including the date originally fixed for the royal visit, and no suggestion had been made to him that he might be required to stay in Paris to receive their Majesties. Therefore it may be assumed that de Valera's first intention was not to be represented at the reception of the royal pair.

When, however, O'Briain refused the invitations, the British authorities, anxious that no discordant element should mar the spectacle of the Empire's unity, considered it necessary to intervene: through the Irish High Commissioner in London they brought pressure to bear on the Irish Government with a view to securing that Ireland should not show itself disloyal or, in the words of the Department of External Affairs, 'singular and discourteous'. The Irish Government yielded under the pressure, and the telephonic instructions mentioned above were given to O'Briain.

But the problem of the Irish public still remained: it was unlikely that it would be convinced of the necessity for so sudden a change, and it was an old nationalist tradition that Ireland's representatives should take part in no act of homage to their Britannic Majesties. So de Valera decided to keep the knowledge of his break with tradition so far as possible a secret from the public. No mention was made in the *Irish Press* of the *chargé d'affaires'* attendance, while an intimation was given to the other Dublin papers that publicity was not desired.

It was not surprising that a couple of months later one of the most important Swiss newspapers, the *Basler Nachrichten,* after pointing out the tendency of South Africa towards greater independence in matters of foreign policy, emphasized the contrast with Ireland in the following terms.

> That the loyalty of the Irish Free State to the Empire does not admit of any doubt, is guaranteed by the personality of de Valera and the recent reconciliation between Dublin and London. If it had come to the test of force, Great Britain would not only have had nothing to fear from this source, but could have relied on valuable moral and material support.

★ ★ ★

I had already protested more than once at the servility of the Irish Government. When O'Briain informed me of his experience and sent me copies of the whole correspondence, after wiring him my congratulations I decided to return to the charge with even greater energy.

I wrote to the Secretary of the Department, pointing out that the presence of the *chargé d'affaires* at the reception of their Majesties appeared to be in conflict with the instructions which I had previously received and inquiring whether those instructions were to be regarded as no longer valid. The ostensible object of my question was to obtain guidance for my own conduct if in the future some similar occasion should arise; its real purpose was of course to ascertain whether the Government would have the courage to stand over its own action. As I expected, my inquiry met with no reply. I repeated my request for instructions: in the end I received a lengthy rebuke from the Secretary. My offence consisted in laying emphasis on the 'anti-English or non-English character of our policy'. Walshe further informed me that it was possible that in the future 'our external policy may coincide even more than now with that of Great Britain'.

It appeared to me that, if we were not to lay emphasis on the 'non-English character of our policy', we might as well be represented by the British Embassy. I therefore took the occasion of my next meeting with de Valera to read him the minute. He listened with obvious impatience. When I had finished, he remarked, 'I hadn't seen that minute.' An embarrassed silence followed; then he added, 'I would perhaps have expressed it in a different way.'

As he had nothing more to say, I thanked him and left. The minute remained the declared policy of the Government. It was a serious moral shock: I thought of the day twenty-four years before when I had read Redmond's speech urging the young men of Ireland to join the British Army. But Redmond had had the courage to declare himself openly before the public, whereas de Valera was keeping his policy dark even from his own followers. There was something repugnant to me in the idea that the policy which I and my colleagues were instructed to carry out was one which could not be avowed before the Irish people.

De Valera's policy was a twofold one: for consumption in Ireland, we were a Republic, since our Constitution did not contain the name of the King; for the rest of the world, we were still a dominion like Canada or Australia, and George VI was the head of our state. Therefore it was essential to him that nothing should be done which would expose the hollowness of his claim to have eliminated the reality of English rule. My object, on the other hand, was to expose the contradiction and make it plain at a later date to the Irish people that our pretended emancipation was a fraud. To this end I bombarded the Department of External Affairs with questions as to my future conduct, whose answers would have entailed a definite statement on our constitutional position.

It would be tedious to give details of the one-sided correspondence – one-sided, because my requests for instructions, however often repeated, were never deemed worthy of a reply. One instance, however, is so strikingly illustrative of the perpetual dilemma in which de Valera was placed by the need of satisfying at once Irish nationalist opinion and the demands of his English patrons that it is worth while mentioning it here.

A new Ambassador of the Soviet Union had arrived in Berlin and had sent me the usual letter announcing that he had presented his credentials. I had previously been informed by the Department that de Valera had more than once refused to receive in Ireland even a Soviet Trade Delegation on account of the anti-Christian attitude of the Soviet Government. On the other hand I could not forget that many years before his zeal for Christianity had not prevented him from making a secret loan to Litvinoff and receiving a portion of the Imperial Crown Jewels as a pledge. Moreover he had shortly before spoken and voted in favour of the admission of Soviet Russia to the League of Nations. Accordingly, I felt it necessary to obtain explicit instructions before entering into social relations with the Ambassador.

My inquiry elicited nothing better than a direction to 'do nothing which might give a reasonable ground for feeling offended to the Soviet Ambassador'. So the question whether we were a dominion or not was left unanswered. In consequence, as I noticed, the responsibility for deciding on the course to be taken was left to me, while the Department apparently reserved to itself the right to disavow later whatever decision I might make by refusing to accept my criterion of what constituted a 'reasonable ground for feeling offended'. I saw no reason to assume a responsibility which should never have been placed on me, and had little inclination to figure as a scapegoat if de Valera should later disagree with my desicion. I wrote, therefore, once more, setting out the situation in the clearest terms: namely, that, if we were a dominion, the Ambassador would have reasonable grounds for feeling offended if I did not pay him the ritual visit, whereas, if we were no longer a dominion and were therefore no longer committed nominally to diplomatic relations with the Soviet Government through the British Ambassador, he would have no such reasonable grounds.

My efforts to obtain a decision remained unsuccessful. I received no information on whether we were still to consider ourselves a dominion or not, no indication as to whether the British Ambassador in Moscow was still to be regarded as a representative of the Irish state, and no instructions on the practical issue of whether or not I should call at the Russian Embassy.

It was not the only question on which I met with a blank wall of silence. During the crisis of 1938, when war might break out at any minute and was averted by a hair's breadth, the Department, apparently as punishment for my insubordination, refused to give me any indication of what measures should be taken for the protection of Irish nationals in Germany, for the securing of communication with Ireland or for any other purpose. Even a purely routine inquiry from the Deutsche Bank as to the position of Irish holders of German loans was left without an answer. It was evidently the intention of the Irish Government to boycott its Legation in Berlin. Even when I was personally in Dublin de Valera and Walshe declined to see me. I could understand the embarrassment at the questions which I might be expected to put to them, but found their attitude difficult to reconcile with the interests of the country.

At times I could not help being amused by the childishness of their conduct, but I realized that the situation was too serious for amusement. I decided to make a last appeal for commonsense and co-operation: after recounting the numerous matters in which the Department was refusing to recognize the existence of a Legation at Berlin, I continued:

I desire to express the hope that you will realize that my requests for instructions are not actuated by any wish to create difficulties for the Department, but by the genuine desire to be enabled to carry out the duties of a Minister in as effective a manner as possible, and by the knowledge that in the absence of the instructions neither I nor any other Minister can do effective work in the interests of the country.

This appeal also remained without answer or acknowledgment.

Relations of such extreme unfriendliness could not continue indefinitely. I could of course easily have re-established, if not friendly, at least tolerable, relations with the Secretary of the Department: I had only to settle down to enjoy an easy life, to avoid asking awkward questions, to acquiesce in a policy which I considered a betrayal of national interests. But insincerity and incompetence are the two qualities which I have always most abhorred, and in the conduct of our foreign affairs by de Valera I found both insincerity and incompetence developed to the highest degree. I could confirm with all my heart the remark made to me by Sean Lester, later League of Nations Commissioner in Danzig; 'Our Department has never even begun to function.' I continued to protest, though naturally without any hope of changing the course of events. The Government retorted by transferring me to the Department of External Affairs in Dublin. As the transfer meant a reduction in rank, I first protested and then sent in my resignation. My last act as Minister was to send a long memorandum to de Valera, beginning with the unconciliatory statement:

Ireland, at the end of ten years' separate representation in Berlin, is regarded by the German Government, as by the other Governments where it has representation, as a British dependency, with autonomy but no real independence either political or spiritual. Hitler in his latest Reichstag speech expressly refers to England's treatment of Ireland as a domestic matter in which he would not be entitled to interfere. President Roosevelt in his open letter to Hitler refers to 'Great Britain and Eire' as *one* of the countries which should be guaranteed.

After giving numerous instances of our lack of independence, I proceeded:

As I have pointed out a number of matters obviously requiring reform, I feel that the Minister has a right to ask for my opinion on their cause. I propose therefore to set out my view with all possible conciseness. The first and most obvious cause of the failure to adopt an independent policy in foreign affairs is what I can only describe by the colloquial term 'inferiority complex'. So long as British institutions (from the system of government down to details of household management) are regarded as the only possible model for Irish Government Departments, so long will it be impossible to expect an objective or independent view on international affairs. Lest it should be thought that I am exaggerating, I desire to refer to a recent correspondence on the payments to be made to the Legation porter during illness: the solution which appeared natural to the officials of the Irish Department of External Affairs was to inquire as to the practice of the British Embassy.

This instance is of course a trivial one though significant: it could be reinforced by many others. The effect produced on the outside world was summed up by a foreign diplomat now no longer in Ireland in the observation, 'Your people from the Minister downwards don't really believe that any other country exists except England.'

The secondary cause of the failure of the Irish Department of External Affairs to function in the manner in which Ministries of Foreign Affairs in other states function is its lack of experience and apparent reluctance or incapacity to learn. In other states one of the first duties of the Ministries of Foreign Affairs is considered to be the instruction of their Ministers abroad as to the policy of their government, and in particular as to the answers to be given to particular inquiries about their policy. The officials of the Irish Department of External Affairs obviously do not consider such instruction as any part of their duties, and indeed resent any suggestion that their present practice could be improved in any respect, with the natural result that Irish Ministers abroad are never in a position to explain the attitude of the Irish Government on any subject to the Government to which they are accredited, and that the Government to which they are accredited assumes that the Irish Government has no policy except that of Great Britain. It is not for me to conjecture whether this outward self-satisfaction conceals an inner feeling of inadequacy or not.

If in fact the Irish Government has no such policy, the officials of the Department cannot be blamed for not communicating it. If on the other hand an independent policy exists, it is difficult to see why it should be kept as a secret not only from foreign governments but from the representatives of the Irish Government itself?

It is of course for the Minister for External Affairs to decide whether his Department shall carry out the duties to which I have alluded. I desire however to suggest the possibility that the practice of all other countries during their centuries of independent national life is not less important than the views held by officials, whose experience began in the year 1922 and has since then for practical purposes been confined to Dublin.

I have no doubt that the Minister is already aware of all the facts enumerated by me in this minute. I am confident, however, that their presentation in tabulated form will be of assistance to him should he in the future contemplate the transformation of the Department into an effectively functioning instrument for the carrying out of a definite policy in international affairs.

I received no answer to my memorandum. Years later I heard that de Valera had read it without pleasure.

EIGHT

A Conversation

'Well, you seem to have made a mess of things,' said Liam, when we were once more together in Dublin. 'I can quite understand your being annoyed with the Department, but why in Heaven's name didn't you keep your annoyance to yourself?'

'It wasn't a question of annoyance,' I explained. 'There was a principle involved. It always sounds, I don't know why, rather pretentious to talk about questions of principle, but, after all, we all have principles of one kind or another, with which we have no right to compromise.'

'The sentiment of all the heroes of the popular stories,' commented Liam, 'expressed in the sturdy though shamefaced manner of the ex-Public School Boy!'

'You're very witty,' I said with slight irritation, 'but the manner, as you know perfectly well, is of no importance whatever. The only thing that matters is the substance, and substantially you must admit that I could do nothing else.'

'With certain qualifications,' said Liam.

'Which are – ?'

'In the first place, are you sure that the principles of which you are so proud were anything more than impatience at the inefficiency or indifference of the people with whom you had to deal, or even the intolerance of opinions with which you disagreed?'

'There was all that,' I confessed, 'but there was more than that. I was morally bound to make a protest.'

'Then there's no use arguing about it,' said Liam. 'But do you think your protest had any chance of being successful, or that it was likely to be of use to anyone?'

'Who can tell? Probably not. If the War had not come, I had intended to publish the whole story in Ireland and America. Now, that is impossible as de Valera has seized the first opportunity of abolishing the freedom of the press and introducing a censorship. But, even if my protest is entirely useless, surely that is a reason the more for making it.'

'Sublimated egoism!' said Liam.

'I hate Freudian jargon,' said I. 'According to you all self-respect is sublimated egoism, and the early Christian martyrs who let themselves be thrown to the lions in the certainty that they would go straight to heaven were nothing more than particularly far-seeing egoists.'

Liam smiled. 'I hope you're not going to see yourself as a martyr,' he observed.

'Not at all. I was only trying to reduce your argument *ad absurdum* by taking an extreme instance.'

'It wasn't an argument,' Liam said mildly. 'It was only a rather obvious comment. However, I won't make any more comments, if they annoy you. Only it seems rather a pity.'

'I don't think so at all,' I retorted. 'I have never felt so sure of having done the right thing.'

'"A far, far better thing than you have ever done!"' he quoted. 'But Sidney Carton was not upholding a principle, he was sacrificing himself for a particular person.'

'Sublimated egoism!' I replied. 'But why do you say it's a pity?'

'I meant,' said Liam, 'that if you had known you were going to be liable to these attacks of untimely conscientiousness, it is a pity you embarked on a career in which you are expected to carry out orders unquestioningly, whether you agree with them or not. Sincerity is an excellent quality in its proper place, but it is not usually essential to a successful diplomat.'

'It depends on what sincerity you mean,' said I. 'I would have had no objection whatever to helping to mislead outsiders in the interests of the country; but I object to joining in a conspiracy to mislead the people whom the Government and I are supposed to represent. No government has the right to conceal its policy from its own people, nor to require its representatives to be its accomplices in concealing it.'

'That is quite unexceptionable as a general proposition,' said Liam, 'but I don't know whether it is applicable in the present case. You seem to have taken the episode in Paris to heart, as if it were an act of deliberate treachery to the nation. Has it never occurred to you that it may have been only the expedient of a weak and flurried Minister, who was obliged to do a thing of which he was ashamed and tried to save his face by keeping it secret as far as he could?'

'It's possible,' I admitted, 'but he had no right to penalize another for acting according to his conscience.'

'If we begin talking about rights,' said Liam, 'we shall never have finished. But you must have realized that you were touching on a particularly sensitive spot.'

'Of course I did. That's why I insisted on rubbing it in.'

'Did it not occur to you that you were making your relations impossible for the future?'

'Certainly.'

'Don't you think your general attitude is slightly unpractical?' he asked.

'I expect most people would consider it entirely unpractical.'

'It's something that you recognize it yourself. Do you also admit that your no doubt well-intentioned campaign against de Valera was unpractical?'

'Unpractical, but inevitable,' I agreed. 'He is an extremely cunning politician, whereas I am in some ways naïve to the border of stupidity. He is in a position of command, whereas I was an entirely unimportant subordinate without the least influence. So that from the first I had not an earthly chance against him. But his ideas on the fundamental aims of Irish policy were so different to mine that I could not honourably continue in his service.'

'I should have thought,' Liam dissented, 'that you had pretty much the same ideas on ultimate aims, but that your obvious differences of temperament had led you to take different paths to achieve them. Are you still in favour of what you used to call a Gaelic state?'

'Yes, I'm still in its favour as the ideal.'

'Well, you can't deny that he is also in its favour; with all his mental reservations and ambiguities on other points he has always declared himself for the Irish language and the Gaelic spirit and all the other high-sounding phrases which appeal to you.'

'Then why does he adopt a practical policy which has the effect of destroying them?' 'Because', said Liam, 'he has to adopt a practical policy. That's not merely intended to be a wisecrack; it's a profound truth, as you'll see, if you'll think it over. Even the Gaels of your romantic visions must eat and drink like the rest of us and have cigarettes and the cinema and a minimum amount of the amenities which make life worth living. If they aren't provided with the necessities and a few of the slighter luxuries of life, they'll die out or emigrate to England or America – which from the point of view of the Gaelic state is the same thing. If he were to insist too rigidly on principles, however justified, he'd find himself left with half-a-dozen surviving Gaels in a sort of Red Indian reservation, making their living by selling little Gaelic souvenirs to tourists. So his policy has first of all to be directed towards enabling them to live, and only after that towards making them Gaelic.'

'That's absurd,' I said. But Liam disregarded my interruption and went on, 'You see, your misfortune is that you don't see things as they are. You have a vision of an ideal Ireland which never can come into existence and probably never existed even in the past. You forget that there is such a thing as human nature. And in the long run human nature is bound to prevail.'

'I never suggested the contrary,' I said.

'But you don't take account of it in your well-intentioned plans for the future of the country. We are living close to the English, we speak the same language, we welcome them as guests – '

' – tourists.'

'Very well, as tourists. Therefore it's inevitable that friendly relations should exist between us and them. You can't seriously want to establish a state of permanent hostility between England and Ireland?'

'"Hostility" is not the word which I would have chosen,' I replied. 'Let us say a sense of being different and an awareness that English influence, whether it be good or bad in itself, can only be harmful to us. In principle the Gaelic Leaguers are right when they refuse to allow English dances and the Gaelic Athletic Association when it expels its members for playing Rugby football. You can call them ridiculous, but no-one ever did anything worth while doing if he was afraid of being ridiculous. And that distrust which they show for English customs, even for those harmless in themselves, is a manifestation of the natural instinct implanted in every people for its own self-protection – '

'Like the instinct of cats that dogs, whether good or bad in themselves, can only be harmful to cats?'

'More or less, though the analogy doesn't help. Over-cordial relations can only harm us, because they will make us tend to forget our own language and our own individuality and to take over a non-Irish way of thought.'

'And therefore, if the Gaelic language is the first line of defence, uncordial relations are the second?'

'You can easily make it sound ridiculous, but it's true for all that,' I retorted. 'Once upon a time the politicians in England used to talk of killing Home Rule with kindness; now they say nothing, but their kindness and tolerance, whether they intend it or not, can only have the same effect – that of killing our national spirit. Their embrace may be fraternal, but if we submit to it, we will soon find out that it is the embrace of the bear or the boa constrictor, which will crush the life out of the nation.'

'That would look well in print,' said Liam with a smile. 'You must have gone to some trouble to think it out. It's a little too elaborate for my taste, but that's not my reason for objecting to it. My objection is to your point of view. You're talking, whether you genuinely believe in it or whether you merely think it picturesque, like the romantic nationalist of a hundred years ago – and very often even he didn't believe what he said. But the time has passed for –

> *On our side is Virtue and Erin,*
> *On theirs is the Saxon and Guilt,* –

which, if my memory doesn't mislead me, rhymes with "dripping with blood to the hilt". The vocabulary and the stage properties belong to an epoch which has passed away and can never return. Assumptions of superiority on the part of a nation are just as insufferable as assumptions of superiority on the part of an individual, and I have never understood why national self-sufficiency should be regarded as any less objectionable than personal self-sufficiency.'

'You're misunderstanding me,' I protested. 'I never suggested that the Irish nation is superior to any other nation – all I said was that it is different. Its contribution to the general good of humanity is different from the contribution of any other nation. And the same applies to the individual. Man cannot think of himself merely as an isolated person: he regards himself also as a member of a community of people speaking the same language, thinking the same thoughts, cherishing the same aspirations as himself. The only thinking which can change him is the loss of his language and of those characteristics which are involved in and flow from the language, and his assimilation to another community whose language and characteristics and ways of thought he adopts. But it is those characteristics and that language which make him and the nation to which he belongs a precious and an irreplaceable part of the mosaic of peoples which compose our world. His renunciation of them is a refusal to carry out that part in the scheme of things for which his Creator sent him into the world.'

Liam looked more impressed than he had done since the beginning of our conversation. 'I see your point,' he said, 'but you seem to expect of the Irish people something that no people has ever done. You want to turn back the course of history.'

'There is no such thing as the course of history,' I said, 'if you mean something inevitably predestined which human effort cannot alter. History is what man makes it, not something obeying a law fixed independently of human actions. And, when you say that no race has ever done what we must do if we are to survive, you forget that another people has set us an example and shown us how nationality can be preserved in the face of difficulties and dangers a thousand times greater than ours. Dispersed through the continents speaking the languages of the peoples among whom they were compelled to live without a home that they could call their own – '

'Oh, you mean the Jews!' said Liam.

' – they have made no concessions. They have had the strength not to let themselves be assimilated; they have taken part in the life of the communities surrounding them; but in their hearts they have remained apart. They have been ready to endure unpopularity and persecution rather than give up their ideal; they have been neither corrupted by prosperity nor daunted by adversity. And finally, after centuries of struggle and privation, they have triumphed. But in the hour of their triumph they have not forgotten that political independence is but a small thing in comparison with the independence of the spirit. And, to maintain that independence, they have imposed upon themselves in the home that they have won at last the language that in the centuries of their dispersion many had abandoned. They are not afraid of turning back the course of history, because they know that only so can they fulfill their destiny in the face of a hostile world.'

Liam was silent: in the end we always agree with one another. It would not be otherwise; for, as the more astute of my readers will no doubt long since have perceived, Liam is nothing else than my *alter ego;* he is as much a part of me as the active self which speaks and moves and comes into contact with the world. He is not my conscience, for the conscience one must always yield to in the long run. I find it hard to describe him: he is the devil's advocate who lives in my brain, who points out the flaws in my arguments and smiles at the extravagances of my enthusiasms. He is commonsense, cynicism, the dread of ridicule, the spirit of compromise, the reaction which automatically follows an activity, the doubt whether things are worth the doing, the fear of the consequences, the faculty of seeing an opponent's point of view, discretion and caution and calculation and sweet reasonableness and agnosticism and much more besides. And therefore, while I always listen to him with the deference which is his due, I seldom follow his counsels: for, if I were to give in to him, it would be the end of action and the doubting of eternal standards and the abandonment of ideals.

'And what Israel has done, Ireland can do!' I concluded triumphantly.

'Who knows?' said Liam.

NINE

South Tyrol in Wartime

To return: my relations with the Irish Government were finally severed, and I was unemployed without even the consolation of a pension, as I had retired voluntarily before completing fifteen years of service. There were two alternatives before me. I could resume my practice at the Irish Bar. But ten years of absence had lost me whatever professional connections I had had, and a new generation of barristers, younger than I, had taken my place. Moreover, my party was in opposition and likely to remain in opposition for years to come, so that I could not rely on any help from official sources. And, above all, I felt myself in violent reaction against the political climate prevailing in Ireland.

In 1914 the mass of popular opinion had been, I could not deny, in favour of England and against Germany. The average Irishman in his simplicity had swallowed English propaganda without a struggle and believed in the stories of Belgian children's chopped-off hands, of violated nuns and soap manufactured from the bodies of those fallen in battle, as if they were gospel truth. Only the rebellion of 1916, the execution of its leaders and the atrocities of the Black-and-Tans in 1921 had shaken his faith in the righteousness of England's cause, while the boasts by English journalists of their successful propagandist inventions had convinced at least some that England's enemies were not necessarily criminals.

But the struggles of Sinn Féin lay far back in the past: to the new generation they were no longer a living reality. De Valera's tactics had produced the effect which had all along been his aim: all that now mattered was 'democracy', and the democratic Irish people rallied to the support of democratic England against authoritarian – and therefore tyrannical – Germany. Few stopped to consider whether an English or a

German victory would best serve the interests of Ireland. One heard once more the inglorious maxim of the first war: 'Better the devil you know than the devil you don't know.' It is true that scarcely anyone would have advocated our entering the War: the only politician who openly proclaimed himself in its favour was expelled from his party, and de Valera himself could only have dragged Ireland into the ranks of the Allies at the risk of his life. But, short of actual belligerence, it was clear that our Government would do everything in its power to assist England, and – as in 1914 – the youth of the country flocked into English regiments.

It seemed to me the negation of even the most elementary national sentiment. I could not forget the executions of Easter Week, the torture of IRA men by English police and soldiers, the shooting of prisoners 'attempting to escape', the courts-martial which condemned their prisoners to death by hanging regardless of the evidence. To employ a hackneyed metaphor, the Ireland of 1939 was like a dog that licks the hand which beats him. I could not face the prospect of remaining in Ireland to witness so unworthy a spectacle. In any event I had a burning curiosity to see the mid-European countries in wartime. Ireland would be a backwater; I wanted to be at the centre of events. And possibly, if Germany won, I might be of some use to Irish interests. So at the beginning of September 1939 I had no hesitation in setting out for Europe.

I had expected difficulties in England and France; to my amazement no difficulty presented itself. The English passport official had obviously no idea what to do in the exceptional circumstances. 'We're all at sixes and sevens,' he kept repeating in a melancholy voice, adding in the endeavour to lend an epigrammatic touch to a banality, 'at sixes and sevens and eights!'

'I have left my furniture and belongings in Berlin,' I explained to him. 'Even my winter clothing is in my old Legation. It's most important that I should get there to look after them.'

He shook his head despairingly. 'I don't know what I ought to do,' he lamented. Then, struck by a bright idea, he said hopefully, 'I don't suppose the French will let you through.'

'If they do,' I asked, 'will you give me your permission?'

'Oh, I suppose so,' he groaned.

It took me half an hour to obtain my visa at the French Consulate; when I reappeared at the English passport office, he seemed surprised.

'I suppose I can have your permission now,' I said, showing him my passport stamped with the French endorsement.

'I suppose it'll be all right,' he said, and stamped his permission to leave England.

The Polish campaign was over, and the War had entered its 'phoney' stage: no-one knew what to make of it. The Berliners were neither down-hearted nor enthusiastic; they were perplexed. Few doubted that Germany would win in the end, but many expected a desperate struggle from which only the Führer's genius would snatch the victory. The anti-Communist theorists of the Party accepted the pact with Soviet Russia only as a deplorable necessity. The man in the street, with the memory of the inflation years after the first War, trembled for his savings. But there was neither fear nor disaffection, still less any tendency to revolt.

Life was normal in Berlin. There was rationing of food, but to one who lived in a hotel and took his meals in restaurants this entailed no privation – and in any event the *Auswärtiges Amt* had allotted me the extra ration cards allowed to the diplomats accredited to the German Government.

'I would never have asked for such a favour,' I said to the Chief of Protocol, when I went to thank him.

'I know that,' he said. 'That's why I sent them to you.'

They were far more than I needed, but I found them useful for distribution to those less favoured than myself. Otherwise we might have been living in peacetime. Prices had not risen – and could not rise without the consent of the Government. The idea of an attack by enemy bombers seemed too fantastic to be entertained for a minute. There was little news from the front and what there was was good: there had been some talk of a French attempt to break through the German lines in order to relieve France's eastern ally but the German wireless quickly reassured us that it had been driven back with loss. There seemed no reason why life should not go on indefinitely in the same manner.

Nor did the problem of money preoccupy me. I had sold my Packard at a considerable profit to one of the numerous Germans who could only obtain an American car from a diplomat, and hoped to live on the proceeds for a year. Although I could not hope for funds from Ireland, I could draw on my account in a Swiss bank. Numerous German friends offered me loans to be repaid after the War was over, but I refused their offers, as I did an offer from Ribbentrop to appoint me to a post in the *Auswärtiges Amt:* I was determined that, if I was to have any influence on the fate of Ireland after a German victory, it was essential that I should keep my independence.

My point of view was understood, and the offer was not repeated, but a little later I was asked my opinion on the value of the Irish Republican Army as a possible ally of Germany. It was such an opportunity as I had hoped for: in a lengthy report I pointed out that the military value of the IRA was non-existent, that any attempt at a rising would be crushed without difficulty by the Irish Government and would only have the effect of rallying the country around de Valera, and that if Germany assisted it by a landing or even by a substantial supply of arms, it would furnish the British Government with the pretext it needed for occupying the Irish ports and possibly the whole country. I did not of course believe that the Germans ever seriously intended to create an Irish front, but it was well to have my opinion on record if events in the future should make it more likely. Two of the Berlin daily papers and a monthly review asked me for articles. I sent them recollections of my past career, including sketches of the American Ambassador Dodd and Sir Nevile Henderson; when these were exhausted, I contributed serious articles on legal subjects and a series of short stories, most of them dealing with aspects of English life – such aspects, that is to say, as were likely to appeal to Germans in wartime. These enjoyed considerable popularity and were well paid. I came to the conclusion that I could always manage to earn my living, even if the War lasted beyond my expectations.

But it had never been my intention to remain indefinitely in Berlin. I did not want to lose the opportunity of communicating with Ireland and therefore preferred to settle in a neutral country from which I could visit Germany whenever I wished.

Only Italy and Switzerland seemed available – and I had no connection with Switzerland except my bank account. Accordingly I made up my mind to travel to Rome in January 1940. To the Berlin friends who came to see me off at the station I said, '*Auf baldiges Wiedersehen!* See you soon again!'

★ ★ ★

On my way to Rome I stayed for ten days with my friends the Marainis in Florence. He was a distinguished sculptor, who had designed the winding staircase in the Vatican Museum and the principal door of the basilica of St Paul's and had been a senator in Mussolini's parliament. His wife Yoi was half-English, half-Polish and an ardent Fascist. On the evening of my arrival they gave a party. It was neutral territory, in which everyone was entitled to his opinion on the War, Mussolini, Churchill, Hitler or Stalin. Yoi introduced me to a well-preserved elderly man. 'This is the head of the British Institute here,' she said. 'Francis Toye.'

'But we know each other already,' I said amiably. 'We were at Winchester together many years ago.'

'I don't remember you at all,' said Toye, looking superciliously at me.

'That's quite natural,' I said. 'I was only a little boy in my first year at school, and you were nearly grown up. There must have been at least five years' difference of age between us. So how could you possibly remember me?'

He said nothing, but I saw him awaiting his opportunity of getting back at me. The occasion soon offered itself. I was talking German to a Russian guest, when he called out from the other side of the room, 'Why are you talking German?'

There was an embarrassed silence. 'Why not?' I asked him. 'Italy is not in the War, and I belong to a neutral country. I see no reason why we should not speak German if we wish.'

'I could talk German if I wished,' said Toye.

'But perhaps not quite so well,' said I.

The conversation dropped, and I had no further encounter with the head of the British Institute. I mention so trivial an episode only as an example of the puerility to which middle-aged men can descend when a contrast of political views is heightened by personal antipathy.

Life in Rome went on much as usual; no-one had the least idea whether Italy would depart from its 'non-belligerence'. Only the number of tourists was sadly reduced: most Americans avoided Europe, and the French and English were not in a position to spend their holidays abroad. A few Germans streamed over the Alps, but their allowances of foreign currency, and consequently their popularity, were extremely limited. A German lady of my acquaintance told me that she and a friend had been sitting in the moonlight in the Borghese Garden, when a couple of young Italians passed by.

'Do you see those Germans?' said one to his companion. '*Stanno godendo la nostra luna!* They are enjoying *our* moon!'

Nor, at first, did the situation change when Mussolini decided to throw in his lot with Germany. After considerable delay food was rationed, but everything was readily obtainable on the black market, and no-one appeared to have misgivings about the future. To my regret, Egypt broke off relations with the Italian Government, and my friend Murad Pasha, the Egyptian Minister, went into exile in Switzerland. I had known him well in Berlin and later in Rome. He was universally known as Bel Ami.

'I have a special mission from the King,' he said. 'He has instructed me to find out who is Hitler's mistress and to send him her photo.'

'I never heard that Hitler had any woman,' I observed.

'There must be a woman,' replied Bel Ami with decision.

He went assiduously about his task, inquiring of every member of the Party he met with even a rudimentary knowledge of French, '*Qui est la femme de Hitler?*'

But he received the invariable answer, 'Our Führer lives only for his Fatherland and the German people.'

Finally one day he told me in triumph, 'There *is* a woman!'

'Who is she?'

'I don't know her name, but she lives in Munich. They would only tell me that she exists, but it is all kept a secret except from a few people. I will find out more.'

It was the first that I had heard of the existence of Eva Braun, and ninety-nine per cent of the population of Germany was in the same condition of ignorance. But the War interrupted Bel Ami's investigations, and he was transferred to Rome, where Mussolini made no secret of his love affairs. In the meantime he had devised a system of government for the Egypt of the future after the victory of the Axis. I asked him its nature.

'First of all,' said he, 'the Parliament must be abolished. It only leads to dissension. Then, we must put an end to the freedom of the press. It is intolerable that newspapers should be allowed to work against the interests of the country. And the Jews must be driven out of public life.'

It was a simple and comprehensive programme, which obviously could only be carried into effect after a German victory. But Bel Ami made no secret of his sympathies. So, when Italy entered the War, he thought it prudent not to return to Cairo, where he anticipated imprisonment by the Powers in occupation, but retired to Geneva to await better times. He had his pension as former Minister of Education in the Egyptian Government in addition to a fund to his credit in a Swiss bank, but the year and a half of waiting must have been beyond all imagination monotonous. But Bel Ami was in his way an idealist and would never have consented to give way in matters of principle. And after eighteen months of waiting he saw his hour approaching.

The African campaign had just started, and Hitler and Mussolini issued a proclamation stating that they would under no circumstances infringe the independence of Egypt. From his Genevan refuge Bel Ami sent enthusiastic telegrams to Ribbentrop and Ciano, placing himself at their disposal for the free Egypt of the future. Ribbentrop sent him a discreet answer that he would not fail to remember the offer when the occasion arose, but Ciano wired that he would be pleased to receive him in Rome. Bel Ami at once took the train and arrived at the Hotel Ambasciatori where I was staying. On the next morning he set off to the Palazzo Chigi, where the Italian Foreign Ministry had its seat.

'Well, how did the interview go?' I inquired.

'He told me to wait here until they have occupied Alexandria, and then he will see me again.'

But week followed week, and Alexandria did not fall. We heard rumours of information given by Italian officers to the Allies of the ships bearing supplies and reinforcements to Africa. Confidence in victory was beginning to sink, and many made no secret of their sympathy for the enemy. Ciano seemed to have forgotten the Egyptian who had come to Rome at his request. Bel Ami's messages remained without an answer. At last he said, 'Do you think I ought to stay longer?'

'No,' I said, 'the programme has obviously been changed by the reverses in North Africa. They can't expect you to wait here indefinitely.'

He left Rome that evening for Geneva. I accompanied him to the station. 'Thanks for seeing me off!' he said. 'They have sent no-one from the Ministry – although I really am a person of some importance. *Ces Italiens – ces ne sont pas des gens sérieux!*'

★   ★   ★

The want was felt of American films and American cigarettes. And the English were *chic* and *signorili,* perfect gentlemen – quite different from the Germans. I was dining in a crowded restaurant with Monsignore O'Flaherty, an Irish prelate who by virtue of his neutral nationality had been entrusted by the Vatican with the mission of visiting the Italian prisoners in English camps, the English prisoners in Italy. An Italian officer in uniform came over to speak to us.

'Have you heard the good news?' he asked in a voice which was clearly audible to the neighbouring table. 'Three English officers have escaped from the camp in Florence.'

To me it was incredible. I could understand and even sympathize with the point of view of a working man who saw and suffered from the incapacity and egoism of Mussolini's ministers. Food rationing had at last been introduced, and food tickets were distributed guaranteeing a sufficient ration of all the necessities of life, but in hard fact the rationed articles were rarely available. The black marketeers made fortunes. In the little restaurants and *trattorie* everything could be obtained if you were prepared to pay the price. Those who could not pay the price went hungry.

But that was no explanation of the upper classes who were certainly feeling the pinch less than their counterparts in the rest of belligerent Europe. The colonel, for instance, who exulted in the escape of enemy prisoners of war, had presumably taken an oath of fidelity to his king and country. Had he and those like him no sense of honour and loyalty? Were they not ready to make the least sacrifice for their fatherland? I asked the Monsignore his opinion, but he only shook his head diplomatically.

It was only later that I came to realize the extraordinary naïvety of the average Italian – a naïvety only partially disguised by his superficial intelligence. During the first years of Fascism he had believed implicitly in the grandiloquent promises of the régime, and the most fanatically Communist provinces of Italy had overnight become the most fanatical supporters of the Party. Then had come the War and the inevitable hardships together with the knowledge of the corruption and incompetence of Italy's leaders. Fascist assurances of victory and prosperity were no longer taken seriously – and in the typical revulsion of public opinion English propaganda, directed on the wireless by the notorious half-Italian Colonel Stevens, became gospel truth. The people firmly believed that all that was necessary to Italy's future happiness was the defeat of Italian arms, after which Italy would be formally adopted as one of the victors and rewarded for her services to the cause of democracy and the triumph of the Allies. When the reality turned out vastly different from the Paradise promised by Colonel Stevens, a large minority of Italian people – and not only of the working class – saw, and still see, salvation in a future Soviet state as depicted by an all-pervading propaganda which a long series of irresolute and inefficient governments has done nothing to counteract.

★ ★ ★

I visited Berlin during the year 1942. Here at least people were taking things seriously, but I could not help recognizing that Germany's war was not going well. The first doubts of ultimate victory had begun to raise their heads with the indefinite prolongation of the Russian campaign. A friend in the SS told me that the *Abwehr,* the Army Secret Service, had assured Hitler that it would be a walkover lasting not more than six weeks, while the more realistic reports of the SD, the Secret Service of the SS, had been disregarded. I did not know whether to ascribe his version to the notorious rivalry between the two bodies.

My friend, Subhas Chandra Bose, the Indian Nationalist leader, had come to Berlin to ask Hitler's help. After months of delay he was losing hope and patience. 'Hitler will never do anything for us,' he complained. 'He wants a separate peace with England, and he would sacrifice India without a second thought if he believed he could conciliate the English. We can expect nothing from him.'

'I have heard exactly the same from others,' I said. 'It is the racial theory pushed to extremes. He has always hankered after the love of his English cousins and refuses to be repulsed, even though they refuse to recognize the kinship. It is impossible to explain except by an inferiority complex which seems to be common to the greater part of the German people. I don't suppose for a minute that he would stir a finger to free Ireland – and indeed Frau von Dirksen said as much to me in Berlin.'

'I'm afraid you're right,' said Bose. Then, after a pause, he added, 'By the way, I saw a countryman of yours the other day whom I knew in Ireland some years ago – Frank Ryan.'

'I didn't know he was in Berlin,' I said. 'The last I heard of him, he was fighting for the Reds in Spain. What is he doing here?'

'That's the curious part of it. I spoke to him in the street, but he seemed in a hurry and went away without giving me his address. So I asked the *Auswärtiges Amt* whether I could meet him. They said they would inquire, but next day they told me it would be impossible to arrange a meeting.'

'Strange!' I said. 'I'll try to arrange it if I can.'

Frank Ryan had been a devout Catholic, but an equally devout Democrat. As is the way with Catholic Democrats, the Democratic element gained the upper hand, and he had felt it his duty to offer his services to the Republican forces in Spain. After a period of fighting, he was taken prisoner by Franco's troops, condemned to death on a charge which was never published in Ireland and subsequently reprieved. Representations by the Irish Government had failed to secure his release. What could he be doing in Berlin?

I went to everyone I knew who might possibly have influence. But my efforts met with the same results as Bose's: a meeting between us was out of the question, Ryan was being held by the Army authorities for a secret mission and was bound to avoid all contact with the outer world. However, I succeeded in eliciting certain facts about his recent career. In Franco's prison he had apparently come to see that a member of the Catholic Church could scarcely continue to support a party which in the name of democracy burned Catholic churches, murdered priests and nuns and openly advocated the abolition of religion. He had the courage to admit his mistake, and after the outbreak of the War asked to be put in contact with the Germans, who, as he recognized, were the only nation likely to give even limited support to the cause of Irish freedom.

The German authorities had brought him to Berlin, and later sent him with the IRA leader Seán Russell on an expedition to Ireland. But Russell had died in the German submarine, the expedition was given up, and Ryan was now once more in Berlin awaiting the further plans of the German High Command. Before the end of the War he died in Dresden sanatorium after a long illness.

I told Bose of my want of success. He shook his head. 'They are going the wrong way about winning the War,' he said. 'It's useless my waiting here any longer, I must go to India. There is no-one there to lead the movement. Gandhi's passive resistance has demoralized the country. No people ever won its freedom by passive resistance.'

'What about Nehru?' I asked him.

'Nehru is not against the English. He was educated in England and has never forgotten it. He has leanings towards Communism. Wherever he goes, he is surrounded by a circle of flatterers who get him to do what they want. No, I must go myself. There is no-one else.'

He gave me a copy of his book on India's struggle for independence and wrote an inscription on the first page. 'And now – goodbye!' he said. 'We may never meet again!'

A month later he had left Germany for Japan. Later, I read in the press that he had appeared on the Indian frontier at the head of an Indian National Army, and, later still, that he had perished in an aeroplane accident. I regretted him deeply as a good friend and a sincere patriot.

Dieckhoff, the former Ambassador to the United States who was now the head of the department for Anglo-American affairs in the *Auswärtiges Amt,* invited me to his office in the Wilhelmstrasse. I had no formal connections with German Government circles, though I was personally acquainted with many officials, and the object of the visit was not clear to me. However, Dieckhoff at once put an end to my curiosity with the words, 'We believe you to be a friend of Germany and we think your knowledge of Irish opinion may be of use to us.'

I assured him that any knowledge I might possess was at his disposal.

'What we want to know', continued Dieckhoff, 'is whether there is any propaganda which might help us to detach the Irish vote from Roosevelt in the coming election. It is of the greatest importance that Roosevelt should be defeated.'

I considered for a moment, then I said, 'There are two possible lines of propaganda which might influence the Irish vote, but I am convinced that you will not adopt either of them.'

Dieckhoff smiled. 'That's possible,' he said, 'but I would like to know what they are.'

'Well,' I said, 'in the first place you could lay emphasis on the fact that the German Army has liberated the Christian Churches in the Baltic states from Communism and restored freedom of worship.'

He shook his head. 'I see your point,' he said, 'but we are not allowed to use that propaganda.'

'I expected nothing else,' I told him. 'Is it worth while mentioning the other possible line?'

'I would like to hear it,' said Dieckhoff.

'You could secure at least a portion of the Irish vote for an anti-Roosevelt candidate if you promised that in the event of a German victory Germany would create an Irish Republic for the whole island including Ulster.'

He shook his head again. 'It is contrary to the policy of the German Government to make any declaration during the progress of the War on its intentions after the victory.'

★ ★ ★

Our experience with Frank Ryan showed me clearly that the various organizations in Germany were almost as much occupied in working against one another as in combining against the enemy. The high hopes aroused by the first triumphal advance of German troops in Russia had yielded to the recognition that final victory was as far off as ever. The enthusiasm of the Russian peasant at his liberation from Communist tyranny vanished when brought face to face with the no-less-brutal methods of the SS in the occupied territories. And the first air-raids in Berlin had taken place. They had done little damage, and the population did not take them seriously, but they meant the end of the security guaranteed by Germany's *Luftwaffe* and were a warning of danger to come.

I returned to Rome, but the landing of the Allies in Sicily, the *coup d'état* of Badoglio and the fall of Fascism convinced me that the climate was no longer wholesome. I left for Meran in the South Tyrol, where I spent the remainder of the War.

Before 1914 Meran had been one of the most brilliant summer resorts of the Austro-Hungarian Empire. It was equipped with a theatre, a Kursaal, radioactive baths and a number of first-class hotels. Numerous members of the Austrian aristocracy owned villas in its neighbourhood. Even in 1943, after twenty years of Italian rule, it was still the Austrian element which set the fashion. Uncrowned queen of this Austrian Society was an elderly lady who went under the name of Frau Burg: in fact she was the morganatic widow of a Habsburg Grand Duke and the possessor of two small castles in the suburb of Obermais – Schloss Rosenstein and Schloss Rottenstein.

Frau Burg and her clique regarded the Italians who had settled in the town – and still more those who flocked into it in the summer months – as middle-class and second-rate. But it must not be imagined that their hostility to Italy implied any friendship towards the Germans. They lived in the atmosphere of Franz Josef and tried to forget that nearly a generation had elapsed since his death. Kaiser Wilhelm they had always regarded as a *parvenu*, and his successors, whether Ebert or Hitler, as vulgarians. At the beginning of the War when Frau Burg's brother, a general in the German Army since the Anschluss, had visited Meran, she had made the concession of showing herself in public in his company in spite of the hated uniform, but now that the tide of war had begun to flow against the Axis powers she insisted on his wearing civil clothes for his promenades with her on the banks of the Passer.

The whole-hearted admiration of the Austrian nobility of Meran was reserved for the English, of whom they knew little from personal experience, but had formed an exalted idea based on the traditions of Edward VII and the rich travelling milord of a previous century. I had at this time published a book of short stories of English life. It was written in German, but bore the English title *Ladies and Gentlemen*. The name proved an attraction to Frau Burg.

'What is it about?' she asked me.

'My first literary venture,' I replied modestly. 'It's intended to open the eyes of the idiots who still believe in the superiority of the English.'

Frau Burg drew herself up to her full height. 'I am one of those idiots,' she proclaimed with annihilating dignity.

'Then I must certainly send you a copy,' said I.

It is unnecessary to add that from that day on the exclusive doors of Austrian Society in Meran were closed against me.

The Tyrolese peasants, on the other hand, were devoted supporters of Germany, and hailed the entry of the German occupying forces with flowers and wine. A hardy race of mountaineers, they had always despised the urbane and effeminate Viennese and distrusted their much advertised charm and insinuating accent: at the bottom of their hearts, they would have vastly preferred Prussian to Austrian rule. Their main passion was a consuming hatred of Italy and the Italians – a hatred which can only be understood when one remembers the deliberate plantation of the South Tyrolese province with

Sicilians and Calabrians who even among their own countrymen do not enjoy the best of reputations.

But of course the dominant element in wartime was neither the Austrian nobility nor the Tyrolese peasantry, still less the Italian settlers. German troops occupied the former Italian barracks, the better hotels, the public buildings. German officials administered the affairs of the community in a number of villas in the surroundings. And in Schloss Labers, outside the town, there was a strong detachment of the SS.

Schloss Labers has since the War been given considerable prominence in the international press: it has been repeatedly alleged that the forged notes with which Germany hoped to flood the Allied countries and destroy the American and English currencies were fabricated in its cellars. In this form, the story is incorrect: the resources of a dilapidated century-old building with no modern conveniences would scarcely have admitted of such an elaborate process as the forgery of bank notes on a large scale. But it is true that the pound and dollar notes which for several years baffled the experts came in great quantities to Schloss Labers from Germany and were thence distributed throughout Italy and the Balkan states.

Head of the local organization was a certain Major Schwendt, whose business it was to purchase supplies for the German army. His emissaries left Meran every week with their cargo of forged notes and returned to report progress at the weekend. In the last days of the War, if I may be allowed to anticipate, Major Schwendt disappeared, leaving his underlings to bear the brunt of Allied reprisals. It was freely stated in Meran that among the American troops who entered the town a few weeks later was a certain Major Clem, who spoke English with a foreign accent and, judging by his appearance, might have been the twin brother of the vanished Major Schwendt. Be that as it may, Schwendt was never arrested, interned or brought to trial by the Allies. A little later it was known that he had escaped to South America, where he was able to live in comfort for nearly twenty years before finally coming into conflict with Peruvian justice for a non-political offence.

SOUTH TYROL IN WARTIME

For some reason not at once evident the Japanese naval attaché had his office in Meran. Under the circumstances his official duties were not heavy, but when the feast of cherry-blossom approached, he sent out invitations to all and sundry to celebrate it in the only hotel not yet sequestrated by the authorities. Invitations of the sort were so rare that no-one refused: for once, persons of every race, creed, political party and class assembled in the hope of consuming the caviare and champagne which were now only available to members of the diplomatic corps.

Looking around the hotel lounge, I saw the heads of the German *Wehrmacht* and SS, who together with their local Tyrolese nominees represented the occupying forces. In their company was the Czech cinema star Lida Baarova, for whose sake Dr Goebbels had wished to divorce his wife Magda, resign his office as Propaganda Minister and retire to the comparative obscurity of Ambassador to Japan. Hitler had refused his consent, but she remained the one serious love of Goebbels' life. As guests of particular regard, Dr Petacci and his wife sat in twin armchairs, while their daughters Claretta and Miriam displayed their furs and jewels to a crowd of admirers. A little group of Austrian nobility did its best to ignore the presence of the German and Italian guests: elderly countesses strove in vain to suppress a look of horror as they realized the strange company in which they found themselves. The Japanese had not brought their wives and families to Meran, and duties of hospitality devolved upon a number of highly oxygenated and *décolletée* young Italian ladies who were presented to us as secretaries and typists.

I was introduced to a quietly dressed girl who talked German.

'I am Hungarian', she told me, 'and am a real secretary.'

'Meaning?'

'Well, I have no duties beyond those of typing and translating.'

'And the others?'

'They don't do any typing.'

I left to the strains of *'O Sole Mio'* rendered with a strong Japanese accent.

★ ★ ★

Meanwhile the news from southern Italy grew more serious every day. The Allies on their landing in Sicily had encountered no resistance worth speaking of. The collapse of the defence seemed at the time inexplicable: only much later did the secret of their facile triumph become known.

Salvatore Lucanio, popularly known as Lucky Luciano, controller of the white slave traffic and the drug ring, head of the Sicilian mafia and its ramifications in the United States, guilty though unconvicted of innumerable assassinations, was doing time for a lesser offence in an American gaol. The American legal authorities from the Attorney-General downwards had toiled for years to have him brought to trial and sentenced. But nations at war cannot afford to be fastidious in their choice of helpers: Churchill had proclaimed that he would make an alliance with the devil himself for the purpose of beating Germany, and it was not likely that the Americans would have many scruples in invoking the aid of their most conspicuous criminal. Advances were made by the authorities, Luciano promised his assistance on certain conditions, and a message from him to the Sicilian mafia was dropped near the house of the head of the organization by an American aviator. The pact functioned to perfection: the mafiosi placed themselves without reservation at the disposal of the invaders, and the whole of Sicily was occupied almost without bloodshed. The Fascist officials were killed or imprisoned: the criminals of the mafia, who had been driven underground by Mussolini's Government, were appointed by the Allied authorities to all important positions in the administration of the island.

German troops were still in possession of Rome: the Jews had mainly been deported, and the rest of the population endured the occupation with passive dislike. There had been few attempts at active resistance, and the German High Command had announced that any murder of German soldiers or officials would meet with reprisals in the proportion of ten to one. It was therefore totally unexpected when a bomb was thrown in the Via Rasella in the heart of Rome which killed some thirty-five of the military police, all of them Tyrolese from the province of Bozen. The reprisals were not long in coming: as the person responsible for the bomb did not declare himself, some three hundred and fifty prisoners were shot at the Fosse Ardeatine.

Some time later I asked an Italian who had been active in the partisans why the bomb-thrower had not admitted his responsibility and saved the lives of hundreds of innocent persons.

He looked at me in surprise. 'But that would have been contrary to our whole policy,' he answered.

'But surely it was no part of your policy to have three hundred and fifty hostages shot as reprisals?'

'The position was this,' he explained. 'We were afraid that the Roman population was getting too friendly with the Germans. We wanted to be sure that they would do their duty if it came to fighting in Rome. Therefore we had to provoke some action on the German side which would lose them any sympathy they might have won among the people. We knew that there would be reprisals and that after the reprisals no-one would dare to show any sympathy with the occupying troops. Everything worked according to plan, whereas, if the bomb-thrower had sacrificed himself and been shot, no-one would have cared.'

To such a statement of strategy I had no answer.

In Meran there was little danger of air-raids, as the town was full of hospitals and the Geneva Red Cross had made representations to the Allies that it should be spared. But it was tedious beyond imagination. The War seemed endless. One waited in vain for something to happen. I wrote articles for the German and occasionally for the Italian press, thus adding a little to the amounts which I was able to draw on my account in a Swiss bank. I told myself that in wartime nothing is so desirable as boredom, as any excitement is likely to be a change for the worse. But in the end I decided that, danger or no danger, I must go to Berlin. I had a valid reason for the journey: my belongings, furniture, pictures, silver, were in packing-cases in the garage of the Legation, and I did not know whether any part of them had survived the bombing of the 23rd of November 1943. So in July 1944 I managed to secure a place in the sleeping-car from Meran to Berlin.

It was a Berlin different from any which I had known in the past. My former Legation lay in a heap of ruins. The entire 'diplomatic quarter' had been wiped out; among the masses of bricks and rubble it was often hard to see where the street had run. The Friedrichstrasse and Unter den Linden showed only isolated blocks; in the working men's districts the destruction was even greater. The bombing continued day and night; only in the early morning and late evening were there a few hours of respite between the attacks of Americans and English. But the food supply was still regular: one could be sure of getting whatever was promised by the ration-cards.

I had gone to the Hotel Continental near the Friedrichstrasse Station; after two days the authorities secured me a room in the Adlon. On the following morning there set in the heaviest bombardment which Berlin had yet known. After three hours in the Adlon refuge I came out on the street: it was two o'clock in the afternoon, but the clouds of smoke from the burning buildings suggested an autumn twilight. The Propaganda Ministry and half the Wilhelmstrasse were in flames. The block in which the Continental had stood was a heap of smouldering ruins. For the first time people said openly that Germany was defeated. There was no panic, but a sense of hopelessness.

A friend from one of the Ministries said to me, 'I want you to come to dinner this evening in the Auslandklub. There's a man there who is anxious to meet you.'

I agreed, and towards six o'clock I made my way to the Leipzigerstrasse. It was the 20th of July, but I did not yet know that it was a day which no-one in Germany was likely to forget. I looked with vague surprise at the cordons of soldiers in the Potsdamer Platz and the Budapesterstrasse.

The Auslandklub was the resort of the foreign journalists who had remained in Berlin. It was not long before I was told of the attempt on Hitler's life, but nobody knew anything for certain. A Norwegian journalist had it on the best authority that Hitler was dead and a triumvirate of Goering, Himmler and Dönitz had assumed supreme power. But he was immediately contradicted by another who knew that the Führer was still alive and by a third who said that the Army had taken control. The only certain information was that no-one could leave the Auslandklub, as all the neighbouring streets had been blocked by the military.

'Come to the bar,' my friend said. 'The man I told you about is waiting there.'

He led me to the bar, where a couple of men were sitting on high stools. 'Let me introduce you to William Joyce,' he said.

I had never met the famous 'Lord Haw-Haw', though I had occasionally listened to him on the wireless, and I had no idea of his origin or his connection with Ireland.

Joyce greeted me warmly. 'I'm delighted to meet an Irishman,' he said. 'It's a long time since I met one.'

'I wonder we never met before,' said I, 'either in Ireland or in Germany. When were you last in Ireland?'

'It's many years ago now,' said Joyce. 'From 1920 to 1922 I was in Galway where my father was born.'

'It's surprising we never met there,' I persisted. 'In those years I was very often in Galway as a young barrister. I used to defend Sinn Féin prisoners before British courts-martial.'

Joyce looked at me with an expression half embarrassed, half amused. 'I was on the other side,' he said simply.

It was the last thing that I expected to hear from him; only later was I told that he had in fact joined the force of Auxiliary Police whose task it was to suppress Sinn Féin by any means, fair or foul. I must have shown my astonishment, for he continued, 'You see, I have always been an Empire man.'

'And now?' I asked.

'Now above all. I always say so on the wireless. Britain has taken the wrong side in the War. Its real enemy is international Communism. It should have joined Germany to defend Europe.'

'And so you came out here?'

'It was the only chance of making my ideas heard.'

'You left Mosley's party?'

'Mosley?' There was bitterness in his voice. 'I left him long before I came to Germany. He could never have been a leader. His vanity destroyed him.'

He continued in the same strain for a while; I did not like to ask him whether the English appreciated the efforts he was making on their behalf – in fact, I felt that there were a number of themes which it was better to avoid. So I said, 'I don't pretend to understand your admiration for the British Empire. I won't speak of Ireland, as you told me that you were on the other side, but what about India? Do you justify British policy in Amritsar? What about General Dyer?' 'General Dyer was perfectly right,' he said. 'He could do nothing else. I have always been for a strong Empire.'

It was a standpoint which amazed me – I had imagined that even in England itself no-one now attempted to defend the General. But I had no doubt of his sincerity. After all, what object could he have in lying to me? We were in Berlin, and Allied bombs falling about us. Nothing that I could do was likely to affect his fate if he fell into the hands of the English; he was far too deeply compromised to have any hope of escape. It gave to his profession of faith the solemnity of a deathbed confession. It had a certain logic, but it was logic run wild, and it had led him into tragedy. However, he fortunately did not ask for my opinion, and soon a messenger came in to say that the streets were now free and we could go home.

Next morning we heard the news. Hitler had survived, the organizers of the plot had committed suicide or been arrested, wholesale arrests were taking place of those suspected of complicity.

I was lunching in the Adlon with a member of the Italian Embassy. Suddenly he said, 'There is Hassell! We'd better go and speak to him.'

I had known Ulrich von Hassell as Ambassador in Rome: in the last years he had been placed 'at disposition' and had taken no part in active politics.

'What a disaster!' said my friend. 'We had the same thing in Italy in the Badoglio revolt, and now it has happened in Germany. I only hope it won't lead to the same result.'

'We must only hope for the best,' said Hassell with a placid smile.

It was only some weeks later that I heard he had been arrested as one of the chief conspirators. At the request of his son Goering pleaded with Hitler to grant him a soldier's death by shooting. 'A man who still has in his body shrapnel from the first War!'

But Hitler would hear no word of clemency, and Hassell was hanged. His jailers on orders from above refused him permission to speak to a minister of religion before his death.

★ ★ ★

SOUTH TYROL IN WARTIME

The end of the War found me in Meran. With the proclamation of the Armistice the German troops silently vanished, and the members of the SOD, the South Tyrolese volunteer police force, burned their armlets and hid their rifles. American troops marched into the town; half the population received them with cheers and garlands. It was hard to know which were the more grateful – the Italians for their liberation from the Germans or the Tyrolese for their liberation from the Italians. The old Austrian barons made no secret of their enthusiasm for the victory, but their enthusiasm was nothing compared with that of the Nazis and Fascists of yesterday.

For anyone with a grievance it was a heaven-sent opportunity to be rid of his enemy by an anonymous letter accusing him of membership of a forbidden party. The denunciations did not run mainly on racial lines: business or personal rivalries were the prevailing motives – and naturally a man's rival belonged to his own race and class. If all the anonymous letters had been acted on, the population of Meran would have been reduced to a handful. I was a neutral and had never transgressed the laws of war. But countless others as innocent as myself were daily being arrested. A good conscience seemed to me insufficient protection if someone should take it into his head to denounce me. But there was nothing I could do except await events.

Professor Petersdorf was a German from Posen who had settled in Meran after the first war: he had conceived an intense hatred for the country of his birth and the army in which he had served, and laboured to pass muster as an Austrian by the employment of such Viennese idioms as *'Servus!'* and *'Küss' die Hand, gnädige Frau!'* He had also conferred on himself the title of Baron.

One afternoon in May 1945 I met him on the road. To my surprise, for I had only twice been in his company, he stopped me with the evident desire of conversation.

'What?' he asked with his habitual short-sighted smile and an assumption of surprise. 'Are you still here?'

'As you see,' I said. 'Is there any reason why I should not be here?'

Petersdorf's smile broadened. 'I thought', he observed, 'that you would have cleared out before the Americans came in.'

'Why?' I asked him. 'In the first place, I am a neutral, and in the second place, I have committed no crime. Why should I be afraid of the Americans?'

He shrugged his shoulders.

'I should have thought', I went on, 'that, if there was any risk in remaining here, you would be in considerably more danger than I. After all, you have a German passport.'

Petersdorf tittered: I could hear in his voice an undertone of pity for my simplicity. 'I have the membership card of the partisans,' he replied.

There had been no partisans in the province, as the country people were to a man in favour of the Germans, but after the Armistice a couple of Italians had declared themselves leaders of the *partigiani* and demanded to be recognized as such by the Allied authorities.

'Since the Armistice all Meran is applying to the partisans for the *tessera*,' I said. 'Only yesterday I was told the current price.'

He made an impatient gesture. 'I am not in the same category as the others,' he rejoined. 'All through the War I was director of the clandestine wireless station in Meran.'

'That is possible,' I said, 'but I can't see that it is a reason why I should disappear. I have my Irish passport.'

'Your passport won't help you,' said Petersdorf. 'Only yesterday they arrested the Hungarian Foreign Minister Baron Kemány.'

'I know. But that has nothing to do with me. He was Minister in the Szalassy Government. His arrest was only to be expected. Whereas I am a quite obscure individual – and I have not done anything but what every neutral has a right to do.'

The Professor tittered again. 'You are not at all so unimportant as you wish people to believe,' he said. 'I can tell you that your name is on our list. We know everything that you have written and everything that you have done. Don't imagine that your neutral passport will save you!'

I had always regarded Petersdorf as a negligible individual, but now all values seemed to be reversed. He must feel sure of himself to speak as he had spoken. I decided to get in touch with the new governing classes.

SOUTH TYROL IN WARTIME

The Italian Committee of National Liberation was working in close contact with the Americans. I called on its President, with whom I was on friendly terms, and asked for his advice.

'I don't even know the person you mention,' he said. 'I will find out how he as a German comes to be a member of the Italian *partigiani*. In the meantime what do you propose to do?'

'I would like to know your opinion,' I said.

He pondered a moment. 'It could do no harm', he said, 'to get into touch with the American police for the purpose of regularizing your position. I would recommend you to visit Major Gordon. If you like, you can mention my name as having suggested the visit.'

I thanked him and made my way to the villa which was serving as Police Headquarters. Here I was shown into a waiting-room occupied only by a sergeant. I took a chair and laid my dark green sun-glasses beside me on the table.

'How much do you want for them glasses?' asked the sergeant suddenly.

'They're not for sale,' said I.

'No?' he asked.

'I'm afraid not,' said I.

My refusal astonished the sergeant: he imagined, no doubt, that everything in occupied territory had its price in dollars. He opened his mouth to speak again, but before he could raise his offer a door was thrown open and a soldier beckoned me into the adjoining room, where an officer was seated at a writing-table. I had already sent in my card; as I went in, I said, 'Good morning!'

'Buon giorno!' answered the officer, and continued in Italian, 'What language do you speak – Italian or German?'

'Both,' I replied.

'Very well,' said he. 'Then we can speak Italian. Well, what was it you wanted to see me about?'

It struck me as strange that an American police officer spoke Italian so perfectly and more especially that he apparently did not wish to conduct our interview in English. He knew who I was, for my visiting-card lay on the table before him. I wondered whether he or his father had been an emigrant from Italy; if he was in fact the Major Gordon for whom I had asked, I could only surmise that his name had been Americanized from Giordano. There was, however, little time to lose in conjectures over his possible origin, and I plunged into my story.

'It's like this,' I said. 'I was in the Irish diplomatic service. From '33 to '39 I was Minister in Berlin. Then, for reasons into which I need not enter, I retired and took to journalism. I contributed to various German newspapers and reviews, and a little later I published a volume of short stories. Do you read German?'

'Fairly well.'

'Then I hope you will read this,' I said, handing him a copy of my book. 'I think it will amuse you, it's not in any way political. They are stories of certain aspects of English life.'

He smiled. 'Aspects, perhaps, which it would not particularly please them to see brought out in time of war?' he suggested.

'Perhaps not,' I agreed. 'Pleasing them was not my chief object in publication.'

'Have you written much against America?' he asked.

'I have written very little about America – only two articles, so far as I can remember. One was humorous: it was about the Ambassador Dodd and his daughter Martha. It was a subject which lent itself to humour even in the eyes of their own Embassy.'

'I know that,' said he. 'You have written against England?'

'Yes, a fair amount.'

'Are you an enemy of England?' he asked with a smile.

I shrugged my shoulders. 'You can't expect an Irishman to be particularly friendly to England,' I replied.

He offered me a cigarette. 'In the States,' he observed, 'we consider the Irish to be some of our best citizens.'

I expressed my pleasure at his good opinion of us. There followed a pause.

'And now,' I said, 'I have come to see you because I have heard that you have received a communication about me, denouncing me for I don't know what. I thought it would be well to explain the facts to you and to regularize my position.'

He echoed my words. 'Regularize your position?' he said. '*Ho capito*. I understand.'

I informed him briefly of my encounter with Petersdorf on the evening before and waited for a comment from him. No comment came: he contented himself with drumming his fingers on the table and looking at me with a faintly amused air. My cigarette had burned itself out; I rose to go. He gave me his hand.

'Goodbye!' he said. 'It is always better to regularize one's position. *Addio!*'

'*Addio!*' I replied.

As I lay in bed that night in the Sanatorium Stefanie, I pondered over my talk with Major Gordon, if indeed it was he.

What I did not understand was his insistence on speaking in Italian. Only after long deliberation did it occur to me that the American police had perhaps been unable to bring their shorthand typists to Meran and had had to fall back on local talent. Was it my fancy, or had there been a curtain not far from the writing-table which might have concealed the door of an adjoining room? And was it not possible that behind the curtain there sat a girl from the neighbourhood with pencil and notebook, intent on taking down any admissions I might make?

The more I thought over it, the more plausible seemed my theory. Only, at the moment, I could see no reason for such procedure. And then I remembered having heard that the Americans were to be succeeded after a short period by British troops and that the English secret police had already taken a villa in the suburb of Obermais. It was possible that the Americans handed over to their British colleagues the records of all interviews of importance. That would at least be an explanation of the desire of the police officer to put our conversation on record.

This new aspect of the case was far from pleasing me: I could not help seeing that I was involved in a more troublesome affair than I had suspected. But my consciousness of innocence once more came to my aid. What could anyone do to me, if I had committed no offence. And that I had committed no offence, I was sure.

'I can only wait and see,' I said to myself, and having reached that satisfactory conclusion I closed my eyes and was soon asleep.

TEN

1945 – Under Arrest

It was some two weeks later, on the morning of the 26th of May, that two policemen walked into my room. The clock on the dressing-table pointed to twelve minutes past ten, and I was preparing to go into the town. One of the policemen was Italian: he was in civilian clothes and wore around his left arm a band with the Italian colours. The other was also in civilian clothes, and it needed no armband to tell me that he was American.

'Will you pack your clothes', said the Italian policeman, 'for two days? You will be questioned about certain matters. After a couple of days you can return here.'

'All right,' said I. 'Is it necessary to take a second suit of clothes and extra underwear?'

'Oh, no,' said the policeman. 'Just what you need for the night.'

I glanced at the American for confirmation, but saw that he did not understand Italian. Then I put a spare shirt, underclothes and money into my suitcase; in addition, I threw in a couple of books and a pack of cards. I did not know where I was going and had no idea of the conditions of prison life, but I had a feeling that, if the worst came to the worst, one could always play patience. Then I locked the suitcase, put the key in my pocket and said to the Italian, 'I'm ready.'

'Take your bag!' said the American policeman in German. I did so; the one preceded, the other followed me down the stairs to the entrance-hall of the Stefanie.

The entrance-hall was full of people – fuller than I had ever seen it. A glance through the glass door showed me that the gravel space in front of the building was tightly packed with military and civilian motors. A voice at my elbow said, 'So you're here too!'

1945 – UNDER ARREST

It was Luis Barcata, an Austrian journalist: he and his wife held suitcases in their hands.

'It's not possible!' I exclaimed. 'Why should you be arrested?'

'I don't know,' she said. 'Perhaps because I am registered as my husband's secretary.'

'Who are all the people around us?' I asked Barcata. 'I have never seen them before.'

'Who knows? Presumably some are our fellow-prisoners and others police-agents. Others are just lookers-on at this interesting scene.'

'And who are our fellow-prisoners?'

'I don't know,' said Barcata. 'I saw Hagemann a minute ago sitting in an armchair. I was rather surprised that he didn't speak to me. I asked him if he was arrested, and he said, "Oh no, I'm working for the Americans."'

'Good God!' I exclaimed. 'Are you sure you're not mistaken?'

'Not the slightest doubt,' said Barcata.

I looked over at Hagemann and noticed that he took care to avoid my eye. He was a native of Bremen and had been sent to Meran in charge of the German military traffic in the South Tyrol. He and his Alsatian wife had always professed themselves devoted supporters of the Hitler régime, out of which he had made a considerable fortune. Now he sat in his armchair and peered round the room with a satisfied smile.

'I'm afraid you're right,' I said to Barcata.

'Are they all here?' asked a voice in English.

I did not hear the answer, but it apparently satisfied the owner of the voice, for he said, 'All those whose names I read out are to go and stand in the porch. Barcata!'

Barcata and his wife carried their suitcases towards the door.

'Bewley!'

I did the same.

'Bloch!'

When seven of us had been assembled in the porch, we were loaded on the motors standing before the door. Barcata and I shared a jeep. We did not exchange a word on the way, as we did not know whether the driver and policeman in front of us understood German or Italian, but as we halted before the gaol-gate, I heard my companion murmur, 'We're in for it all right!'

We were led into an office, where the Italian functionaries registered our names and particulars, placed our money and valuables in sealed envelopes and assured us in a whisper that they would take any messages we wished into the town. We were then led upstairs.

'Cell number seven!' shouted the warder.

A door was opened, and I was pushed into the cell. Originally intended for two prisoners, there were now crowded into it six pallet beds with straw mattresses. Five were occupied; the gaoler indicated the sixth to me and went away, locking the door behind him.

'What? You here!' said a voice from the bed beside mine.

It was the Dutch president of the Meran branch of the International Red Cross; he had been living with his wife and son in the Stefanie, but I had never spoken to him except for a greeting on the stairs.

'As you see,' I answered, 'but why have you been arrested?'

'I have no idea,' said Van Vliet. 'I have been here for two weeks, but no-one has told me what I am accused of.'

At this moment there was a noise of excited voices outside; Van Vliet sprang to the door and looked through the aperture. A warder unlocked our cell. We all thronged into the corridor.

One of the other cells was open. Two boys in their early twenties were standing outside the door; they were obviously in a state of intense excitement. They alternately embraced an elderly man who had apparently come to visit them and munched the provisions which he had brought. The head warder looked on with a benevolent smile. Finally the boys fetched their bags out of the cell, seized their father by the arm and disappeared with him down the staircase.

One of the warders had remained to lock the cell-door; someone asked him what had happened.

'They are being released,' he answered, 'in order to make room for the political prisoners.'

'And what was their offence?'

'They broke into a farmer's house and stole his food and money,' said the warder.

The day passed slowly: I struck up a conversation with Van Vliet.

'You're Dutch, I believe?' I said.

'Yes,' he agreed, though in a tone without conviction.

Ik heb ook een beetje Hollandsch geleerd,' said I. 'Perhaps you wouldn't mind speaking a little Dutch with me?'

He consented without enthusiasm, and for a few minutes we carried on one of those banal conversations which take place when both speakers are only moderately familiar with the language in which they are endeavouring to express themselves. For Jan Van Vliet, in spite of his exaggeratedly Dutch name, had no greater command of the language than myself.

It was not altogether a surprise to me, for, when members of the Dutch colony had visited him in the Stefanie, I had noticed that their conversations were conducted in German. Moreover, he had been on markedly friendly terms with the SS in Schloss Labers – and, although as head of the Red Cross it was his duty to cultivate friendly relations with all persons in authority, it had been commented that his friendship had gone far beyond the necessities of official intercourse.

But perhaps I was wronging him: when the SS had evacuated Schloss Labers, Van Vliet had taken possession of it in the name of the Red Cross, and in the interregnum between the departure of the Germans and the arrival of the Americans he had assumed the command of Meran. Nor could his enthusiasm for the German cause have been so great as we imagined, since he had gone to the bridge to welcome the American armoured cars with a small star-spangled banner in his hand, and from that day onwards American and English officers had been his daily guests in the Stefanie until his removal to Meran Gaol.

'I suppose you know Berlin well?' I said, relapsing into German.

'I had business there until the War made it impossible.'

'And you had no difficulties with the authorities?'

'No,' he said, 'they gave me no trouble. I remember, when Hitler came into power, my old friend Max Friedländer coming to me and asking me what we should do. "You, Maxi, as a Jew should leave Germany at once," I told him. "I will stay!"'

I took silent note of his implied Aryan descent. 'So you never had the slightest trouble with them?' I asked.

'On the contrary, they thought highly of me as an art expert. They asked me to become a member of the *Reichskulturkammer*, but of course I refused. "Leave me in peace!" I told them. "Why should I join your ridiculous institutions?" So I stayed in Berlin until things became too difficult. Then the Red Cross appointed me its representative in Budapest. I was able to save the lives of twelve thousand Jews there who had been arrested by the SS.'

'But why should the Allies have arrested you now?'

'God knows! But it can't be for long. I have sent an urgent telegram to our Headquarters in Geneva protesting against my arrest. They will certainly send some of their people to have me set free. I am expecting them at any moment.'

One of the prisoners mounted on his bed and began to explore the corners and crevices of the wall.

'What are you doing?' I inquired.

'It's easy to see that you have only arrived today. I'm looking for bugs.' As he spoke, he removed something from a crevice, crushed it between his fingers and smeared it on the wall.

'Are there many?'

He laughed. 'Wait till the lights go out, and you'll see!' He stepped down from the bed, took up the straw mattress and examined the seams and holes in the canvas. From time to time he removed a bug and crushed it on the floor. 'That makes the thirty-eighth today,' he remarked. 'Yesterday I killed sixty-five.'

'Does it do any good?'

'Not the slightest. The bug is a highly intelligent animal. It is capable of crossing the ceiling to a certain point and then letting itself fall on the bed below. In consequence it is useless to stand the feet of the bedstead in buckets of water. They get there all the same. Not that we have buckets of water here,' he added pensively.

'I have often wondered why the bug was ever created,' observed another prisoner. 'I completely fail to see its utility in the scheme of things.'

'One theory is', said Van Vliet, 'that it was put in the world in order to stimulate man to cleanliness. If there were no bugs, he would never wash himself; their presence ensures a certain rudimentary hygiene.'

'Forty-seven . . forty-eight . . forty-nine . .' counted the searcher.

I decided not to undress for the night, but to put on my overcoat and gloves and hope for the best. The lights went out at eleven o'clock. I waited anxiously for further developments.

After a quarter of an hour, in spite of my upturned coat-collar, I felt an irritation on my neck. I slapped my neck with my open hand. Nothing there!

'Imagination!' I thought.

But the irritation grew worse, all around my neck, at my wrists, at my ankles. The flesh seemed to have grown stiff and hard. I got up and seated myself on the bed.

'Now,' I thought, 'even if I don't sleep, I will at least be free from further bites.'

It was a pathetic illusion: as I sat on the bedside, I felt the same itchiness at one point after another. It was not only the sensation; it was the horror of thinking that in the darkness the bugs were climbing up my coat, wandering over my shoes, descending my sleeves to find the exposed portions at my wrists, and that I could do nothing. I could not even walk up and down; there was no room between the bedsteads. Van Vliet was snoring sonorously; some of the others, to judge by their heavy breathing, were fast asleep. From a corner of the wall I heard a stealthy noise.

'*Bist du noch wach?*' I asked, 'Are you awake?'

'Yes,' said a voice. 'These damned bugs never let me sleep.'

It was an elderly man from Leipzig who had been a railway employee. That was, so far as he knew, his only offence.

'The dawn can't be far off,' he said. 'Once we have daylight, they are less troublesome.'

The light gradually increased; by five o'clock it was fairly clear in the cell. I took off my shoes and laid myself on the bed. I had two hours' sleep before a warder flung open the door and shouted, 'Get up and wash!'

★ ★ ★

Next day Van Vliet was busy writing his *curriculum vitae* for the authorities; as his English was deficient, he asked me to correct it.

'I must let them know who I am,' he said. 'In all this time they haven't interrogated me once. As soon as the Red Cross in Geneva gets my wire, they will have me released, but it takes so much time to get in touch. If only my poor friend Franklin Roosevelt were still alive! If once he heard of my arrest, it wouldn't take long. Some of those American officers would be in trouble, I can tell you!'

'Do you think they are likely to interrogate me?' I inquired.

'How can I tell? No-one has been questioned yet, but so many have been brought in since yesterday that they must do something.'

In the course of the afternoon I heard the name 'Barcata' called by a warder and the sound of feet coming down the stairs. 'Interrogation!' said someone. 'I should be the next in alphabetical order,' said I. And, sure enough, a few minutes later the warder called my name.

I was led down to a small garden, where a young officer was sitting under a little tree. In front of him was a small table covered with papers and beside it an empty chair. He motioned me to sit down.

'Why are you living in Meran under the protection of the Red Cross?' he demanded.

'What do you mean?' I asked. 'I am not living under the protection of the Red Cross – I did not consider that I needed anyone's protection. Mr Van Vliet lived in the sanatorium where I was staying, but I had never even spoken to him till I met him here.'

'We have been informed that you placed yourself under the protection of the Red Cross,' said he.

'You have been misinformed,' said I.

'I would like to know about your career,' he said. 'Give me the main facts.'

I gave him the main facts.

'Were you ever in the English service?' he asked.

'Certainly not. I have always been an Irish nationalist.'

'You have no reason for your attitude, then?'

'Yes, a great many. In 1916 they destroyed the chief streets of our capital and shot our leaders.'

'I see. And that is your reason for being against England?'

'One of them.'
'And then you wrote against England in the German press?'
'Certainly. As a neutral I was entitled to.'
'What do you know of the SD?'
'Nothing.'

The officer looked at me intently; I could see that he had promised himself good results from the unexpected question. Possibly he had read one of those little manuals for the use of cross-examiners, in which an abrupt change of subject was recommended for the purpose of startling the accused into an admission.

'Do you know what SD means?'
'Of course: *Sicherheitsdienst*, Security Service.'
'What else do you know about it?'
'Nothing.'
'What members of it do you know?'
'None.'
'You have heard of some?'
'Only the gossip going round here.'
'What have you heard?'
'I have heard of a man called Schwendt who is said to have become a millionaire through his activities, but I have never met him.'

My interrogator must have known of the activities of Major Schwendt alias Clem for he dropped the subject. 'Is that all you are willing to say?' he asked.

'That is all I know.'
'Our informants say that you can tell us a great deal more.'
'I would like to know who your informants are.'
'You have nothing to add?'
'Nothing.'
'Than all I can tell you is that it is highly probable that you will stay in here for an indefinite time.'
'If I stay the rest of my life here, I can't tell more than I know.'
'Why do you think we brought you here?' he asked suddenly.
'I haven't the faintest idea,' I answered. 'That seems a question that I might more appropriately put to you.'

The cross-examination continued its weary way. The officer repeated time after time the questions he had put to me. Finally he asked with an air of importance, 'Can you tell me any reason why we should let you loose on the community?'

'I would have thought', I answered, 'that it was for you to tell me whether there is any reason why I should be deprived of my freedom.'

'You can go.'

'One moment,' said I. 'I am a neutral and have the right to communicate with the representatives of my country in Italy. Will you please arrange to have a letter sent for me to the Irish Legation?'

'You must ask the Italian authorities,' he replied. 'Such matters are entirely in their hands.'

I returned to the cell where my comrades were drowsing on their beds. Only Van Vliet was busy with his *curriculum vitae;* he had reached the seventeenth page. It appeared that those who had been arrested on the previous day had been examined. 'You're lucky,' said one of the prisoners. 'You'll probably be released tomorrow.'

'I wish I could think so,' said I, 'but the officer who examined me seemed to be of quite a different opinion.'

In fact I had little hope of being speedily released; the general atmosphere was definitely hostile, and in particular the refusal to allow me to communicate with the Legation was a bad sign. I had been informed by the Italian chief warder that no letters could be sent without the express consent of the American authorities.

As soon as the warder had darkened the cell, I got up, put on a second pair of socks, turned up my coat-collar, put on gloves and seated myself on the bedside. Vain hope! No more than a quarter of an hour had passed when I felt the same sensations as on the previous night. The bugs possessed an instinct which led them infallibly to the few centimetres of bare skin between coat-sleeve and glove, between coat-collar and hat. Only the double socks more or less protected my ankles. In his corner I could hear the Leipziger scratching his feet.

'If by any chance I am really released tomorrow,' I said, 'I will give you a pair of socks.'

When I rose, face, neck and wrists were even more swollen than before.

'I don't think I will be able to stand this life for long,' I said.

'You'll get used to it,' said Van Vliet. 'One gets used to anything.'

I doubted it, but it was not worth while contradicting him. Fortunately I was not put to the test. The warder's voice sounded once more from below.

We heard Barcata's steps on the stairs, then the warder called out once more, 'Bewley! Get your things ready!'

The others crowded around me as I prepared my suitcase and offered me their best wishes.

'I'm not so sure,' said I. 'He told Barcata he was free. He only told me to get my things ready.'

'What difference does that make? Of course you're free. What does it matter what the warder says?'

I took my two spare pairs of socks and handed them to the Leipziger. 'You can't possibly stay here without socks,' I said. I said good-bye to everyone and went down the stairs. Below, Barcata was standing with his suitcase, near him were a couple of American soldiers. 'Ilse is free!' he said. 'So is Bloch!' I was going over to him, but a soldier motioned to me to stand at the other side of the room; it was clear that I belonged to another category. Time passed; the soldiers smoked cigarettes and chuckled over American humorous papers. Finally another prisoner from the Stefanie came down. One of the soldiers called a sergeant. He looked at Barcata. 'You can go!' he said. 'Bewley!'

'Yes.'

'Ebers!'

'Yes.'

'You two go into that office and get your money back!'

We did so and paid the chief warder for the food sent in to us.

'Are you ready?' asked the sergeant.

'Yes.'

'Get into the car!'

We got in; an armed policeman seated himself beside the driver.

'God knows where they're taking us,' I said to Ebers.

'Not very far, I imagine, otherwise they wouldn't send us in so small a car.'

'In any case, it can't be much worse than the prison.'

'Scarcely.'

'We must hope for the best.'

★ ★ ★

'You will stay here,' said the American policeman in his painful German, as the car turned towards the former barracks, now employed as a *Campo di Smistamento* or Transit Camp. It was the same policeman who had entered my room the morning before; I did not consider it necessary to make any reply to his remark, but my companion thought otherwise.

'You speak excellent German,' he said.

'*Ich spreche wie ich spreche,*' replied the policeman severely. 'I speak as I speak.' The conversation came to an abrupt end.

We were ushered into a room where a number of German officers had been entrusted with clerical work. A lieutenant made a note of our names and led us to our sleeping quarters. he was a Viennese in his fifties and a commercial traveller in private life.

'I have arranged for you to sleep in the officers' quarters,' said he. 'Strictly speaking, you should as civilians sleep with the ordinary soldiers, but no-one will know.'

'What will they do with us?' asked Ebers. 'It looks very bad that we are here when so many others have been set free.'

'*Es wird nie so heiss gegessen wie gekocht,*' said the Viennese consolingly. 'Nothing is ever eaten so hot as it is cooked.'

But Ebers was not comforted by such pieces of proverbial philosophy; as we walked up and down the barrack yard, his mood was one of unmixed gloom. It began to get on my nerves.

'I don't think it was necessary to compliment that policeman on his German,' said I.

'It's never any harm being polite,' he retorted.

'Polite, yes; but I don't see the need of being effusive. And, judging by the answer he gave you, he didn't much appreciate your politeness.'

'What can we do? We are in their hands.'

'Everyone must decide for himself. Personally, I don't propose to speak to them at all except when it is necessary. After all, we are their prisoners, arrested without a shadow of justification. The ordinary rules of politeness don't apply.'

As we walked up and down, we talked of our cases at interminable length: every detail of the arrest, of the examination in the prison, of the demeanour of the examining officer was repeated, analyzed, sifted in the hope of discovering some favourable feature, but neither of us could find much consolation.

Suddenly Ebers said, 'Shall we make a dash for it?'

'*Um Gottes Willen!*' I exclaimed. 'Are you mad? It would be impossible to get out of the camp, and, even if we got out, where could we go?'

'If I was once over the Austrian frontier,' said Ebers, 'I would be all right. I could stay in some peasant's hut in the mountains, where they would never think of looking for me.'

'It's a long way from here to the Austrian frontier,' I objected, 'and we are neither of us as young as we used to be. And, even if you got there, it wouldn't be quite so simple as you think. Suppose the Allies imposed the death penalty on anyone harbouring escaped prisoners?'

'It won't come to that,' he said. 'I'm sure I could get through all right.'

'How do you propose to get out of the camp?'

He pointed to a low shed built against the camp wall on the side remote from the river. 'Nothing easier than to jump over the wall and get away. I am sure there are no sentries there, and in the twilight no-one would see me go!'

'Of course there are sentries there,' I said, 'probably with machine-pistols. You don't seriously think the Americans would be such bloody fools as to leave so easy a passage unguarded. And, assuming they didn't shoot you on the spot, if they once caught you and brought you back, your prospects would be a hundred times worse than before.'

'Then there is nothing left for me', he said dramatically, 'but to open a vein in my wrist and make an end of it all!'

I laughed. 'Nonsense, man! We're not reduced yet to such extremes. In another few months we'll look back on this evening and wonder how such ideas ever entered our heads.'

He saw that his effort at drama had failed to impress me. 'I suppose you're right,' he admitted. 'But my case is really a serious one.'

It was clear that he felt the need of confiding in someone, but was not sure how far he could trust me. 'What did you do?' I asked.

'What have you heard about me?'

'Only that you belong to the Organization Schwendt. And of course I know that Schwendt had given orders in the Stefanie that you were to be supplied with everything you asked for, regardless of cost. I used often to envy you the French brandy that ordinary mortals couldn't get for love or money.'

'That's correct,' said Ebers. 'Schwendt provided the notes and I travelled for him. I speak the Croat language, so I used to go down that way. But how could I know that the pound notes were forged? I was only a small employee. They never told me their secrets.'

'You told them that when you were examined?'

'Yes, but I don't know whether they believed me. And now that swine Schwendt had gone over to the Americans and will give us all away to save himself!'

'He can't give you away if you didn't know the notes were forged.'

'But how can I prove that?' said Ebers despairingly. 'You see, my record's not so good. If they take the trouble, they can find out my other sentences.'

'But not for passing forged notes?' I asked.

'Oh no! Only for currency smuggling. You see, there was a lot of money to be made out of that. But it was risky.' He became more confidential, as he thought of his past adventures. 'However, I often got away with it.'

'How did you manage it?' I inquired. 'That is, if it's not giving away a trade secret.'

'There are a lot of ways,' said Ebers. 'Of course we had to change them from time to time. Often I got through by rolling up the notes inside the blind of the railway carriage. Some used to hide them under the seats, but I always thought that unfair, because they arrested whoever happened to be sitting over them. Besides, they always looked under the cushions.'

We strolled up and down the courtyard, and he went on, 'The Regina Coeli in Rome is the worst gaol I've been in, worse than Zagreb or the Albanian prisons. Far and away the best are the Swiss prisons – the cleanest and the best food. I thought all that was forgotten, and now that dirty bastard Schwendt will give us all away to save his skin!'

'You can't tell,' I said in a futile manner.

'Of course he will, man. There's so much against him that he'd inform on his mother just to get out himself. It was he who got the notes from Berlin and stored them in Schloss Labers. Then he used to distribute them to agents like me. How could we be expected to ask for a guarantee that they were genuine? We'd have lost our jobs.'

We were joined by the Viennese and another lieutenant, who hoped to hear from us news from the outside world. 'Just finished our work for the day,' he remarked.

'You're lucky,' I said. 'Regular work, regular meals, not waiting like us to be transported God knows where.'

'*Scheisse!*' he said explosively. 'So long as there is work to be done, they make use of us. Afterwards, when this camp is evacuated, we will be interned like all the rest.'

'A pleasant prospect!' I remarked.

He shrugged his shoulders. '*Es wird nie so heiss gegessen wie gekocht!*' he repeated.

'Our only hope', said the other lieutenant, 'is that they will recruit us for the war against Japan.'

'Do you think that likely?' I asked incredulously.

'An American colonel made a speech to the prisoners in another camp, asking them whether they were prepared to join up. The terms were good: the same pay as American soldiers, food for their families in Germany, three hundred dollars when they leave the service and the option of becoming American citizens.'

'The war against Japan won't last much longer,' I objected.

'No, but they need us against Russia. Japan is only an excuse,' he answered.

'Would you join up yourself?'

'Of course. I have nothing left in the world. My whole family was killed in the raids on Dresden. The house is destroyed. I have nothing but the clothes I stand in. What can I do except join up? In the end perhaps I can start a new life in the States.'

It was my first experience of the fantastic rumours – *Scheisshausgerüchte*, latrine reports, the German soldiers called them – which circulate in all concentration camps, so I did not contradict the story on the spot – besides it would have been cruel to destroy his illusions.

'When do you think they will interrogate us?' asked Ebers.

The Viennese shrugged his shoulders. 'Who knows? The Major told someone he wished to examine you two himself, but he is away at the moment.'

'Can he talk German?' asked Ebers.

'No, he has an interpreter. Our people call him Isidor Kohn; I don't know his real name, but he was born in Tarnopol and is now a New York business man. An amiable type – the Major follows his advice in everything.'

'Yes, most friendly,' chimed in the other lieutenant. 'I think he would like to boil every German alive, judging by the way he looks at us.'

But the time passed, and the Major showed no desire to examine us. On the following afternoon, however, a young German officer told us that he had orders to lead us to the sergeant-interpreter.

We followed him down a long corridor and into the Major's room. The interpreter was sitting on the Major's writing-table and smoking a cigarette. The officer motioned us to stand in front of him at a couple of yards' distance; he then saluted and said, 'These are the prisoners.'

The interpreter made no reply, but continued to smoke his cigarette and to scrutinize us in silence. Two minutes must have passed; then the officer asked nervously, 'Is anything needed?'

'No,' said the interpreter and went on looking us up and down. After another minute he said, 'So these are the two, are they? I just wanted to make sure I'd know them again. Take them away!'

'What do you think he meant by that?' asked Ebers when we found ourselves once more in the courtyard and I had translated the interpreter's remarks. 'Do you think he can do anything to us?'

'Of course not,' I said. 'He is only a sergeant: what influence could he have? It was just an attempt to intimidate us; probably it amused him to have us brought before him.'

'I didn't like his look.'

'No more did I, but we'll certainly have to get used to worse things than that before we're finished.'

'I suppose so,' said Ebers with a sigh.

On the next morning some hundreds of prisoners were brought in – Germans, Italians, soldiers in uniform, civilians young and old. We were ordered to take our baggage and form rows in the barrack yard. I found myself next to a good-looking young man in officer's uniform.

'Erlanger!' he said. 'Brazilian.'

'Bewley!' I said. 'Irish.'

'Why are you here?' he asked.

'I really don't know. Possibly something I wrote in the papers didn't please the Allies. And you?'

'My mother was Austrian. You've probably heard of the bankers Erlanger. I kept her name and nationality so as not to lose the family property. Then I was called up for military service.'

Our conversation was cut short by the command to get into the motor-lorries standing at the side of the courtyard. The police searched us for revolvers, while the interpreter walked up and down in front of the lorries and directed the proceedings.

'Do you think he is coming with us?' whispered Ebers.

'Of course not. He has his job here as interpreter.'

The lorries set themselves in motion and passed in single file through the camp gate. They were a dozen in all. As we drove by, we saw the Viennese lieutenant waving from an upper window. He appeared to be shouting after us, but the noise of the motors drowned his words. I turned to Ebers.

'I wouldn't mind betting', I said, 'that he is telling us, "*Es wird nie so heiss gegessen wie gekocht!*"'

Then the lorries turned into the road to Bozen, and he passed from our sight.

Towards midnight we reached our destination, the Transit Camp of Bassano. The lorries drew up on the side of the road; a couple of American soldiers stood by each to prevent any attempt to escape under cover of darkness. Erlanger, who was very proud of his English, engaged the nearest one in conversation.

'Whence come you?' he asked.

'From Texas.'

'Are there nice girls in Texas?'

'I'll say there are – the finest girls in the States!'

'Also Italian girls are fine girls,' said Erlanger, but the Texan seemed unconvinced. 'Not so bad,' he said, 'but our girls are better class, I reckon.'

'Why come you over to Europe?' asked Erlanger.

'Well, you see, it's this way. We in the States don't give a damn for what happens over here, but old Hitler was gettin' a bit too fresh. Well, of course we couldn't stand for that. We had to come over to clear things up.'

'I understand. And when you have cleared things up, I suppose that you will return to America?'

'When we're satisfied that everything's goin' on all right over here,' said the soldier, 'we'll go back home, you bet! Of course, we can't allow no goddam Hitlers. We got to see that none o' them guys don't start no rackets in the future. See what I mean?'

'I see,' said Erlanger.

A German on my other side whispered to me, '*Mein Gott!* That a German officer should talk in such a way!'

Inside the camp we were herded into a large building which appeared at one time to have served as a theatre. Erlanger was no longer with us: his proficiency in the English language had earned him an immediate engagement as interpreter. The rest of us were ordered to stand round the wall and open our bags. Our pockets were searched; I trembled when my wrist-watch was taken out of the pocket where I had concealed it during the journey, but the soldier glanced at it and replaced it in my suitcase.

'Any money?' he asked.

I handed him a roll from my inner pocket; he gave it to the officer. I made an involuntary movement.

'That's all right,' said the officer. 'We'll give you a receipt for it as soon as there's time to count it.'

1945 – UNDER ARREST

He proceeded on his way along the row of prisoners; when the examination had been completed, he called me to a desk in the middle of the hall.

'I'll count your money now,' he said, and took up the roll of thousand lira notes. 'One, two, three . . .' he counted. 'Fourteen, fifteen, sixteen . . .' A sudden thought struck him. 'Oh, those are thousand lira notes, are they? You got too f—— much money!'

I said nothing, he went on counting. At the end he said, 'One hundred and twenty-four thousand two hundred and sixty-nine lire, fifty-one English pounds. Is that right?'

'I presume so.'

'I'll let you have fifty dollars, that's five thousand, and the chicken-feed. You'll get a receipt for the rest.'

'When do I get it back?'

'When you leave here.'

He filled in a receipt in block letters, signed it Donald Van Horn, Lieutenant, and gave it to me.

But it was over a year till I saw my money again, and by that time the lira had lost nine-tenths of its value.

The camp of Ghedi in the neighbourhood of Brescia consisted of a number of flat empty fields dotted by a few tents occupied by the American forces and a number of open pits which, as we soon discovered, served as latrines for the prisoners. We dismounted in the middle of a field, and the lorries departed in the direction from which they had come.

An American officer instructed the interpreter, 'Tell the Germans to come this side of the track, the rest the other side.' The interpreter repeated the order in German. Then he added, 'Those whose names I call out are to step forward and wait on the track.'

He took out a paper and called out, 'Bewley!'

I stepped forward and waited on the track.

'Ebers!'

Ebers and seven others joined me. The interpreter said, 'Go over to that black tent and wait till I come.'

Obediently we made our way across the field towards the tent. When we arrived, we were joined by six young men in shorts and military shirts: all had scarlet scarves around their necks and scarlet bands on their arms: two wore broad-brimmed hats adorned with red ribbons and feathers. They looked like a chorus of bandits in *Fra Diavolo;* one expected them at any moment to break into song.

'What in the name of God are they?' I asked my neighbour. 'Partisans?'

'False partisans,' said he.

'What are false partisans?'

'German deserters. Communists dressed as Italian patriots.'

The interpreter joined us and drove us into the tent. 'You are to stay inside,' he said. 'There will be a guard before the entrance. If you wish to go to the latrines, he will get someone to accompany you.'

There was scarcely room for fourteen of us to spread our blankets and lie down with our feet pointing towards the centre, while the fifteenth made himself comfortable as best he could around the tentpole. I found myself between Ebers and one of the false partisans. In front of the tent-opening sat a little Chinaman on a chair with a rifle. Judging by his perfect American he must have been born in New York or San Francisco. When one of us appeared at the tent-opening, he smiled benevolently and nodded. It gave him particular amusement when he accompanied one of us to the latrine. From time to time he shouted remarks in Chinese to his countrymen or in English to the white Americans. It was obvious that he was inordinately proud of calling them Tom or Sid or Elmer.

'*Wo kommst du her?*' I asked my partisan neighbour.

'*Non capisco,*' he answered. 'I don't understand.'

I repeated my question in Italian. 'Where do you come from?'

'I am Polish,' he said. 'Patriot Anton Grabowski.'

'You were with the partisans?'

'After the Armistice,' said the young man beyond him in German, 'we waited to see how things would go. When we saw that the partisans everywhere were forming Committees of National Liberation, we decided to come down from the mountains and look for jobs. So we came to Brescia, left our bags at the station and presented ourselves to the Allied authorities. I don't know why they have arrested us; they wouldn't even let us bring our baggage from the station. I thought they would have recognized our services to the Allied cause. If you speak English, you might ask them about it tomorrow.'

I have no sympathy with Communists, and least of all with German Communists. I therefore disregarded him and turned to Patriot Anton Grabowski. But, before I had time to speak, the other interrupted me.

'Do you speak English?' he persisted.

'I do.'

'They will probably interrogate you tomorrow. You might tell them about me. They are doing me a great injustice.'

'So you belonged to the Garibaldini?' I asked Grabowski in Italian. 'They are Communists, aren't they?'

'Yes,' said he, 'but Italian Communists are good. They are fighting for Italy. Many of them are good Catholics. They want a war against Tito.'

'And you yourself – what do you want?'

'I want to go back to Poland to fight against the Russians.'

★ ★ ★

The camp of Modena, like that of Ghedi, consisted of several enormous fields; unlike Ghedi, it was crowded with humanity. There were few tents, and we camped out under the stars with the blankets provided by the Americans. The Communist partisans had been allotted to another section of the camp: Patriot Anton Grabowski was recruited for General Ander's anti-Communist Polish Army. I joined a group of Germans who were exchanging recent experiences.

'I don't understand', said a fifty-year-old civilian, 'why they want to revenge themselves on us like this. Never was a people treated after a war as they are treating us now. What had I to do with war crimes? I was a customs official on the Italian frontier. Is that a crime? We worked for the Ministry of Finance. Then an order came placing us under the SD. We knew nothing about it, it was purely an administrative change and we went on doing the same work as before. And now we are treated as criminals, as if we had no rights of any kind.'

'I was in the SS,' said another. 'Last October I was transferred into it without even being asked. What could I do? It was SS or KZ. I'd like to know who would have chosen the concentration camp. Besides, I wanted to do my duty to my country.'

'The whole thing was a mistake,' said a third. 'Adolf should never have declared war on Russia. We couldn't fight against the whole world.'

'Not only that, but we made enemies everywhere – Jews, Catholics, Protestants.'

'And when he declared war on Russia, he should have done it in a different way. The Poles and the Ukrainians and the majority of the Russians themselves were only too glad to be freed from Bolshevism. I served a year on the Russian front. When we occupied a village, the people brought us flowers and food. Nothing was too good for us. But of course it didn't last. It only took them a couple of months to find out that the SS was no better than the Bolsheviks – and then it was finished as far as we were concerned. A pity!'

'That was Adolf himself,' I remarked. 'When anything wrong was done, they always put the blame on the others and he knew nothing about it. Of course that's absurd: he knew all about it, it was his policy. It came from his ridiculous contempt for the Slavs – Russians, Poles, Ukrainians alike. That is what has ruined Germany!'

My neighbour nodded assent. 'You're right,' he said. 'But why do you say only his contempt for the Slavs? It was much more than that.'

'His *Vernichtungswille,* if you like. His desire to annihilate them.'

'That's more like it. He wanted to wipe them out. I saw it the whole time on the Eastern front. And now we have to suffer for it.'

'I sometimes think', said the SS man, 'that it was a pity the plot of the 20th of July didn't succeed. Of course I didn't think so then, but now we know more about it.'

'What do you think', one of them asked me, 'of the reports of atrocities in the foreign press? Do you believe them?'

In Ghedi I had seen for the first time an American paper with lurid accounts of Buchenwald and Dachau. I had known of course that there were concentration camps, as there were in every belligerent country, but I knew as little of atrocities as ninety per cent of the German people and had put down to enemy propaganda the vague rumours which had reached my ears.

'I don't know,' I said. 'I suppose there are always atrocities in wartime in every country. I certainly wouldn't assume that everything is true that appears in the press. We all know that both sides have their propaganda. We must only wait till we know more before we can form an opinion. I'm afraid it looks as if some of the reports were true.'

'If they were true,' said one of the group, 'our Government had a terrible responsibility. They have ruined Germany.'

'If they had only been successful on the 20th of July!' sighed the SS man. 'We would not be sitting here now.'

'*Ja, ja,*' agreed the customs official, 'you are right. But it turned out differently, and now Adolf is out of it all – *und wir sitzen noch hier in der Scheisse!*'

There was a silence: it was clear that the last speaker had expressed the sentiments of all, and that no-one could find anything to add to his summing-up of the situation.

An Italian with a haggard face and five days' beard sat down beside me. 'I have just come from the prison in Pallanza,' he said.

'Under the Americans?' I asked.

'Under the partisans. I'm thankful to be under the Americans now.'

'Was it so bad?'

'You can't imagine it. We were over three hundred – mostly elderly men. I am a retired colonel: for the last five years I have been living quietly with my wife. They kept me there for a month.'

'Why did they arrest you?'

'Because I belonged to the Fascist Party. They give us watery soup and a small piece of bread once a day – just enough to keep us alive. Every day we were knocked about and beaten – even the old men over seventy.' He pointed to the bruises on his own face.

'And now you have all come here?'

'All who are still alive. Every night they used to call out some of us. We knew what that meant; we never saw them again. Sometimes we heard shots, sometimes not. Once we saw some of the bodies. It is the same everywhere – if you are a Fascist, you have no right to live.'

'I heard that eight thousand were murdered in Milan, but I didn't know if it was true.'

'Quite true,' he said, 'and in other cities it was no better. I didn't think our people could be capable of such cruelty. I am ashamed of being Italian.'

I lent him my safety-razor, brush and soap: he had been allowed to bring nothing with him from Pallanza. 'They took our pocket-books, our money, everything,' he said.

'And you have nothing at all now, not a lira?'

'Nothing.'

'Colonel,' I said, 'let me lend you a thousand lire. If you are released tomorrow, you will need money for a railway-ticket.'

'No,' he said, 'I'm very grateful, but I can't take it. I don't know when I would be able to pay it back, and you probably haven't much yourself.'

'I have plenty,' I said, 'and I would be unhappy if I thought you had nothing. Besides, it would be a poor thing if we didn't try to help each other when we are all in trouble.'

He shook hands with me and went off to shave. Later that evening we resumed our conversation. A former Major had brought a sensational report from the camp gate. 'I have just heard that the Government has resigned,' he told us, 'and Prince Umberto is forming a new Government with the Christian Democrats. The Communist Party has been declared illegal; Grazia is to be a member of the new Government, and all former Fascists will have the right to inscribe themselves on the lists of the Christian Democratic Party.'

I had no idea of what had happened in the world during the last week, but the rumour seemed too absurd to have the least foundation. The Colonel shook his head.

'It's too good to be true,' he said. 'Our time hasn't come yet. The people are still swept away by propaganda; they have had no time to think.'

'Do you believe the time will ever come?' I asked doubtfully.

'I believe it, because I believe in Italy. It may take ten years, it may take only five or it may take twenty, but sooner or later the Italians will know that the man they murdered, whose body they insulted and mutilated was the greatest Italian of all time.'

He pointed to the Italians sleeping on the grass not far from us. 'Do you see these men around us?' he asked. 'Poor men, all of them – peasants and workers. They were Fascists in the first days of Fascism, because they believed in it and because they believed in Mussolini. Many of them suffered for their faith, but they remained faithful. Every one of them believes in Fascism today, as he believed in it twenty-five years ago, and, whatever they may suffer, they will remain true to the end.'

There was a silence, then he asked, 'Do you believe in God, Major?'

'Yes,' said the Major. 'And you?'

'They called me out of the cell one night in Pallanza,' said the Colonel. 'I was lined up with two others to be shot. I prayed to God to save me or at least to give me the grace to die with courage. And then for some reason they sent us back to the cell. And, just as He saved me, so I believe that God will save Italy.'

Ebers and I were called to the camp gate and driven to the Town Hall for interrogation.

'Perhaps they will tell us this time what we are accused of,' said Ebers.

'I hope so,' said I.

But our hopes remained unfulfilled. I was shown into a room where a non-commissioned officer sat at a writing-table, a sheet of paper covered with writing in front of him.

'Sit down,' he told me. 'Why were you living in Meran under the protection of the Red Cross?'

'I had no connection with the Red Cross, and I had no need of protection.'

'H'm,' said he. 'In what German papers did you write?'

'In the *Deutsche Allgemeine Zeitung,* in the *Berliner Lokal-Anzeiger*, in a monthly review called *Die Aktion* and in some other papers.'

'How did you come to write in the German papers? Did you approach them or did they approach you?'

'They approached me in the first place.'

'Who?'

'Mr Silex, editor of the *Deutsche Allgemeine Zeitung*.'

'Why do you think he approached you?'

'Probably because he knew me.'

'Where did you meet him first?'

'At a cocktail party in the Embassy of the United States of America.'

'Did the Germans tell you what to write?'

'Certainly not. I wrote what I thought fit.'

'Could your writings have been used as German propaganda?'

'Of course. Almost everything can be used as propaganda.'

'Do you think it would have been good propaganda?'

'Without question. I write well.'

'Very good,' he said. 'That will do. I am really only concerned with military questions. You will be examined in a couple of days by the officer who deals with civilians.'

'Can I communicate with my Legation?' I asked. 'I have been arrested for nearly a fortnight and have not yet been allowed to tell them where I am.'

He looked embarrassed. 'You had better ask at your next examination,' he said.

* * *

I was not further questioned in Modena; instead, I was sent by myself on a lorry laden with packing-cases to Verona. The lorry drew into a courtyard; I climbed down and was told to open my suitcase. A sergeant removed my scissors and razor-blades, remarking with a grin, 'Danger of suicide!' He then led me to a room on the third floor with an empty window-frame and told me that it would be my quarters of the next few days.

The house had been occupied by the SS before being taken over by the CIC. It was divided into apartments of three or four rooms. The other prisoners in my apartment belonged to the German Army. I had been placed with the non-commissioned officers and soldiers, the officers slept in the adjoining room. There were no bedsteads, but the officers had their fur-lined sleeping-bags.

The window looked out on the Adige. Some twenty yards to the left there had been a bridge; now, only a pylon rose out of the water surmounted by a recumbent female figure. Her head had disappeared, and an iron spike rose from the middle of her decapitated neck, creating the effect of an early Chirico. I went to the window and looked out on the flowing water and the couples strolling along the Lungo Adige.

'Why have they brought you here?' The inevitable question came from a man in corporal's uniform. I told him that I did not know, but that I suspected that it had to do with my writings in the press.

'So you did propaganda for the Nazis, did you?' asked the corporal.

'I wrote articles,' said I. 'You can call them propaganda if you like.'

'If you succeeded in inserting yourself in the Nazi propaganda machine,' said he, 'you deserve all you get. Anyone who did propaganda for National Socialism or Fascism deserves to be punished.'

I looked at his uniform with surprise. 'Everyone who had to do with the Party', he continued, 'must be punished. The Allies have been far too lenient.'

I was on the point of giving him an appropriate answer, when I saw one of the soldiers winking at me and held my tongue. After the other had gone away, the soldier said, 'That is no corporal!'

'What is he then?'

'An officer in disguise.'

'Why has he disguised himself?'

'I don't know. He must have his good reasons. It's better not to talk to him. With a *Scheisskerl* like that you can't be too careful!'

Existence in Verona was as tolerable as could be expected under the circumstances. The food was excellent – good coffee and milk, fresh bread and butter, fresh meat. One of the guards brought us fruit every day when he came back from his afternoon outing. The greatest inconvenience was the lack of sleeping accommodation: I felt stiff in every joint after lying on the floor with only a blanket under me. I envied the officers their sleeping-bags: I had not imagined that wooden flooring would be so much harder than the field at Modena.

As I went downstairs to my third interrogation, I felt inwardly certain what the first question would be. I was not mistaken: the sergeant sitting opposite me with the usual paper in his hand shot the question at me. 'Why were you living in Meran under the protection of the Red Cross?'

'I have already explained in Meran and again in Modena that I had nothing to do with the Red Cross. I knew no-one belonging to the Red Cross, and in any case I felt no need of protection.'

'So?' said he. 'Well, it's possible there may have been a misunderstanding?' He glanced at the paper in his hand and continued, 'In what German papers have you written articles?'

I told him.

'You have also written in the *Bozener Tageblatt*,' he stated.

'No, never.'

'Do you tell me you have never contributed to the *Bozener Tageblatt*?'

'Certainly not. It was a little local rag full of news of stray cows and hotel-keepers' silver weddings. It would have never entered my head to write for it.'

'Our informants state definitely that you wrote for it.'

'Your informants have misinformed you again,' said I.

'For what papers in the north of Italy have you written?'

'I have published an article in the *Adria-Zeitung* of Trieste.'

'What was it about?'

'Ernest Hemingway.'

'My God!' He seemed genuinely startled. 'What did you say about Hemingway?'

'The article was entitled 'As they see themselves'. There was an extract from Aldous Huxley about the English and one from Hemingway about the Americans – especially about their conduct in the last War.'

'We'll get hold of it,' he said and consulted the piece of paper again, but before he could put the next question a piece of stucco detached itself from the ceiling and fell to the floor behind my back with a loud crash.

'Well, what about your book?' he asked. 'What sort of a book was it?'

'Short stories,' I said. 'Mostly about life in England.'

'Was it a success?'

'Twenty-four thousand copies were sold in two months – we could get no paper for more.'

'Do you write in German?' he asked. 'Or do you write in English and get it translated?'

'I write in German.'

'Have you published in the Italian papers?'

'Very little.'

'Can you write Italian?'

'I'm afraid you'll consider my answer highly compromising: I can.'

He smiled. 'Oh, no,' he said, 'we're not so ignorant as to think it compromising if anyone speaks or writes in different languages.' Was it my fancy, or had he laid emphasis on the word 'we', as a warning that others might not take the same enlightened view?

As he appeared to have no more questions, I said, 'I wish formally to apply for facilities to communicate with the Irish Legation in Rome. It is my right to inform it that I have been arrested, but so far I have not been permitted to write.'

He looked at me coldly. 'We regard Ireland as an unfriendly country,' he said.

Once more the summons came to prepare for a journey. I came downstairs with a general and a major of the SS. We climbed into the jeep.

I had paid no particular attention to the guards accompanying us, but something unfamiliar in the timbre of their voices made me look at them with more interest. Their uniforms were of another shade of khaki than the American; they were neither so well-cut nor so clean; the men were wearing on their heads not American forage-caps but shapeless tam-o'-shanters. I had seen nothing like them since the days of the Auxiliary Police in Ireland, who had been responsible for the shootings and burnings in their campaign against the Irish people. We had been handed over to the British authorities.

It was not altogether a surprise: I knew that the British police had occupied a villa in Meran, presumably for the purpose of arresting those suspected of unfriendly sentiments towards the British Empire. Much that I had not previously understood became clear to me – the continual transfer from one camp to another, the casual nature of the interrogatories, my treatment as 'special prisoner' in the tent at Ghedi. The Americans, I inferred, had no interest in me personally; they had merely arrested me at the request of the English and had no other concern than that of holding me until they could deliver me into English hands.

Having reached this conclusion, I composed myself to listen to the conversation of the two English soldiers. The discussion seemed to turn on the problem whether vermouth was wine or something else undefined; I had not imagined that an apparently academic question could be debated with such warmth of conviction. I transcribe their dialogue word for word as I heard it.

'I'm tellin' you,' said one of the soldiers, 'f—— vermouth is f——wine.'

'Naow!' said his companion with contempt. 'F—— vermouth ain't f—— wine.'

'Wot is it then?' asked the first soldier.

'Wot is it?' repeated the second. 'It's f—— vermouth!'

The first soldier was far from satisfied with his companion's verdict. 'Garn!' he said. 'You don't know f—— all abaht it! We'll arsk old George!' He leaned over to the driver and asked, 'Wot you say, George? We was talkin' abaht f—— vermouth. Is it f—— wine or ain't it?'

George, who appeared to be a man of few words, looked at him vaguely and said, 'It ain't!'

'Wot is it then?' asked the other.

'It's f—— vermouth,' said George.

My interest in their conversation died down. We climbed the mountain-pass of Porretto and descended through a zone of chestnut forest. The green shade was a blessing to our eyes wearied by the blazing sunshine. In the silence left by the closing-down of the engine I could hear the harsh cry of a jay.

1945 – UNDER ARREST

Suddenly a dragon-fly whirred through the air over our heads and came to rest on the floor of the jeep. I had never seen one to compare with it for size and beauty: from one emerald-green wing-tip to the other it must have measured six inches. As it rested to gather strength for a new flight, I could see the vibration of the slender body, of the delicate transparent wings. It seemed to have strayed by misadventure from some Eden into our everyday world.

I was not the only one to have noticed the dragon-fly. One of the soldiers regarded it with interest. A knowing grin overspread his face. He drew his sidearm, and, before we had realized his intention, he sliced it neatly in three pieces and with his boot crushed the remains into the floor of the jeep. Of the beauty and grace, of the quivering life of a moment before, nothing was left but a dirty green smear. He replaced his sidearm with an air of satisfaction.

'That's settled the bugger!' he exclaimed.

★ ★ ★

We arrived in Florence in the afternoon. The lorry passed the Porta Romana, followed the tramline up the hill, drove up an avenue and halted before the door of a villa. In front was a colonnade strewn with pieces of paper and the butt-ends of cigarettes. Half a dozen young men in khaki shorts strolled up and down; from somewhere in the back regions a radio filled the air with jazz.

A soldier led me to a room on the second floor and locked me in, always without saying a word. The window and balcony were filled by a barbed wire entanglement, and the room itself was empty save for a small table and a couch. It was my first experience of solitary confinement. Half an hour later the same soldier opened the door and beckoned me to follow him. He led me to a room in which an individual in khaki trousers and shirt was seated at a table: he wore no badge from which I could discover his rank.

'Sit down!' he said.

I did so. There followed a silence during which I had time to study the Englishman who, I assumed, was about to submit me to the first serious cross-examination on the hitherto undefined crime which I had committed. He had a flat expressionless face and wore pince-nez. His unhealthy white complexion and unwieldy figure made it clear that he had not been for long exposed to the Italian sun and was more accustomed to the stuffy atmosphere and sedentary life of an office. I concluded that he had been sent out from London after the Armistice, and therefore that he belonged, not to the regular Army, but to the police with temporary Army rank. As regards his social origin, his pronunciation of the word 'down' – neither completely Cockney nor completely upper-class – showed that he came neither from the public school nor from the proletariat. Probably the son of a small shopkeeper or clerk, I thought, who passed his examinations with distinction in a Board School, joined the police and hoped to better his position through the War.

The man sitting opposite me raised his head, looked me up and down, and said in a voice which he strove to make impressive, 'Why were you living in Meran under the protection of the Red Cross?'

I could not resist a smile. 'I have already explained in Meran, in Modena and in Verona,' I said, 'that I have never had anything to do with the Red Cross as I did not consider that I needed the protection of anyone.'

'We shall see,' he said. 'Did you sympathize with Germany?'

'Certainly,' I said. 'I sympathized with Germany.'

'And do you still sympathize with Germany?'

'Of course. I would have thought that everyone must sympathize with the Germans in this immense human tragedy.'

He noted my answer carefully on a blank sheet of paper.

'Why did you retire from the service of the Irish Government on the 1st of August 1939?'

'I had differences of opinion with the Irish Government.'

'Does it not seem strange that you retired on the 1st of August 1939 immediately before Germany made war on us?'

'The date was not fixed by me, it was fixed six months earlier by the Irish Government.'

'When did you go to Rome?'

'In January 1940. I stayed there till 1943.'

'Then your case is that you wished to settle in Rome like so many other retired diplomats in a perfectly innocent manner?'

'It is not my case, it is the fact.'

'Do not your actions lend themselves to another interpretation?'

'I can only tell you the facts, I cannot account for other person's interpretations.'

'And then you began writing against England?'

'I wrote as a neutral in the German press. Some of my articles were against England.'

'Do you still insist that you know nothing about the activities of the SD?'

'I know nothing whatever about them.'

The examination dragged on interminably and, so far as I could see, without any particular system. Finally he cleared his throat and began to speak with the air of one about to make an important statement.

'I should advise you in your own interest', he said slowly and emphatically, 'to tell us everything. If you imagine that you can hide anything from us, you are making a terrible mistake. There is no hole or corner that we shall not investigate; there is no possibility of keeping everything a secret from us. It is in your interest to tell us everything, you will be more leniently treated if you make a full confession.' He paused expectantly.

'I'm glad to hear that your investigation is so thorough,' I answered, 'because you will be able to convince yourselves that I have done nothing whatever to justify arrest.'

'You are aware,' he asked, 'that we only bring to this house people in whose cases we take a particular interest?'

'Really?' I said. 'Am I to take that as a compliment?'

'As you wish,' he replied.

As I sat in my solitude, I thought over the interview with a feeling of relief. I had nothing to conceal, but I had feared that some fantastic story of espionage or the like might have been attached to my name, which I might have difficulty in disproving. Now I saw that they knew nothing whatever to my detriment. My fifteen years' experience as a lawyer told me that no advocate with the least degree of competence makes an appeal to the accused to make a clean breast of his crime save as a counsel of despair in default of proof.

A guard threw open the door and beckoned me to approach. I did so; he handed me a tin plate covered by a repulsive-looking grey substance, on which some pieces of broken biscuit were floating. I deposited the plate by the door and ate the contents of one of the tins of food which I had received in Modena.

The guard opened the door again with a can of tea in his hand and beckoned once more. I remained seated. He had obviously been instructed not to speak to me; he deposited the can by the door. Half an hour later he returned, took the full plate and can and departed still without a word. The same process was repeated three times on the next day; he placed the utensils in the corner by the door, whence he removed them some half hour later. On the third morning I was told to prepare for a journey.

My travelling companions were, as before, an SS general and major. Most of the day was passed in silence. I felt no inclination to start a conversation. The SS general thought otherwise. He had brought with him an abundant supply of cigarettes. Either from a desire for human intercourse or in an attempt to ingratiate himself with his captors, whenever he lit a fresh cigarette, he offered his cigarette-case to the guards, who as regularly refused it.

'But they are good cigarettes,' the general said. 'Will you not smoke one?'

'Tell 'im 'e needn't try to come over me with 'is f—— stuff!' said one of the others. 'I know too f—— much abaht it!'

The general seemed at last to understand that his conversation was not desired; he subsided meekly into silence.

It was after seven o'clock when we arrived in Rome. Without stopping in the city the jeep turned westwards and drew up before a building in Cinecittà, the film town which the Italian Government had constructed between Rome and Ostia. An English sergeant showed us into an empty hall and told us to submit our luggage for inspection. But before I had time to open my suitcase, a soldier shouted my name 'You are to go at once to the Captain!'

I followed him into an adjoining room, where an officer sat at the usual writing-table. He had precise features and an old-maidish air, and gave me the impression of being a schoolmaster in civil life.

'Oh, Mr Bewley!' he said, as I came in, with somewhat exaggerated courtesy and an Oxford accent. 'We don't often have people of your quality here. There must have been some misunderstanding. We'll make that all right as quickly as possible.'

I looked at him coldly: it was barely three days since the police official in Florence had told me that the authorities took a particular interest in my case, and I saw no reason to doubt his word.

'I am sure you must have many friends in the Vatican,' continued the Captain with thin-lipped geniality. 'Now, whom do you know there?'

I mentioned a name.

'Splendid!' cried the Captain with enthusiasm. 'You could not have mentioned a better man. We know the Monsignore, he has visited this camp more than once. Well, that will be all right. I shall ring up the Vatican City at once and make all arrangements for having you transferred there.' He looked at his wrist-watch. 'I'm afraid though it's rather too late to get onto anyone today; the offices will be closed. I'll ring them up first thing in the morning.'

I remained silent.

'I'm afraid I must ask you to stay with us for the night,' said the Captain. 'I'm sure you'll understand. Unfortunately it will have to be in a cell, but you shall have the best cell here. You will be alone except for one other.' He glanced at a slip of paper. 'There will be a Dutchman with you – yes, a Dutchman, an excellent person, I assure you. I hope you will be as comfortable as possible. In the morning I shall ring up the Vatican City at once. Will you bring your belongings, please, so that I may send someone to show you the way.'

The cell was fairly commodious and seemed clean. I took it to be a sleeping room for the workmen employed in Cinecittà. On one of the two pallet beds a man in shirtsleeves was lying. He stood up as I came in: it was the German-speaking soldier who had accompanied us from Florence to Rome.

'I suppose you are astonished to see me here,' he said in German, as the door clanged behind the departing guard.

'I have ceased to be astonished at anything,' said I.

The cell appeared to have been occupied by prisoners from half the countries of Europe. A life-sized caricature of the comédienne Dina Galli dated surely from a period before the English occupation. On the opposite wall was a prayer in Polish and under it a long Fascist manifesto. Over the Dutchman's bed was a musical phrase:

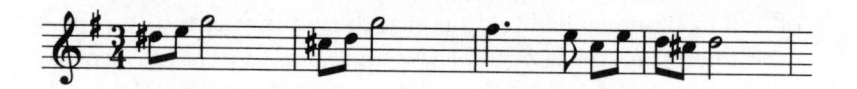

'That must have been an Austrian,' I remarked.
'Why?' asked the Dutchman perplexed.
'Don't you know the *Fledermaus*?'
'No.'
'*Glücklich ist, wer vergisst, was nicht mehr zu ändern ist*,' I recited. 'Happy the man who forgets what can't be changed. Only an Austrian could have written it, and only an Austrian could have written it here. It contains the whole philosophy of Vienna.'

'I will write something in Dutch,' he said, and traced in bold characters on the wall, '*Hier woonde Hollands glorie*'. 'It's the title of a Dutch book,' he explained.

On the second morning at six o'clock a soldier opened the cell door, but the summons was for me. I was put into a jeep with an armed guard. It is superfluous to say that I had no second meeting with the amiable captain nor received any information about his telephone call to the Vatican City.

I expected to be transferred southwards to Naples or Brindisi, whence I could have been shipped to England. But, to my surprise, after we had passed down the Corso to the Piazza del Popolo, the jeep pursued its way along the Via Flaminia and over the Ponte Milvio towards the north. The road was familiar to me: I had driven over it times without number in my own car. And when, two hours later, we turned into an enormous square surrounded by barbed wire, I knew that I had arrived at my journey's end, the Concentration Camp of Terni.

ELEVEN

Meeting John Amery

One camp is like another – blocks of buildings, barbed wire enclosures for the various classes of internees, soldiers and military police with an air of mingled boredom and superiority, a barbed wire surrounding fence three yards high punctuated by towers in which sit sentries with machine-guns. So large a proportion of the inhabitants of the world have made the acquaintance of a camp in the last generation that any further description would be superfluous.

I was placed in Cell No. 22. Its floor was of cement, its walls whitewashed. A large window-frame without glass was covered by a close iron grating: through it I could see barbed wire and beyond the wire a heap of earth left by the workmen after the work of excavating the foundations. Above the mound I could see a small patch of sky.

Soldiers passed occasionally up and down the corridor; then footsteps sounded outside which did not seem to me those of a soldier. I went to the peep-hole and looked out. An elderly man in prisoner's clothing was sauntering by; when he came to my door, he halted. 'Want a cigarette?' he asked in English.

I thanked him and took the cigarette.

'I hear you're Irish,' he remarked.

'I am.'

'What are you in for?'

'No-one has told me yet.'

He looked at me appraisingly. 'I can only give you one piece of advice,' he said. 'If you have something to hide, don't!' And he strolled on.

While I was pondering on his remarkable behaviour, an officer passed down the corridor accompanied by two soldiers. I asked him when I could expect to receive a bedstead and a blanket. He seemed thunderstruck at my effrontery in venturing to speak to him unaddressed. For a moment he looked at me in silence; then he said, 'Oh, so you're not satisfied with the accommodation we're giving you? I can only tell you that I served six years in the desert and that it was a bloody sight worse there.' He sniggered and went off down the corridor.

In the course of the afternoon the door was again opened; I was sitting on my suitcase and did not look up.

'It's time you learned that it is your duty to stand up when a British officer comes in,' said a familiar voice. It was the officer to whom I had already spoken; he wore a kilt and carried a little cane like Charlie Chaplin, which he had the habit of twisting nervously in his hand when he talked. I learned that his name was Captain Oakshott. I shambled to my feet.

'This cell is in a filthy condition,' said the Captain. 'Has no-one told you that it is your duty to keep your cell clean?'

'No,' said I.

'Well, I'll tell you your duties now. You sweep out your cell every day.'

He went over to the window and looked at the sill. 'As I expected, filthy!' he exclaimed. 'See that you clean that up before I come again.'

I said nothing; my silence appeared to displease him.

'Your age and rank will not in any way be taken into account,' he went on. 'We shall see that you perform your duties: if not, it will be the worse for you.'

I looked at him with interest: it was the first opportunity I had had of seeing a British officer carrying out his official duties. The thought occurred to me that in the past other British officers had spoken in the same way to Pearse and Connolly, to Gandhi and Bose and a thousand more, and that yet others were probably instructing ex-Ministers and Generals of the Axis Powers in the duty of keeping their cells clean. Not an abusive tone, be it understood: merely a voice and attitude which make it clear to the non-Briton that he belongs to an inferior race, to one of the 'lesser breeds without the law', as the English national poet has phrased it.

As if he had read my thoughts, Captain Oakshott continued, 'This camp is not a prison. It is not a concentration camp. It is an institution for civil internees under British management. That

MEETING JOHN AMERY

means that you will get justice.' And with this satisfying assurance he left my cell.

Next morning, a sergeant told me that I would have the privilege of going for exercise and taking my meals with the other 'special prisoners'. It occurred to me as strange that there should be 'special prisoners' in an institution which Captain Oakshott had expressly stated not to be a prison. But I joined the others without comment for our hour's exercise in the barbed wire enclosure.

The special prisoners were ten in all, of whom five were Englishmen charged with collaboration with the enemy. If they had collaborated, they were now doing their best to atone for their offence by their determined efforts to ingratiate themselves with the British soldiers and their exaggerated deference to Captain Oakshott. One was reported to have spoken on the Berlin wireless and afterwards to have given detailed information on the activities of his English and American colleagues to the British authorities. I judged it prudent to avoid all intercourse with them during our meals and exercise hour. The only exception was John Amery.

From Amery there was no danger of delation. In my frequent talks with him I gained the impression that he was entirely sincere, though his point of view seemed to me fantastic. Equally fantastic were the accounts of his career which he gave me in the barbed wire enclosure.

'I could not stand the atmosphere of the English public school,' he told me, 'so I ran away at the age of fifteen. I knew they would bring me back if I stayed in England, so I got over to France and hid myself. I had no money. I worked as a housepainter. I had a variety of jobs, and when they discovered me, they could do nothing about it.'

I wondered whether the house-painting had been suggested to him by Hitler's original trade, but I showed no signs of disbelief.

'The greatest misfortune for England', he argued, 'was Edward's abdication. I shall never forget that last evening when I and his other friends waited with him for something to happen. We sat there all through the night. He was firmly convinced that the people would never let him down. Every moment we expected to hear of a popular rising in his favour; then all he would have to do would be to put himself at its head, and Baldwin would be swept away by the force of public opinion. But of course nothing happened, and we let the last opportunity slip, sitting and waiting instead of going out and rousing the country. We should have known that the people never does anything of itself without a leader.'

With the details of his immediate past he was more sparing, although he never denied the part he had taken in helping the Germans. 'It won't be long', he repeated, 'before the English people realizes that everything I have done was in its best interests.'

'You can't expect them to be enthusiastic about your recruiting English prisoners for the SS,' I pointed out.

'Why not?' he asked. 'When they saw that the only result of the War was to strengthen Communism, it was in their interest to join the Germans in fighting Russia. They didn't understand it before the Armistice, but they're bound to see it now. My policy was the only one which could save England.'

'And if they put you on trial?'

'I only wish they would! When they hear my defence, it will do more to convince them than a hundred political meetings.'

His fellow-prisoners were far from sharing his optimism. One of them suggested to him that he ought to make an attempt to escape, but Amery refused even to consider it. 'They will never do anything to me,' he said, 'because they know that I am right. When the war comes, I shall be known as the man who did his best to save England!'

Immediately across the road from the camp rose a wooded hill with on its summit the village of Collescripoli. It was my greatest regret that from my cell I had no vision of the landscape. But, as I continued to gaze through the holes in the grating, I discovered that on the mound behind the barbed wire among the coarse grass and burdocks which had taken root, was growing one of those low branching plants, so common in the Italian fields, with a small blue flower at the end of each long grey stalk. In certain lights it was practically invisible, but during part of the afternoon, when the air no longer dazzled the eye, the diminutive blossoms shone like tiny blue stars against their dingy background.

I stood at the window every day with my eyes fixed on the plant. Its luminous blue recalled to me the waters of the Mediterranean on a summer morning, the myosotis that grows by certain Alpine streams, the feathers on a kingfisher's breast. Only when the sun had descended behind the block of the building and the shadow had wiped out the radiance, did I leave my post, asking myself how it was possible that a few bright spots of colour could give me such pleasure and wondering whether my fellow-prisoners had found some similar comfort outside their cell-window. But I soon remembered that every day during our exercise hour Amery gathered the stunted blossoms which struggled towards the air and light between the stones of our pen and arranged them in a broken cup beside the photographs of his wife and child . . .

Poor Amery! The *Union Jack,* the newspaper issued to the British troops, had published his photo with such comments as it hoped would be to the taste of its readers: it referred to him as a 'cur' and a 'rat', stated that he had been guilty of forgery and bigamy, and hinted that it would have been in a position to make other disclosures if it had not been restrained by the British spirit of fair play and the desire not to influence his trial. The soldiers giggled over the paper and made humorous remarks as he passed them; some of the English prisoners referred to him in his absence as the 'rat' and avoided him ostentatiously at mealtimes. Scarcely anyone besides myself was willing to be seen speaking to him.

He behaved with simplicity and even a certain dignity. Never for a moment did he admit even by implication that anything he had done was not in the best interests of his country; on the other hand, he complained that the Germans had not followed his advice in their propaganda for the British public.

'I was always trying to induce them to hold a parade of the British SS in Paris,' he told me. 'They could have marched up the Champs-Élysées and laid a wreath on the grave of the Unknown Soldier. It would have produced a tremendous effect in England: at bottom the English people are fair-minded, when they are not led astray by politicians like Churchill. And not even Churchill could have suggested that so many of his own soldiers were traitors. If I am ever brought to trial, I will tell them so to their face!'

But in his inmost heart I do not believe that he expected to stand his trial: he looked on a war between the Western democracies and Russia as inevitable in the near future. I did not share his opinion, and after the victory of the Labour Party it became clear that history was not going to be made so rapidly as he imagined. Two days after the election a police sergeant came into his cell and told him to prepare for a journey. He was permitted to speak to none of us before he left. I could only call my best wishes after him as the sergeant hustled him down the corridor. That afternoon we heard that he had been taken by car to Rome and thence by aeroplane to England.

In the meantime I had inquired about the elderly prisoner who had given me the Gold Flake cigarette and the enigmatic warning.

'Be careful what you say to him,' I was warned. 'He's not healthy.'

'Who is he?' I asked.

'He calls himself Salazar – Count Salazar.'

'But he seemed to be English.'

'Oh, yes, he's English all right, and he was in the English service. Sometimes he claims to be Irish – Sarsfield Salazar. He says he is a descendant of Patrick Sarsfield.'

'Sarsfield Salazar,' I repeated. 'It's not a convincing combination. Like Murphy Hohenzollern. What is he here for?'

'Nobody knows exactly. They say he was in the Secret Service in Italy during the War. Then after the occupation, when supplies to the factories were rationed, an Italian firm took him on as technical adviser. The factory got extra supplies for some months, but then the English got wise to it and arrested him.'

'But why is he in the cells and not in the general camp?'

'He was in another camp. Some Italians were caught attempting to escape, and people said he had informed on them. So they transferred him here for his protection. Even here he might be killed in the general block, so they keep him in a cell. They make things as easy for him as they can.'

I had already noticed and wondered at the indulgence shown to Salazar. In his cell I had seen a real bed with sheets and pillows; Oakshott used to bring him tobacco and the latest numbers of *Punch* and *Tatler* and chat with him in his cell; he was able at all times to have the door opened and stroll about the premises. But the name Salazar had awakened a dim recollection in my mind. One day, as he passed me in the corridor, I asked him, 'Did I not meet you in Ireland before the first War?'

He did not answer, but walked on as if he had not heard my question. I looked after him in surprise, but his silence was the best answer. About 1913 I had met in Dublin a Count Salazar: he had not then been Irish nor, to the best of my recollection, had he claimed the name of Sarsfield. It was the time when the Irish Volunteers were beginning to be active and the IRB (though then I did not know it) was contemplating the possibility of an armed rising in the event of a European war. I wondered what a foreign count had been doing in Dublin at so critical a period of our history.

Shortly afterwards I met him in the corridor. 'Good morning!' I said.

Salazar turned away his head and walked past me without acknowledging my greeting, nor did he take notice of my existence during the months I spent in the punishment block.

A week later I saw a young Italian who had been put on the job of sweeping the corridor. No soldier was in sight, and we could exchange a few words.

'I oughtn't to be seen speaking to you,' he remarked.

'Why, Mauro?' I asked.

'Because you are a *persona pericolosissima*, a most dangerous person, and it might damage my chance of being released.'

'Who says so?'

'Salazar,' said Mauro. 'And he is so friendly with the English that everybody says he has it from them. But', he added consolingly, 'nobody minds what he says. Only I thought I'd better tell you.'

★ ★ ★

I do not in my life remember any moment of such unmixed joy as that in which, suitcase in hand, I descended the four steps of the punishment block and crossed the twenty yards which separated the barbed wire entanglement from the precisely similar entanglement surrounding the general block. A police sergeant announced 'Number 671!' to the internee who kept the register, and departed. It was my first moment of freedom from supervision.

Marini, a London Italian who like myself had been transferred from the cells came up. 'I'll show you round,' he said. 'Come and have a drink.'

We passed through the great central hall: the current issue of the *Union Jack* was painted on the wall, and an Italian with some knowledge of English was translating it to his countrymen. Notices on the board announced that I had been transferred to Squad Six B and that two Italians had been sent to the punishment cells for two weeks for offences against discipline.

'Not much of interest,' said Marini. 'The bar is over there.'

'I have no money,' I said. 'I paid one of the painters 1500 lire to smuggle out a letter to our Legation. Not that I believe for a minute that they will make the slightest effort to do anything for me, but at least they can let my brother know where I am. I haven't been allowed to send any letters.'

'That's all right,' he said. 'I earn a little by giving English lessons – fifteen lire a week per pupil. And you can always sell some of the cigarettes from your ration and buy a little fruit and wine. It doesn't go far, but it's always something.'

We drank a glass of the local wine: it seemed to me freedom compared with life in the cell. Then he said, 'This door leads to the chapel. We have two interned priests here – a Capuchin and a secular. Fascists, of course. One of them says Mass every morning. You'll like the chapel. Everything in it was made by the prisoners.'

We entered and stood in front of the altar. Under the altar-cloth I could see the bricks left over from the construction of the buildings and the wood from abandoned packing-cases. The candlesticks were made of the remains of metal discovered somewhere in the camp precincts. For gold leaf the tabernacle was covered with tinfoil. On either side stood tins which had once contained food; now they were filled with wild flowers from the fields around the camp. The lanterns hanging from the ceiling appeared to be made of wrought iron. Marini followed my glance. 'All made from odd bits of iron they found lying around,' he said.

He drifted away, but I remained in the chapel. Three Italians were kneeling on the altar-steps. Above the tabernacle was stretched a canvas with nearly a life-sized Madonna and Child, the work of an internee. On either side of the altar the windows had been decorated with the mysteries and emblems of our religion; I found myself gazing at them as if I had never seen them in my life before.

To the right was the Lamb, and, rising behind it, the Standard of the Faith; above the Lamb, a Monstrance displayed its radiant burden, and beneath hung from the Vine a bunch of purple grapes ripe for the wine-press. In the windows farther to the right were the Ladder on which the Roman soldiers had mounted, the purple robe that Christ had worn, the Dice with which the soldiers had cast for their plunder. Left of the Madonna was a hand holding the sacred Host over a Chalice; over it stood an open Gospel and the Cruet with wine and water, and under it an Ear of Corn bursting with the grain which would one day be transformed into the Bread of Life. In the windows to the left were the vinegar-laden Sponge and the Spear, the Pincers, the Hammer and Nails. Round the corner, in the side-wall of the chapel, were two more windows: on the first I saw the Crown of Thorns with an ear of corn passing through its centre, and at its side a bloodstained hand holding a Scourge; on the second, the Column to which Christ was bound and the Cock that crowed when Peter denied his Lord.

The colours were gaudy and the drawing childlike; the man who had painted them was certainly no skilled artist; but, as I looked at them, I felt that never in any cathedral, not in St Peter's itself, had I so clearly understood their significance. I thought of the craftsmen who for nearly two thousand years had painted similar emblems, and I knew that the humble painter in Terni Internment Camp was one with those who had traced Host and Spear and Dice on the stones of the Roman catacombs and with those others who had depicted them on the walls of timber churches in distant continents, when the Church of Christ went forth to carry the Gospel to the farthest recesses of the earth. I thought of those countless others who in prison or in the line of battle, in savage lands and under persecution, had gazed on the same symbols, and I felt that we in our imprisonment were but an infinitesimal part of those who had called on God in their distress with the sure knowledge that their prayers would not be in vain.

Tears came into my eyes, which I did not try to check. I knew that, however long I might live, I would never more see the symbols of the faith without thinking of the humble chapel of the camp of Terni, which the prisoners in their need and poverty had erected from the poor material rejected by their captors as a shrine for the King of Heaven. No phrase that I could devise was capable of giving expression to the emotion which I felt: only later, when I opened my prayer-book, did I find the words I sought:

> *Te aeternum Patrem omnis terra veneratur:*
> *Te per orbem terrarum sancta confitetur Ecclesia.*
> *Sanctus, Sanctus, Sanctus Dominus Deus Sabaoth:*
> *Pleni sunt caeli et terra majestatis gloriae tuae.*

★ ★ ★

My first meeting with Freiherr von Buttlar took place in the lavatory of the 'calabush', as the punishment block was called. Before we had time to exchange more than a few commonplaces, a soldier looked in and beckoned him to return to his cell.

'Who is he?' I asked.

An Austrian told me, 'He says he is the head of the Buttlar Chemical Works.'

'Don't you believe him?'

'He looks very young. We'll know sooner or later whether he has told the truth.'

'How?'

'He says he was one of the first to enter into relations with the Americans; he is in negotiation with them about the secrets of his factories.'

'But if so, why is he here?'

'That's what doesn't convince me. He says the Amis brought him from Germany to Rome in a special aeroplane and that he was perfectly free in Rome to go about as he liked, until the English asked for the loan of him for a few days. He says it must be due to some misunderstanding and the Amis will reclaim him as soon as they know where he is.'

But the days and weeks passed, and no summons came for Buttlar. He had been in the normal course of events transferred to the general block: two months later, when I myself was transferred, he was still there. The Americans appeared to have completely forgotten his existence, and he seemed equally to have forgotten them, if one could judge by his silence in their regard.

When I met him again, he had given himself the trouble of finding out who I was, for he remarked gaily, 'I can claim to be a countryman of yours.'

'How is that?' I asked.

'My ancestors, the Barons von Buttlar, came originally from Ireland.'

I was aware of the fact, but I could not feel any strong desire to claim him as a fellow-countryman. There was something spurious about him; his manner seemed to me a compound of impudence and servility – qualities which were scarcely in keeping with a baron and industrialist.

His favourite topic of conversation was the vexations which he had suffered under the Nazi régime and the efforts which he had made to prevent his chemical formulae from falling into official hands. The fact that, as he informed his friends with pride, he had been a member of the leading industrial organization of the Reich had not saved him from menaces and persecution. We listened to him with slightly sceptical patience; only once after the conclusion of one of his elaborate narratives a worthy citizen of Meran said to him with the most innocent air in the world, 'Herr Baron, I see that you suffered terribly under Nazi tyranny. There is only one thing you have forgotten to tell us.'

'What is that?' asked Buttlar.

'You forgot to tell us how they put you up against the wall and shot you.'

Like many of his countrymen, Buttlar was an enthusiast for order and discipline and never tired of inveighing against the Italians for their habit of talking and laughing during the roll-call, as soon as the sergeant's back was turned. 'If I was the sergeant,' said Buttlar, 'I would stop all cigarettes for a month. That would teach them a lesson!'

'But in that case we would lose our cigarettes too!' objected a German.

'It would be worth it,' said Buttlar, 'for the sake of teaching those Italians what discipline means!'

Nevertheless, though he could have wished for greater strictness on the part of the British, he approved in general their conduct of the camp and looked anxiously for an opportunity of collaborating with them. In the end he was successful in finding what he sought. He approached me one evening with a smile in which I imagined I could trace equal proportions of satisfaction and embarrassment, and observed, 'I have been thinking lately that I ought to learn some English; I know practically none. I wonder if you would be so kind as to give me a lesson?'

'A lesson?' I echoed. 'You could learn nothing in one lesson.'

'All I need,' he explained, 'is to learn the English names for the most important articles of food.'

'Whatever for?'

'Well,' he said, 'I have had the offer of a position over there,' and he waved his arm vaguely in the direction of the officers' quarters, 'and I would need to understand some of the simplest names.'

'What sort of a position is it?' I asked.

'I will have to wait at table at the officers' mess, and of course it would be an advantage to know what they are asking for.'

'I'm sorry,' I said, 'but I have no time.'

It was a curious aspiration in a baron – that of serving the officers' mess as a waiter. So I was not surprised when strange rumours began to circulate about him – that he was not the Freiherr von Buttlar at all, but one of his employees, a valet or secretary, who had assumed the identity of the Baron in the hope of better treatment. The other Germans used to discuss the subject at length.

'What do you think?' one of them asked me. 'Is he genuine or not?'

'I have always suspected him,' I said, 'ever since he told that ridiculous story about the Amis having lent him to the English. Also, he doesn't speak a word of either French or English and he doesn't know how to play bridge – all of which are accomplishments which one would expect a baron to possess. But a couple of days ago, when I saw him pressing his trousers, I became absolutely certain that he is not a baron.'

'But why should a baron not press his trousers?'

'No reason in the world,' I said. 'but the genuine Baron von Buttlar would scarcely have been in the habit of pressing his own trousers, and if he had to start doing it here, he would show a certain want of practice. Whereas our friend, in spite of the primitive conditions here, knew exactly what to do. He got hold of a table of exactly the right size, he sprinkled the amount of water in the right places to take the bags out of the knees, he had a lump of metal as substitute for an electric iron, and his movements were so sure and automatic that it was quite evident that he had been ironing trousers all his life.'

Eventually the news later leaked out that the 'Baron' was neither a baron nor the head of a chemical factory, but only a minor employee with social ambitions. But by that time I had left the camp.

★ ★ ★

There was a crowd round the pillar in the refectory where the *Union Jack* was posted up for the benefit of the internees. I went up to see what news could be of such interest. For a moment I could not get near enough to see the paper, but someone said to me, 'John Amery is condemned to death!'

'Impossible!' I said. 'There was nothing about his trial in yesterday's paper, as there would have been if it had commenced the day before. The report today is the first that has appeared, so the trial cannot be over yet. It should last at least a week.'

'It lasted eight minutes,' said my informant. 'Look for yourself!'

I elbowed my way through the crowd; to my amazement I found that he was correct; Amery had pleaded guilty and had been condemned to death on the spot. I hurried upstairs to find Marini.

'Look at this, Stefano,' I said, 'you're the only person except myself who knew Amery. What do you make of his pleading guilty?'

'I don't know,' he said. 'I never thought they would condemn him to death. What do you think yourself?'

'I don't know either. I thought his family connections would save him.'

'I thought he was in the British service all the time,' said Marini. 'You never can tell.'

'I never thought that; he always seemed to me sincere. But his pleading guilty is the most extraordinary thing I have ever heard of. I can only imagine it in the case of a man who was overwhelmed with remorse, he might plead guilty for reasons of conscience. With Amery that was obviously not the case; you heard him talking, and you know he was sincerely convinced he had acted throughout in the best interests of England. I can't imagine him admitting now that he was wrong all the time and practically inviting them to hang him.'

'Especially as we saw a few weeks ago that he claimed to have been naturalized as a Spaniard, and the trial was adjourned so that his brother might look for the necessary document. I still can't help thinking he was a spy.'

I was far from convinced, but I could think of no explanation. I remembered my conversations with Amery – how he had talked of the speech he would make if they put him on trial, his enthusiasm for the cause he had supported, his certainty that the England of tomorrow would share his view. I could not believe that it was all a carefully thought-out scheme, that even in the prison cell he was playing a part. And if he was not playing a part, it could only be explained by a complete moral and mental breakdown. But the paper reported him as being perfectly calm and collected. It was inexplicable.

But on the next day I knew even less what to think, when Marini hailed me with the cry, 'Well, you see, I was right!'

'I'm sure you were,' I said. 'What about?'

'About Amery. He's not to be hanged after all. They have discovered he is tuberculous and has only three or four months to live, and the paper thought that England is too chivalrous to execute a dying man. The net result is that he is going to get off. I don't believe for a minute that he is tuberculous, he showed no signs of it here. Of course he was in with them all the time.'

I thought of James Connolly, wounded to death in the Rising of Easter Week 1916 and carried on a stretcher before the firing party. I still did not believe that Amery was a spy. 'It doesn't necessarily follow', I suggested, 'that he was in with them all the time. Possibly they offered him his life if he would agree not to defend himself. His defence might have caused them some embarrassment. Personally I don't believe he was a spy.'

'You're too simple,' said Marini.

'Possibly. But I suppose now we'll never know.'

However, it was not long before we learned something more about Amery. A short paragraph in the *Union Jack* stated that the Home Secretary had rejected the petition for reprieve, and at the same time that the doctors had ascertained that, in contrast to their previous diagnosis, he was not suffering from tuberculosis.

'A strange coincidence!' I remarked to Marini. 'What do you think of it?'

'I don't know. It seems more of a mystery than ever.'

'I'm not sure,' said I. 'I'm beginning to see a possible explanation.'

'I'd like to hear it.'

'It's quite simple. It's obvious from all that we hear that the English people are discontented. They showed that by kicking out Churchill and electing Labour. But of course it's clear that things will be no better under Labour than under the Tories. The authorities are afraid that a reaction against the War might set in if it was allowed to express itself. The last thing any English government wants is to have people asking whether they might not be better off if they had made peace in 1940 or 1941. So far no-one has had the opportunity of conducting a campaign on those lines: in the country of freedom of thought it's very easy to silence dangerous opinions. But if Amery had defended himself at his trial as he proposed, that would have been his main point. He would have pointed out that, if England had followed his advice, it would be in a far stronger position today than it actually is. It's an idea that might appeal to some of the discontented elements in the population, fed up as they are with rationing and strikes and the want of decent houses. And naturally anything he said from the dock would have had a hundred times more publicity than the speeches in a public meeting which can be boycotted by the press.'

'Possibly,' said Marini. 'And what then?'

'Well, isn't it possible that they gave him to understand – somebody quite unofficial, of course, who promised nothing, because he was not in a position to guarantee anything, but undertook to do his best – that, if he gave the authorities no trouble and pleaded guilty, they would do what they could to have him reprieved. Nothing binding, only a gentleman's agreement. It may be that neither the judge nor the prosecution knew anything about it: I would not like, unless I had clear evidence, to suggest that they would deliberately break their word. So, perhaps, Amery agreed and withdrew his defence, and they did their best to obtain a reprieve, but the Home Secretary for reasons of state and in deference to public opinion could not reconcile it with his duty to grant it. So, as a result of it all, poor Amery will be hanged tomorrow.'

'Do you think that's what happened?'

'I have no idea. It fits in with the facts as we know them.'

The execution took place next day with the approval of the English press of every shade of political opinion. A distinguished authoress in a report of the trial referred to him with exquisite taste as a 'poor young idiot' who had committed the 'classic type of treachery' and asserted that 'at the end of his muddled and frustrated existence' he had seen the vanity of his ideas and welcomed death as the only way out of a hopeless situation. I thought of the John Amery I knew in the cell at Terni – courageous in adversity, without regrets for the past, hoping against hope for the future. I could hear his voice once more as he spoke of his wife and daughter, I could see the broken cup with the half-withered flowers before their photographs, and I remembered how his wife had been brought from the prison in Milan too late to see him for the last time.

TWELVE

Dispersal

It was a cold and sunless day in the first week of December. I had finished my midday meal in the refectory and returned with my tin plate and spoon to the *camerata*. To my astonishment I found it occupied by a large force of soldiers and military police with rifles; a number of them had taken up positions at the end of each row of beds, others were engaged in bustling the internees out of the room. I made my way to my bed.

"Urry up, you there!' barked a soldier. 'Get out of 'ere!'

I laid the utensils on the bed, snatched a blanket and joined the stream of prisoners on their way down the stairs.

'What is it all about?' I asked my neighbour.

'A search for arms!' said he. 'As if anyone here could possibly have arms after all the searches we have had!'

We made our way downstairs and into the compound; many of those who had been disturbed at their meal had not even a jacket over their shirts. After a few minutes a dozen non-commissioned officers followed us into the compound.

'Get over to the far side!' yelled the sergeant in command.

We did so: the English grouped themselves in twos at intervals of some fifteen yards, and the search began. What they expected to find, I know not; it was obvious that, if anyone had really been in possession of a revolver or hand-grenade, he would have had ample time in the minutes before their arrival to deposit it under a stone at the far end of the compound or in the long grass outside the barbed wire. They did not themselves appear to ascribe much importance to the proceedings; the perquisition of our pockets was purely perfunctory. In half an hour the search was over; the only objects which they removed were a couple of bunches of keys. The non-commissioned officers left the compound and returned to the block; two sentries remained at the entrance to prevent us from approaching the building.

DISPERSAL

In the meantime we could see through the windows: they appeared to be carrying out a far more thorough search of the beds than of our persons. A lorry drove up to the door of the building: from time to time soldiers came down the stairs with wooden trays, which they placed in the lorry. It was too far off to see the contents of the trays. We strolled up and down over the sharp stones of the compound in the vain attempt to keep warm.

'What does it mean?' asked Klissura, an elderly Albanian. 'Surely they don't think anyone keeps weapons in his bed!'

'Of course not,' I said. 'Weapons are the very last thing that they expect to find.'

'Then what are they doing it for?'

'They will find lots of other objects which interest them far more than weapons – money and cigarettes and all sorts of little things which might be useful to them.'

Klissura seemed rather shocked. 'But you don't really suggest', he objected, 'that English soldiers would steal from their own prisoners?'

'I think it's just possible,' said I.

'I believe you are mistaken,' said Klissura. 'With us in Albania the English have a reputation for absolute honesty.'

'Have you had much personal experience of them?' I asked.

'No,' he admitted, 'we have never had them in our country, but I have heard a lot about them. The party I belong to has always relied on English help. We were against the Germans and Italians. We also fought against the Communists and King Zogu. We are the National Democratic Party of Albania, and we have always hoped to form a democratic government in Albania on English lines.'

'Well, now you'll have an opportunity of seeing English democracy in action,' I assured him.

There was a sudden movement, and we saw a number of internees running towards the gate of the compound. 'Come on!' I said to Klissura. 'The sentries must be gone. We'd better go and see what has happened upstairs.'

We made our way out of the compound and joined the throng which was struggling up the narrow stairs. In a few minutes we stood in the dormitory.

'Great God!' said Klissura. 'Have you ever seen anything like it?'

It was a scene of the wildest confusion. The blankets had been dragged off the beds and flung haphazard on the floor. Here and there one saw a boot without its fellow. Shirts, towels and underwear had been trampled underfoot. Suitcases lay open and empty on the beds: examination showed that they had been broken open – evidently by hands skilled in the forcing of locks. A German on the other side of the central passage came across in our direction.

'What are you looking for?' I asked him.

'My wife had just sent me new shirts and underwear. It's all gone!'

Few of us had been in possession of any articles of clothing with a market value, but nearly everyone had lost what scanty possessions he had had. Packets of cigarettes, money, fountain pens, toilet articles of leather or metal, shirts and underclothing had been systematically abstracted. A watchmaker from South Tyrol had obtained permission to carry out his trade in the dormitory: his tools and the watches lying on his table for repair, even including some belonging to the British officers, had disappeared. There could be no doubt what the soldiers had carried downstairs on their trays and loaded on the lorry.

'Have you lost anything?' I asked an Ukrainian.

'I had nothing to lose', he said, 'except twenty cigarettes – they are gone. And you?'

'I had nothing at all,' said I. 'They forced open my suitcase and threw it about, but there was nothing in it for them to take.'

'My things have not been touched,' remarked another German. 'It is just another proof of what I have always believed, that there are good and bad among the English, as there are in every other race.'

At the roll-call next morning only one police sergeant was present. We heard afterwards that the colleague who usually accompanied him on his rounds had remarked to one of the internees, 'I couldn't face them after what our fellows did yesterday.' Such considerations obviously did not trouble the sergeant. As he passed by, someone shouted, *'Ladri! Ladri inglesi!'* But the sergeant pursued his way, smiling and undisturbed.

★ ★ ★

One afternoon, just before the hour when we were summoned for tea, one of the Frenchmen in our squad came in and, seeing me sitting on my bed, asked me, 'Have you heard what they have done?'

'Who?' I inquired.

'The English.'

'No. What have they done?'

'The prisoners in the cells were out at exercise from three to four. One of them was wearing a cap he had made himself. When he went indoors again, he kept the cap on. A sergeant shouted to him to take it off. It seems he didn't take it off at once; but when the sergeant shouted to him the second time, he took it off and went on to his cell. The sergeant followed him and, when the door was opened, he hit him on the head with the butt of his revolver.'

I remained sitting on my bed, immersed in my thought. A new regulation had been introduced a short time before, providing that all internees sent to the cells as a punishment should in addition have their heads shaved. The fact that a measure hitherto applied to criminals convicted of a serious offence should be applied to civilian internees in peacetime had created much bad blood in the camp: the intention of the British authorities to humiliate their prisoners was evident. If 'offences against discipline', such as the failure to wear the identification badge in a prominent position or a contemptuous answer to the abuse of a British soldier, were to be punished as criminal offences, it was obvious that the elementary rules of justice had ceased to have any validity for us – and now apparently those so victimized were regarded as fair game for the brutality of the British soldiery.

All that evening the camp was in a turmoil: everyone was agreed that something must be done, but no-one knew exactly what we could do in our helpless situation. Innumerable self-appointed committees deliberated on an adequate protest. Speeches were made in the refectory, encouraging the internees to resist – it was not clear how or when. Finally the *Capo Campo* Colonel Invrea undertook to go early next morning to the cells and ascertain how the matter stood. The internees accepted his proposal.

On the following morning there was no roll-call: the authorities evidently feared an incident in view of the prevailing excitement. Towards eight o'clock the Camp Leader returned and made his report; there was little in it to soothe the excited spirits of the camp. When the cell door of the wounded man Ferrari was opened, he was found lying unconscious in a pool of blood. Other prisoners gave evidence that he had been beaten in the course of the night. No doctor had been called. The guards refused to allow him to be carried to the infirmary.

It was at once decided that all camp-workers should declare a strike. A series of demands was formulated for submission to the authorities. The Colonel in command of the camp was absent on leave, so Invrea and the deputation requested to be received by his substitute. When they had left our block, they were conducted to the punishment block, handcuffed and locked in a cell. A notice appeared on the order of the day stating that they had been punished by a week in the cells for offences against discipline.

The rage of the internees rose to boiling-point. It was resolved to refuse all work of any kind, including that of the kitchen, and to decline the provisions sent to our block. The morning was passed in a series of public meetings in the refectory: the speakers denounced the conduct of the English police and soldiers and called for a determined resistance to their efforts to break our spirit. Unfortunately, in the absence of Invrea there appeared to be no-one capable of assuming the leadership, and the programme was of necessity limited to the strike, with which (in my opinion, regrettably) they associated a hunger-strike.

The lead had of course been taken by the Italians, who formed the vast majority of the internees. The Germans with few exceptions were opposed to the protest: they were mostly elderly men who did not want to be disturbed more than was unavoidable. In the course of the morning I met Langenfeld. 'What do you think of the strike?' he inquired.

'We had to do something,' I said. 'If we let it pass without protest when one of our comrades is half killed by an English soldier, it would mean that we admit their right to bully us in any way they please.'

DISPERSAL

He held out his hand. 'Congratulations!' he said. 'You're the first person I've met this morning who says they are right.'

'Don't you agree with me?'

'Of course I do.'

'Who have you been talking to?'

'My countrymen of Six A. Some of them seem to think the sergeant was justified in assaulting the prisoner in the maintenance of order. Others agree that it was a brutal assault, but don't feel inclined to do anything about it.'

'Have they joined the strike?'

'The South Tyrolese in the kitchen have all laid down their work.'

In the meantime it was clear that the news had arrived in the female block. From our windows we could see a number of Italian girls in the compound; it was too far off to hear their voices, but they appeared to be protesting to the guards. Suddenly, without the possibility of knowing how the struggle originated, we saw a number of girls in handgrips with two or three soldiers. The door of their block was composed of glass panes: one after another these were smashed from the inside and fell with a crash on the stone pavement. Amid the hooting and jeering of our block the soldiers drove the girls into the building with the butts of their rifles.

'Bravo!' cried an Italian. 'Our women have shown what they can do!'

'Hysterical creatures!' remarked a German.

The morning dragged on until dinner-time. We sat on our beds and ate the bread or biscuits which we had saved from previous meals: those who had no provisions received from their neighbours. It looked as if the afternoon would pass in the same futile agitation as the morning. Towards three o'clock Marini came to me and said, 'It's no use going on like this. We're not getting any further. There is a committee in the Camp Leader's room trying to establish some order. They propose to write a formal letter of protest and want to know if you will draft it.'

'Certainly. I'll be delighted to do anything I can to help.'

We went together to Invrea's room, where we found a dozen Italians engaged in discussing the situation.

'It's a difficult position,' one of them explained to me. 'You see, now that Invrea is imprisoned, every second internee thinks he has a right to lead the rest.'

'The democratic spirit!' I observed.

It was not easy to distinguish the precise facts from the innumerable rumours floating round the camp, but I jotted down what seemed to be the salient and incontrovertible points and asked for a few minutes to adapt them to a formal letter of protest. My deliberations were interrupted by shouts outside the window. 'Don't touch them!' I heard. 'Leave them where they are! We don't want them!'

'*Santo Dio!*' groaned one of the Committee. 'The supplies for our supper! It was a terrible mistake to start the hunger-strike.'

'In any case,' I remarked, 'a hunger-strike of over a thousand is a sheer impossibility. With, say, a dozen it might be possible, but with a larger number there will always be a minority, or more probably a majority, which will insist on eating when it feels hungry.'

It was a melancholy conclusion, but there was nothing we could do. I went on drafting the letter: it was soon ready. After setting out the facts in as objective a manner as possible, I presented the demands of the internees for the punishment of Sergeant Thomas Campbell, the removal of Ferrari to a hospital where he would be treated by Italian doctors and the immediate release of Colonel Invrea and the deputation. The committee expressed its approval, and the letter was translated into Italian for the benefit of the other prisoners, after which it was transmitted through one of the guards to the authorities.

On the next morning it had become clear that the hunger-strike was on the point of collapsing. On all sides we saw discontented faces and heard murmurs that it was useless to continue. By tacit accord the provisions were carried to the kitchen, and the workers resumed their interrupted duties. In the course of the morning Invrea and the deputation were released: he reported that Ferrari had been removed to the infirmary and was receiving proper medical treatment. At our midday meal there were double rations. The evening roll-call was held under normal conditions. The strike was at an end.

Three evenings later, as we were preparing to go to bed, we were startled by the noise of shots. There was a rush into our dormitory by the Italians from the adjoining room. 'They're shooting into our windows!' they said.

'From which side?'

'From the north side.'

There was a terrace to the north of our *camerata*; consequently we were in no danger and could interest ourselves in their story.

'Who is shooting?'

'Renzetti saw an Indian aiming at the windows with his rifle. No-one else has gone near the windows.'

'Have they fired into the rooms on the first floor?'

'I think so, but it is better not to go downstairs at present. You could easily get a shot on the way.'

The firing continued at intervals for ten minutes, then it ceased and we went to bed. On the next morning we crowded into the other room to see the damage: nearly all the windows at the far end beyond the terrace were shattered; I could count seventeen places in the ceiling where the plaster had been brought down. On the first floor it was the same: nearly all the windows on the north side had been fired into.

'Che farabutti!' said someone. 'They are trying to intimidate us. They want to show us what they can do if there is any more trouble in the camp. *Vigliacchi! Ladri fottuti!'*

'I heard', said another, 'that somebody emptied a bucket of water over the Indian.'

'No,' a third contradicted him, 'that is not true. The Indian was drunk.'

'The sergeant says he was mad,' volunteered a fourth. 'It seems he has been taken to an asylum.'

A wave of sympathy for the unfortunate Indian seemed to be spreading through the camp: no-one cast even a glance at the bullet-marks in the ceiling or the broken windows. I reflected sadly on the simplicity of human nature.

'Has anyone here ever heard of Sheehy-Skeffington?' I asked.

No-one had ever heard of Sheehy-Skeffington.

'He was a journalist in Dublin. After the rebellion in 1916 an English officer had him arrested and shot. He was rather well known, and everyone knew that he had nothing whatever to do with the rebellion. So the British Government sent over a commission to inquire into the case. After hearing the evidence the commission could not suggest that there had been any excuse for the shooting – in fact it was a murder in cold blood. But of course a British officer could never commit a murder. So they found unanimously that the officer had given the order to shoot in an access of insanity and sentenced him to an asylum to be there detained during His Majesty's pleasure. It was in all the papers at the time, and the world was duly impressed by British justice. On the other hand, it was in none of the papers when they released him six months later.'

★ ★ ★

Silbermann was blond and blue-eyed, and, when I met him without knowing his name, it never occurred to me that he had Jewish blood. The only peculiarity which I noticed in him was his affection for the French language, which he spoke with a fluency and correctness quite exceptional in a German.

'But I served for five years in the French Foreign Legion,' he explained in answer to my question. 'It's only natural that I should speak French well. After all I am a naturalized Frenchman.'

'I took you for a Rhinelander,' I said.

'You're not far wrong. I come from Frankfurt. But in 1933 I made up my mind that life in Germany was going to be intolerable for Jews, so I left while it was still possible.'

'I would never have thought you were a Jew,' I faltered.

He laughed. 'Non-Jews often don't recognize it,' he said, 'but of course a Jew would know at once, just as I always know another Jew when I meet him. After I left the Legion, I set up as a watchmaker in Algeria.'

'But why did the Allies arrest you?'

He shrugged his shoulders. 'I'd like to know myself. They arrested a number of Jews after the landing in Africa.'

'But why?' I repeated. 'Surely they can't have suspected you of sympathizing with the Nazis?'

'Whoever wins in any war,' he answered, 'we are usually the victims. Of course I wouldn't suggest that they are likely to exterminate us like the Germans, but at bottom there's not so much difference in their attitude. They used us for propaganda – which was perfectly justified – but they are not going to do anything for us. It's not surprising that so many of our young men in their despair are joining organizations like the Stern Band.'

'Are many of them joining it?' I asked.

'I don't know in what quantities they are joining,' he said. 'I had never heard of the various secret societies until quite lately. In Padula I met two young men who I am sure were members.'

It would have interested me to know his personal opinion of the extreme wing of the Zionist movement, but I did not like to put the direct question.

'I haven't altogether made up my mind about them yet,' he continued, as if he had read my thoughts. 'But, whether all their methods are justified or not, one thing at least cannot be denied – they have helped to give us back our self-respect.'

'In what way?' I inquired.

'You know the propaganda against us – that we profit by the wars between the nations, but that we take care not to risk our own lives. You could read it every day in the press – and not only in Germany. There were very few countries where you didn't hear the same kind of sneers. It wasn't the fact, of course; we have neither more nor less courage than other peoples: in the other war there were Jews who died fighting on both sides. But it's true that many of our young men didn't see why they should sacrifice themselves in a war which we didn't make and in which the Jewish race could only be a victim. And so by degrees we came ourselves half to believe what the rest of the world said about us – even though in our hearts we knew it was a lie. It's hard to understand, but that was the result.'

'I can quite understand it,' said I. 'Something of the same kind happened to us in Ireland in the years before our rebellion.'

'But now,' he went on, 'at least that lie has been exposed. Whatever anyone may think of the Stern Band no-one can say in future that Jews are not prepared to give their lives for what they believe to be their duty. And, after all, that's the most important thing for a nation, just as it is for an individual, isn't it?'

'I have always believed it,' said I.

'I want you to come tomorrow to my wedding,' said Max Brandli, the oversized Swiss from Zurich.

'Your what?' I echoed in surprise.

'My wedding.'

'And who is the happy lady?'

'She is called Gerda Stumpf. She is in the women's block.'

'But how did you get to know her as well as that?'

'We worked together before we were arrested,' said Max cautiously. Then, throwing aside his reserve, he added, 'We were in the same branch of the *Abwehr*.'

I knew already that he had been in the *Abwehr*, the counter-espionage branch of the German army and the enemy and rival of the SD: the scene of his activities had been the Middle East, from which he had been brought to Italy for internment. I regarded him as a lineal descendant of the picturesque Swiss adventurers in the Middle Ages who, with spirits still uncontaminated by the hotel industry, had sold their loyalty to popes and kings and emperors.

'Congratulations!' I said. 'Who is going to conduct the ceremony? Padre Gabriele?'

'No,' said Max. 'I am reformed and Gerda is Lutheran. We could scarcely be married by a Catholic priest. A notary is to come from Terni.'

So on the following afternoon two guards escorted Max and me and three Germans to the women's block, where the celebration was to take place. The bride was waiting with four German female friends in the room which the authorities had made available. She was a large-boned and sturdy woman in her late thirties, who outside the camp might have appeared comely, but the months of imprisonment, the lack of facilities for bathing, the entire absence of cosmetics, made her look drab and grimy. I wondered for the hundredth time how any man could find anything sensually attractive in the dingy figures which we saw walking in the women's compound.

General introductions were made. I found myself sitting next to a Frau Grünberg, who set herself to impress me with stories of the Thüringian nobility. As I had for several years before the outbreak of war spent the Whitsun week in a castle in Thüringen, I was able to test her accuracy; she seemed genuine, but I had learned by now to distrust *a priori* all stories told me by strange members of the camp. But I cannot deny that a little society gossip was a welcome change after so many months of the usual camp conversation.

Our talk was beginning to wear a little thin, the other guests appeared to be in the same situation. Max turned to me.

'Would you mind asking him', he said, pointing to the soldier in attendance, 'what has happened to the notary?'

I translated the question, but the soldier knew nothing about him. He went outside to inquire, but soon came back saying that nobody had any information.

'I wonder if they notified him at all,' said Frau Grünberg.

'I have come here to get married,' said Max, 'and I am going to be married before I leave this room. *Nicht wahr*, Gerda?'

Gerda blushed and smiled: it was evident that she too was determined not to leave the room until the words had been spoken uniting her with her friend.

'We'll give him another ten minutes,' said Max. 'Then, if he doesn't turn up, someone else will have to perform the ceremony.'

The ten minutes passed, but the notary had not arrived. Max turned to me again, and said, 'It's no use waiting any longer. He can't be coming at all. Will you marry us? Here is a copy of the New Testament.'

'*Aber, lieber Max!*' I protested. 'I have no licence to marry people. Besides, we're in Italy, and I'm not Italian. No marriage I celebrated could possibly be valid.'

Max did not seem to judge my objections of excessive importance: he had told me beforehand that couples who married in the camp were allowed one night together, presumably from some idea on the part of the authorities that marriages were not valid without consummation: he had also told me that a bed with real sheets was placed at their disposal.

'Besides,' I added, 'I am a Catholic. How can I marry two Protestants?'

It was not much of an argument, but it seemed to convince him. 'What about you, Professor?' he asked, turning to one of the Germans.

'I will celebrate the marriage with pleasure,' said the Professor. Whether he had already performed similar ceremonies or not, I had no means of knowing, but he appeared to have no doubts about the procedure. He took the New Testament and told the bride and bridegroom to kiss it; then, taking it back from them, he asked, 'Wilt thou, Max, take Gerda to be thy lawful wife?'

'*Ja!*'

'Wilt thou, Gerda, take Max to be thy lawful husband?'

'*Ja!*'

'I declare thee, Max, and thee, Gerda, to be man and wife according to the law,' said the Professor.

It seemed almost too simple, but what more could be done? No register could be signed, because no register existed; no rings could be exchanged, because all jewellery and objects of value were sealed in envelopes bearing the letters OHMS in the police office awaiting their owners' liberation; no wedding presents could be given, because bride and bridegroom and their friends were as completely devoid of private property as the citizens of the most proletarian of Communist states.

The wedding feast began. Max had ordered wine and fruit from the camp bar; his funds did not admit of further additions to the camp food. The healths of bride and bridegroom were drunk. I was asked to make the speech in their honour; as I had refused to perform the marriage ceremony, I felt that it was the least I could do. I thought of the last speech I had made – at a farewell dinner given for me in the summer of 1939 in the Berlin Garde-Kavallerie Club. The last thing that I could then have anticipated was that my next appearance as an orator would be at the wedding of two prisoners interned for espionage in a disused Italian factory, that I myself would be wearing prison clothing, and that an English soldier, bored and uncomprehending, would be sitting at my side to preserve decorum.

★ ★ ★

The days passed slowly by; I wondered how much longer I was likely to remain in the camp of Collescipoli. But unexpectedly one morning I heard my name called.

'You are wanted in the office,' said a messenger.

I went downstairs; the messenger escorted me across the camp square and delivered me to a police corporal, who led me upstairs to a small office, where a sergeant was standing behind a writing-table.

'Bewley, Number 671?' he asked.

'Yes.'

'You will be released on Monday December 17th,' said the sergeant. 'You will report 'ere for papers and belongings at eleven o'clock.'

I looked at him in silence – I had made it a rule never to address a word to a British soldier except in case of absolute necessity.

'Where do you want to go?' he asked.

'To Meran where I was arrested,' I said. 'My clothes are still there.'

He wrote down my address in Meran. 'You will be given a pass for the military trains,' he said. ''And over your camp money to the store. The amount will be given back to you 'ere in Italian money.'

As he seemed to have no more to say, I went back to the block. No-one had ever told me why I had been arrested, and now no-one told me why I was being released. The only clue I had consisted in the date December 17th: I remembered that my interview with the English policeman in Florence had taken place on the 17th of June. It seemed probable that I had been sentenced by a policeman to six months' internment without a legal process or a formal charge or any opportunity of defending myself.

It would be of little interest to recount in detail the events subsequent to my release. It will suffice to say that an Italian visitor to the camp offered me a seat to the station of Terni, and that after two days in Rome for arranging my financial affairs I returned to Meran. Here I found that my typewriter, a new leather suitcase, two suits of clothes, fur gloves, an electric torch, a pair of shoes and various sundries such as bottles of brandy and playing-cards had been removed by the Allied police entrusted with the task of searching my room for compromising documents. In compensation, however, I found that I had only to mention to anyone I met, whether Italian or Tyrolese, that I had been a prisoner of the English to find myself the object of every possible sympathy and attention. The presence of the British troops of occupation in Meran (they had succeeded the Americans shortly after my arrest) had done more to make the German cause popular than ten years of Goebbels' propaganda.

Nor was it difficult when I came into contact with the local authorities. One morning I received a telephone call from the *maresciallo* of the *carabinieri* asking me to come to the police station. 'This means my expulsion from Italy,' I thought. 'But there is nothing I can do. The citizen of any other neutral state could apply to his Legation for help and protection, but the Irish Government and its Minister in Rome have made it quite plain that they will do nothing to help anyone who did not support England in the War. I must only submit.'

My distrust in the Irish authorities was not unfounded. I had managed to smuggle a letter out of the camp, which, as I afterwards heard, had reached the Minister MacWhite and by him been forwarded to de Valera. MacWhite's only comment had been, 'He deserves all he's getting for being a pro-German.' And de Valera had been so nervous that he might be expected to do something on my behalf that he did not even communicate to my family that I was still alive.

But, when I reached the police station, I found that my fears were entirely unfounded. A pleasant-looking official in civilian clothes was sitting at a table with a file of documents before him. He got up and shook hands with me.

'The English have sent us your file', he remarked, 'and asked us to keep you under observation as a suspicious person. but of course we have nothing whatever against you; we regard it as a purely English affair. They want to penalize you because you're Irish.'

He glanced at the dossier. 'Have you a daughter in Rome?' he asked with a grin.

'I have no daughter in Rome or anywhere else.'

'Then it is incorrect when they say that your daughter in Rome was doing propaganda for the Germans?'

'Quite incorrect,' I assented.

The police official turned over the leaves of my dossier, smiling occasionally at what he found in it. Then he appeared to have come to a decision. 'I know very little English', he said, 'and there are some expressions which I don't understand. Perhaps you would look through it and tell me what they mean.' He shoved the file across the table to me, so that I could see the heads of the charges which the English had brought against me. I read, 'Irish journalist who has written many articles against England and America. Suspected of being member of the SD.'

The *maresciallo* did not bother to ask me for any translations; instead he asked, 'Do you know who denounced you?'

'I have always assumed it was a certain Petersdorf,' I answered, and told him of my meeting with the Professor.

'You're quite right,' he said. Then with a smile he added, 'Well, I needn't waste any more of your time. I am usually about the town. If I meet you there I hope I may have the honour of offering you a drink.'

I thanked him and we shook hands. It was the official close of my career as a criminal.

When I left Terni, I imagined and hoped that my friendship with some at least of my fellow-prisoners would continue undisturbed. My wish has not been fulfilled: though it is always a pleasure when one or another of them greets me in the street, our ways lie too far apart to admit of frequent meetings, and correspondence without the vivifying effect of personal contact sooner or later becomes a mere formality and dies a natural death. It may however be a certain interest to mention the subsequent fate of a few of those of whom I have written in this book.

Kemény was handed over by the English to the Hungarian Communists and sentenced by a revolutionary tribunal to death by hanging. At his execution, which took place on one of the public squares of Budapest, he and the other Ministers condemned with him were hailed by the Communist crowd with jeers and curses. According to the press he continued to pray until the moment of his death.

Vrancic, the former Croatian Minister, was delivered by the English to Tito's Communists. His execution would have been inevitable if he had not succeeded in escaping during his transport to Yugoslavia. So far as I know, he is now in South America; the Yugoslavs assert that he was furnished by the Vatican with a forged passport.

Klissura, the elderly Albanian, was cured by one afternoon in Terni of his hopes of English help towards the liberation of his country. He resumed his life of exile and conspiracy in Rome and Cairo. It is not long since he died.

The marriage of Max and Gerda was, as might be expected, invalid, and the whole episode may be regarded as no more than the adventure of a night. Gerda has, if I am rightly informed, found another and, I hope, more durable husband, while Max, unable to return to Switzerland except at the risk of a heavy sentence for evasion of military service, has settled down, as far as his roving temperament will allow him to settle down, in northern Italy.

Hahn has found religion in the form of the Oxford Group or some similar German organization. I am informed that he preaches in its interest in the cities of the Bundesrepublik. As he is connected by marriage with the owner of a noodle factory, I imagine that his material needs are reasonably well provided for.

I met Van Vliet shortly after his and my release: he was more cheerful than I had seen him before, and as exuberant and indignant as ever. His chief complaint was against the Americans.

'Do you know that they took twelve million dollars from my room in the Stefanie?' he asked me.

'Twelve million dollars! For God's sake!' I responded politely. I did not like to inquire whether they had been printed in Germany and distributed from Schloss Labers.

Professor Petersdorf is, so far as I am aware, still in Meran. It turned out that his claim to be a baron was no more justified by the facts than his pretence of being a *cameriere segreto* of His Holiness. At a trial in the post-War years for the murder of a South Tyrolese peasant who committed the crime of entertaining sympathy with Germany, he gave evidence that, as 'military adviser to the South Tyrolese underground movement', he had approved the killing as an 'act of war'. He was not, as he might have been, prosecuted for incitement to murder: the elimination of persons with German sympathies was still regarded as legitimate if the eliminator claimed to belong to the 'partisans'.

On my return to Meran I was walking with a friend on the Promenade when we met Petersdorf. As he went by, I said in German, 'I see that the race of informers has not yet died out.'

Petersdorf turned round and overtook us. 'What did you say?' he asked me.

'You heard me.'

'Did you hear what he said?' he asked my friend.

'*Non ho sentito niente – non capisco il tedesco*. I heard nothing, I don't understand German.'

He turned to me again. 'I'll take an action against you for slander,' he said.

'I hope you will. You couldn't do anything which would give me greater pleasure.'

Petersdorf walked away. I am still awaiting the writ.

Camp Literature

AFTERWORD

Camp Literature

Near the close of his memoir, Charles Bewley is looking out of a place of detention near Verona; the time is early summer 1945:

> Some twenty yards to the left there had been a bridge; now, only a pylon rose out of the water surmounted by a recumbent female figure. Her head had disappeared, and an iron spike rose from the middle of her decapitated neck, creating the effect of an early Chirico. (p. 237)

In these two sentences, the reader finds concentrated all the glosses, ambiguities, distortions, elisions, silences, and assumptions which characterize the remarkable narrative which is *Memoirs of a Wild Goose*. Is the figure that of an actual human being – the victim of a brutal killing – or is it that of a depicted human being, a statue of some sort? The sentences are slow to resolve the uncertainty. Indeed, when the comparison with the art of a flamboyant modernist painter is made, the effect can only be to nudge the reader towards acceptance that the figure on the bridge is a corpse. As the sentences in question are promptly followed up by an indirect account of Benito Mussolini's execution by partisans – this registered in the prose by reference to a photograph – the assumption that the prisoner is looking out at a corpse is all too reasonable.

Yet somehow the average reader will conclude otherwise. Bewley is not a writer about whose memoirs the reasonable assumption is always justified. By an odd coincidence, he was born in the same year as Giorgio de Chirico, whom he cites. He was to reside for perhaps longer continuous periods of his life in the painter's homeland than in any other place, Ireland included. The eldest son (of four) born to a prosperous doctor, Henry Theodore Bewley, and his wife Elizabeth Eveleen Pim, Charles Henry Bewley first saw the light of Dublin on the 12th of July 1888. Thus by the time we encounter him in post-war detention, he had travelled from the comfortable environment of a Protestant bourgeois home, by way of English public school and Oxford college, conversion to Catholicism and adherence to cultural nationalism, to find himself – a compulsorily retired diplomat of the Irish Free State – interrogated by British and American officers as a suspected collaborator with German and Italian fascism.

A fellow detainee in one of those Italian camps, writing to Colonel Duggan in 1986, described Bewley as 'peevish, clever, self-important, snobbish, and not really very nice'. To one who has only the written record to go on, that seems judicious, eminently fair. In his assessment, James Clark went on to point out how revealing it was that Bewley 'should see himself as something as romantic as a Wild Goose'. Even in choosing this epithet, Bewley displays an odd ability to yoke the incongruous together; he cites Oliver St John Gogarty as fellow wild goose, unaware that the term's denomination (of emigré aristocrats and soldiers and their immediate descendants) rebuffs the latter-day eccentric. Only an ill-disguised anti-Semitism links Bewley to Gogarty, and nothing links either to Patrick Sarsfield. It is fully emblematic of the book that, when a *soi-disant* descendant of the last-named crops up in *Memoirs of a Wild Goose,* he is an identikit Count Salazar, sometimes English and sometimes Irish, his immortality a mere half-page.

Lucky to escape formal court-martial or trial in Allied-occupied Italy, Bewley subsequently wrote up his experiences while living in Rome. Eamon de Valera, John Amery, Sarsfield Salazar, Freiherr von Buttlar's butler posing as von Buttlar, and other increasingly absurd figures proliferate. But the unknowns and the world-famous are alike reduced in the process, as if the author transmitted to each of them something of his own incompleteness. This is not to argue that some completeness of personality is possible or desirable; on the contrary, it is Bewley's egoism, his unreflective integrity, which generates the dissolution one observes through his characterization. His characters proliferate *and* auto-destruct at the same time. In this context, the execution of Amery is central, not so much as a point of political reference but as an exemplar of character as such, with the off-stage execution of the Hungarian Kémeny added to deprive the book of any symmetrical or focused order. (The typescript ends with the author's unfulfilled commitment to getting even with a fellow suspect whom he has cast as his betrayer, and at every point the reader is made aware of unfinished, untold business.) Though many of these wretches and rascals are all too typical of the flotsam drifting idly in the immediate aftermath of the Second World War, the scope of the book goes well beyond pen-portraiture.

The net is thrown wide; we are introduced to the contrasting behavioural codes of Winchester and the Sinn Féin courts; we read of diplomatic high-jinks under the Third Reich, followed by luscious incidental vignettes of a prison chapel and a few flowers. Of the fifty-odd years covered by his *Memoirs,* Bewley spent only half a year (six months to the day as he nonchalantly complains) in the various detention camps of the American and British victors. The pages devoted to this period are wholly disproportionate in number, especially given the repetitive, even serene, existence the author (by his own account) sustained throughout it. His book is therefore describable as camp literature in two senses. On the one hand, it associates itself *scandalously* with the writings of Bruno Bettelheim and Primo Levi, or the diary of Anne Frank, victims, survivors, or temporary survivors of the Nazi concentration and extermination camps. On the other, it veers reelingly towards Curzio Malaparte, in whose *Kaputt* Himmler is observed in his sauna and corpses in the Warsaw ghetto are compared to paintings by Chagall. One would classify the book as an exercise in self-pity, were there evidences of either self or pity to be found unambiguously in its pages.

One pauses at glimpses of a landscape seen through a grid, tempted to call them phony or forced. As if turning then to rebuke the author, the reader discovers that somehow it is the author himself who has succeeded in eluding the net. The narrative is richly verifiable in relation to Bewley's English academic achievement and his professional career as an Irish diplomat, not to mention those major incidents of the war to which he alludes. And yet it is manifestly *unreliable.* Or, to mitigate that admittedly prejudicial term, one has to say that any attempt to assess these *Memoirs* as a historical source has to be conducted in the light of a separate assessment of the author himself. Yet who is Bewley, what kind of person might he have been? Answers to these questions do not come to mind easily.

Historians are frequently obliged to make judgments about documents based solely on internal evidence or on such evidence measured against banally established fact. By these standards, our man immediately emerges as a commentator grotesquely biased in his general view of Eamon de Valera whom he casually parallels with Hitler. Readily convicted as an unreliable judge of character, Bewley is not wholly dismissable as a witness to de Valera's behaviour where – as in the amusing if malicious account of the Irish leader's manipulation of press photography – he reports on individual actions which he personally witnessed. *Memoirs of a Wild Goose* has its use as a historical source, but only in instances which the author would probably have regarded as peripheral to his main purpose.

That purpose is justification. Of course, a man who adopted successive allegiances strikingly different from those to which he was born and trained may find himself called on to justify his adjustments. Bewley converts to Catholicism from the inherited Protestantism of his family. To that, he adds political conversion from the conventional values of his childhood home (essentially British and imperial values) to Irish nationalism in one of its most militant and military phases. While serving a democratically endorsed nationalism at the elevated level of a diplomat with consular and even (to a degree) ambassadorial status, he gravitates rapidly towards the values of those totalitarian régimes to which he was posted as diplomat. Psychologically, it is a remarkable odyssey and sufficiently controversial to require justification. At this level, justification involves demonstration by the subject of the essential rightness of his actions, considered against the evidence of appearances, misrepresentations, misunderstandings and other non-essential factors. Even pathological liars and fascists consider themselves justified in having done whatever they have done – indeed, such personalities are especially sure that they have been right.

In Bewley's case, justification should be regarded at a further level. According to certain forms of Christian theology, justification is 'the action whereby man is justified, or freed from the penalty of sin, and accounted or made righteous by God'. Traditionally, a theological dispute revolves around the rival arguments for justification by faith or by deeds, with Lutheranism insistent that 'faith alone' justifies. The subtle varieties of theological position adopted on this topic need not concern us. What is central, however, is the necessary prerequisite of sin, evil, wrongdoing to this action. And, however blindly or dishonestly or self-deceivingly, *Memoirs of a Wild Goose* does aspire to be the author's justification in this second and deeper sense.

According to these memoirs, Bewley left Oxford 'more than satisfied with second-class honours' (p. 37). According to the prefatory matter in his biography of Hermann Goering, he had taken a first-class degree. It is quite possible to reach, in the manner of the professional historian, an objective answer to this question of conflicting evidences. (The records show that he had obtained first-class marks at the mid-point of his undergraduate career, but that the final degree result was indeed second-class.) Less immediately reconcilable to such a notion of objective fact is Bewley's description of *Ladies and Gentlemen* as 'my first literary venture'. Despite the title, the book (published in 1944) was in German and comprised a series of short stories written by Bewley to illustrate the inadequacies of English society: it was, of course, part of a desperate campaign of Nazi propaganda to bolster up the collapsing morale of the German people, a campaign to which at least two other Irishmen – William Joyce and Francis Stuart – had contributed in their different ways.

Bewley, however, had published a poem of pamphlet length while still at Oxford, and as the poem won the prestigious Newdigate Prize (for 1909) it is unlikely that its author had wholly forgotten it any more than he had forgotten the pieces contributed to *The New Ireland*. One can simply note that the *Memoirs* specifically do not admit evidence of success or achievement in England. Not that 'Atlantis' can be rediscovered as a masterpiece of Anglo-Irish poetry. Apart from its liquorice all-sorts of Swinburne, the early Yeats and Tennyson, the poem is remarkably confused as to whether the mythical location is an island or a plain. His other literary activities in fascist Europe including hijacking passages from American and British authors which, in the cluttered isolation provided by the *Adria-Zeitung* of Trieste, mocked the Allied war effort. All in all, his literary activities are characterized by a chronic or extreme approach to the question of how parts of a thing might relate to its entirety: he appears to have grasped imperfectly the logical category of proportion or relationship.

Yet he also appears to have had a highly developed talent for learning foreign languages, as if translation from one language to another were more congenial than ratiocination from one premise to another. In a freakish or exact way, he embodies a transition from the determinist world of Victorian thinking, in ethics, philology, biology, physics, to a world in which the endlessly relative and the random will dictate terms as best the relative and random can. Or to be more precise, he is in part a transitional figure, in part an anachronism. It is not in jest that one would see Dracula as his avatar. Bram Stoker, though older than Bewley by forty years and more remotely linked to the Dublin medical profession, created his monster of endangered orality and glib fluency in 1897, a monster whom Bewley's Europe took to its heart through innumerable translations and cinematic adaptations. In a more up-to-the-minute demonology, the dance of death of post-structuralist signifiers should be able to find a place for a comfortably off and Quaker-descended Belial.

From even his earliest days, Charles Bewley had difficulty in reconciling things to their mundane actuality. It is pointless seeking some explanation for this state of affairs, its origins by now untraceable in the case of the particular individual under discussion. But the evidence of his psychological condition runs right through the *Memoirs,* from his defiance of parental opinion on the Boer War to his fatuous claiming of diplomatic immunities years after he had been obliged to resign from the Irish service. Less particularly, his characteristic strategy was to adopt a position which could not merely be accommodated, compromised, or moderated. While he evidently thrived in the labyrinthine implications of dinner- and house-party intrigue under the Nazi régime, and revelled in his own ability to translate backwards and forwards among the international clientele of detention camps, Bewley needed to be 'over against something' in order to be assured of his existence. Intransigence towards others was a form of self-assurance. It is not surprising that, in writing of his conversion to Catholicism, he quotes approvingly Saint Athenasius's position, *contra mundum*. And in keeping with this preference for the total, he fails to notice that the work on *Infallibility* recommended and lent to him by an anxious Anglican (p. 35) was written by a fellow Dubliner, George Salmon. Such casual, actual, local, even personal relationship eludes Bewley again and again.

The conversion to Catholicism was similarly absolute. Without military experience in the Irish Republican Army, and it's clear lacking even a rudimentary knowledge of the Gaelic language, he associated himself with the Irish people, historically and ideologically, through their religious experience. Interned after the war, he declined to perform a marriage ceremony for two other prisoners, citing their Protestantism as an obstacle. The set-piece description of the altar in the detention camp at Terni recalls in some respects Francis Stuart's magnificent novel *Redemption*, with its delicate juxtaposition of Irish provincial Catholicism with the sublime terrors of the Russian advance on Berlin. Like Bewley, Stuart spent the war in Axis territory; but while the former was taking cocktails with Japanese dowagers in the South Tyrol, Stuart was sharing a Berlin flat with the dying Frank Ryan. Brutalized in Franco's prisons, deaf, and politically disoriented by the Nazis' springing him from Burgos gaol and fêting him in occupied Paris, the sometime leader of a left-wing faction in Irish republicanism is mentioned in passing by Bewley – but without reference to Ryan's socialism or to his Irish flatmate.

The failure to mention Stuart is another instance of the *Memoirs'* unreliability, for an Irish ex-diplomat continuing to reside in Germany and Italy can hardly have been unaware of Stuart's broadcasts on German radio. (Lord Haw-Haw's typist became Stuart's second wife.) Also missing from Bewley's recollections is any reference to Daniel A. Binchy, his predecessor at the Irish legation in Berlin. Binchy of course was a brilliant Celtic scholar, a shrewd analyst of fascism, and an admirer of many aspects of British policy – three adequate grounds upon which Bewley could exclude him. On the general topic of missing persons, note the almost total absence of women, the successful exclusion of any reference to Hermann Goering with whose family he was elsewhere happy to claim a certain intimacy and whose biography he was to write – in German. Finally, some allusion to the activities of Ezra Pound in wartime Italy might have been expected. Only the dead John Amery challenges for the reader's attention.

But the irony of his silence on Francis Stuart goes beyond personalities. Stuart's *Blacklist Section H,* first published years after Bewley's death, provides a remarkable parallel to the career summarized in *Memoirs of a Wild Goose.* At the biographical level, the duplication can be observed in a number of formative moments. Both men were born into well-to-do Irish Protestant families, each was a first (or only) son. Both were sent to public school (Winchester and Rugby) in England, where they greeted news of international crisis with positive excitement – the Russian Revolution in Stuart's case. Both converted to Catholicism and to Sinn Féin, and felt disillusioned by the result of the Irish War of Independence. But there the resemblance ends – for the moment. Bewley adhered to his bourgeois training by becoming a servant of the state, whereas Stuart chose a republican *ressentiment* leading on to juvenile poetry, a first novel written in Lourdes water, and a self-conscious literary career in Dublin and London. Then, at the end of the 1930s, that 'low, dishonest decade' of Auden's phrase, the resemblance begins again when both men opt for residence in the Axis countries, in Berlin particularly.

Nevertheless, the differences are more revealing. Stuart was an accomplished novelist even before he chose to take up a university post in Berlin in 1939. And between 1945 and 1972 (when *Blacklist* was published), he had explored the imaginative and moral implications of his decision in a number of impressive novels, notably *The Pillar of Cloud* (1948), *Redemption* (1949), and – more problematically – *Victors and Vanquished* (1958). Therein lies a drastic cleavage, and a paradoxical one. For all that

Francis Stuart champions the imaginative realm over and against the claims of morality and convention, he remains a moralist in a sense perhaps more familiar to the French (Baudelaire, Rimbaud, Jean Genet) than to the Irish. And it is a revealing distinction that Stuart, after the war, found precarious refuge with a Jewish writer in Paris and a Jewish publisher in London, while Charles Henry Bewley lived in Italy on a private income of which we know nothing.

Some readers of Stuart's novels may find the claim for him of moralist surprising, even scandalous. Yet in the fifty-first chapter of *Blacklist, Section H,* the author's ciphered representative argues strenuously with the English Captain Manville in favour of an approach to life in which one deliberately aligns oneself with the guilty, the unacceptable, the rejected. In my own view, it is a seriously flawed morality not unlike that of the trendy missionary. But one cannot – ultimately Francis Stuart cannot – deny that it is a moral attitude, a search for justification. By comparison, *Memoirs of a Wild Goose* never approaches the moral dimension. While the authorial voice sedulously protects its protective, echoing shell, there occurs a proliferating evasion of judgment. Nothing in the *Memoirs* indicates the casuistry, the disintegration of language as a criterion of truth, more clearly than Bewley's report of his reply to an equivalent of Captain Manville:

> 'And do you still sympathize with Germany?'
> 'Of course. I would have thought that everyone must sympathize with the Germans in this immense human tragedy'. (p. 242)

This inability to distinguish between the pre-war German state and Germans who survived the war – isn't it a semi-conscious attempt to give the former something of the humanitarian appeal of the latter? – conforms to Bewley's larger outlook as encapsulated in his choice of title. *Memoirs of a Wild Goose,* but as title only, assimilates an individual to a general, historically validated endorsement. By comparison, Stuart's *Blacklist, Section H* draws attention to the problematic status of character as such, both in its title and in its unfolding narrative. The two books deserve further comparative examination, particularly in the light of current discussion in Ireland concerning the status of the self. Declan Kiberd, speaking from the Irish Republic, and John Wilson Foster, speaking for Northern Ireland, have in their different ways argued that the Irish personality is incomplete. This condition of impoverishment at once material and psychic they ascribe to a voracious colonialism (Kiberd) or nationalism (Foster), agreeing (by implication) that completeness, roundedness of character would be desirable in an ideal Ireland of bourgeois individualism.

One does not simply mean that Bewley suffered from some crisis of identity, onset of insecurity, leading him to seek refuge in the whirlpool of flattery and indifference which he reveals the fascist *beau monde* to have been. He does of course also deserve consideration alongside those tweedledum and tweedledee figures of Thomas Kilroy's play, *Doublecross,* William Joyce and Brendan Bracken. But the issue goes well beyond matters of social displacement seen either as the cause or consequence of a psychological crisis in the individual.

The year of Bewley's severance of official relations with the Irish state (1939) is notable enough, God knows, in political and military terms without supportive reference to the annals of literature. Yet, in the same year, Joyce's *Finnegans Wake,* Yeats's *On the Boiler* (including the play 'Purgatory'), and Flann O'Brien's *At Swim-Two-Birds* were published. Samuel Beckett and Francis Stuart opted for residence in Europe, the one to become a fugitive in German-occupied and Vichy France, the other to lecture on English literature to Berlin undergraduates. Elizabeth Bowen was moving towards involvement in low-level espionage in the country of her birth. Louis MacNeice left for the United States, but returned to wartime London. Whether as text or gesture each of these items on the calendar negatives any self-defining, integral notion of the Self. Within this drastically relativized and pluralized context, one can certainly read Bowen's *The Heat of the Day* and even Yeats's 'Purgatory' as justification. But Charles Bewley is, in a sense, the illiterate and revealing obverse of a heavily embossed literary medallion.

Yet one should not be hasty to dismiss the *Memoirs of a Wild Goose.* For a start, it makes a change from the high-stylistic seriousness of a Bowen and the earnest delinquency of a Stuart, and there is something to be said on behalf of fascist hyenas who don't wear borrowed plumes. More seriously and earnestly, one should anticipate that the book may yet earn a place in that relatively neglected genre in which Irish authors have specialized, the fictional autobiography or autobiographical fiction. (In addition to some of the authors referred to already, consider George Moore and *Hail and Farewell,* Sean O'Casey's six-volume autobiography, and especially Brendan Behan's *Borstal Boy*.) Yeats's own *Autobiography* is of course of a different order, as are Joyce's fictions of Stephen Dedalus, but neither body of work is irrelevant to the question of self and of self-authoring.

If one is tempted in this latter company to dismiss the *Memoirs* as incompetent or unpolished, there is an early scene to be recalled. It occurs at the close of the first chapter, when Bewley has gone to the west of Ireland as a barrister appearing before one of the underground Sinn Féin courts. The hearing takes place in a burnt-out Big House with the broken relics of its classical aspirations in casual attendance:

> On the floor of the hall stood at regular intervals plaster casts of Roman emperors and the gods and goddesses of Olympus. Many had lost their heads or arms: nearly all showed traces of burning at some date in the near past. The missing parts lay on the wooden floor where they had fallen or been kicked into a corner . . . the litigants and witnesses strolled about among the statues, and smoked their pipes and cigarettes and from time to time spat furtively on the floor. (pp. 69–70)

When Jimmy MacGovern is reported 'striking a match on the backside of the Apollo Belvedere', he becomes the symbol of a future Ireland peopled by red faces and codfish eyes.

In Irish terms it is a telling moment: Oxford-educated republican recoiling from a vision of the petit-bourgeois future he is bringing into existence. A similar frisson was audible in Yeats's work at least as early as 'September 1913', while Bewley's piece of stage-setting is remarkably apt for a recovered historical reading of 'Nineteen Hundred and Nineteen'. In all of this one might miss Bewley's shrewd emphasis on the spurious, or at least suspect, quality of the classical heritage now in shattered disarray, the second-rate Dresden china, the odds-against 'genuine'

AFTERWORD

Canaletto, the mockery of the name Apollo Belvedere attaching to some plaster copy. For Yeats this ambiguity is material for tragic poetry, for Bewley it presages a general nihilism.

Nevertheless, the scene has a formal organization which nearly disguises its own final admission, that the one language Bewley is fated not to learn is Irish, the very basis of the cultural nationalism he otherwise recommends at every opportunity. One does not expect of the Bewley of 1919 that he relate the fragments of plaster-cast anatomy to the casualties of the Anglo-Irish war – by his own admission he was a non-combatant and the conflict was not one which generated many instances of gratuitous dismemberment. But the revelations of fascist atrocity without precedence in scale, intensity, and systematic planning were well authenticated by the 1960s in which Bewley is writing. Without effect on Bewley, it seems, whose casual solecism about 'the missing parts' now indicates the violence of his own writing. And while there is a resemblance between the mutilated Roman emperors and decapitated Olympian goddesses of Bewley's west of Ireland and the Italian bridge which he later compares to a modernist painting, no European place of interpretation can be alternated with the Irish context to provide exoneration or justification.

Giorgio de Chirico spoke of how

> every object has two appearances: one . . . which we nearly always see and which is seen by people in general; the other, a spectral or metaphysical appearance beheld only by some individuals in moments of clairvoyance and metaphysical abstraction.

From this Lucy Flint has argued that, in de Chirico's most enigmatic paintings, 'traces of concealed human presences appear in the fraught expanse of [the] work'.* Bewley remains an author who simply cannot *tell* the difference between statues and corpses, while evidently knowing it.

---

* *Handbook: The Peggy Guggenheim Collection* (New York 1983), p.90.